APERTURE ALIKE

Lucas Roman
Foreword by Michael Kennedy

Aperture Alike is published under Catharsis Books, sectionalized division under Di Angelo Publications INC.

CATHARSIS BOOKS
an imprint of Di Angelo Publications.Aperture Alike. Copyright 2021. Lucas Roman in digital and print distribution in the United States of America.

Di Angelo Publications
4265 San Felipe #1100
Houston, Texas, 77027
www.diangelopublications.com

Library of Congress cataloging-in-publications data
Aperture Alike. Downloadable via Kindle, iBooks and NOOK.

Library of Congress Registration

Paperback

ISBN: 978-1-942549-80-2

Cover Photograph: Jeremy Bishop
Cover Design: Savina Deianova
Layout: Kimberly James
Words By: Lucas Roman

1. Sports & Recreation—— Outdoor Skills
2. Biography & Autobiography—— Sports
3. Sports & Recreation—— Extreme Sports
4. Travel—— Adventure

United States of America with int. Distribution.

APERTURE ALIKE

Lucas Roman
Foreword by Michael Kennedy

///

DEDICATION

This work is dedicated to the youth of today. To Miles, E.J. and Violet, to those born in these times. May you return to the source. May you follow the path of the indigenous peoples, and in so doing may you find what is most holy. There, may you free all that is most wild. There, may you find the most of your humanity.

///

ACKNOWLEDGEMENTS

To the women. To my grandmothers, each, for their love. To my mother who birthed me, who painted cartoon figures over smashed-in doors to make beauty from pain, who always longed for freedom. To the mothers who have cared for and adopted me as their own son. To the men. To my grandfathers, each, for the grizzled, promising smiles they forced out despite lives constitutionally forged by suffering. To my father, who showed me the boundless potential of finding bottom, and who taught me to find the Holy in the rising glide of circling hawks and the cast of shadows across sacred lands. To the men who have loved me as their own son. To my sisters, who have taught me the power of unconditional positive regard toward another. To my brother, for taking those leads without having the right gear, long before we climbed anything, so I wouldn't have to. For the years on the Wilshire porch and Mulberry rooftop, and for all the foundations we built together. To the Boustani family, for May 2nd, for taking me into your fold, for all the expressions of undeserved love and invitation.

To the boys, to Brendan, Nate, Nathan, Jordan, and Johnny, for the Nights staged in Fullerton learning how to bleed on the page and slosh freeform riots, until truth was found voice-boxes ran dry.

To the friends in these chapters, whose lives and actions have fundamentally inspired me to wake up each day and try to toe the line a little further. For allowing me the chance to see in each of you, something you may or may not have seen within, and for granting me the chance to open that light to anybody who would turn the next page.

To the community of outside seekers. To all who practice a craft and have shown me how. To those who seek truth in outside spaces. To the fellowship of men and women in the rooms. To John Rosendahl, for all the drops of sweat and the graceful smiles behind them. To Bobby, for the couch and shoulder to cry on in the trenches, then and still now. To Matt, and Dave, for lessons in partnership.

To Michael Kennedy, for your unwarranted, bountiful kindness, for your wisdom, for always sharing from the heart, and doing so in such generous fashion.

To Jeremy, for a companionship greater than the oceans between us. For your gargantuan embrace, for your untamable spirit, for your light.

To Nathalie, for everything words cannot contain. For the sacred moments, for naked acceptance, for an unfathomable journey to the edges of life itself. For your love, not only because I see it, but because through it I see all things.

For you, my salt.

///

FOREWORD

How is your heart these days? The question, clear and direct, comes towards the end of a spontaneous conversation aside a quiet country road in western Colorado as the afternoon enfolds us in crystalline late autumn warmth. The sun arcs down towards a nearby ridge top, foretelling the shadow to come. My friend and I have been talking politics and the pandemic and how we've weathered this strange year of 2020, each of us thankful to be in a place in our lives where we could ride out the waves of economic and social insecurity that have devastated communities all over the world. Thankful for this small mountain town with trails and open space close by. Thankful for friends and family and good health. Thankful for life.

She and I have known each other for decades and although we see each other infrequently our encounters are always marked by kindness and a sense of deep connection. Her question is not at all unwelcome, yet it takes my breath away. *Broken*, I tell her. *My heart is still broken.* She probes further, her eyes radiant with concern and curiosity. I tell her that I see the world through a different lens than before; I seek a peace that may never come and within that yearning find lengthening moments of clarity, of understanding, of wonder. *I no longer assume a right to happiness.*

///

Such matters preoccupy the author of the volume you now hold. Lucas Roman explores them not only with the eclectic cast of characters portrayed herein but within himself, and in doing so he encourages the reader to explore that which we hold in common with the misfits, madmen and mystics who walk among us and with us and whose visions and struggles mirror our own. "The broken among us teach us how," he writes of Ghazaly, who despite the tremors of Parkinson's revisits his own "before" on Cathedral Peak in the high country of Tuolumne. "They have the key. They know deeply what it is and what it feels like to be human. They know pain and loss, they know frailty, and darkness. They know fear. They know the paralysis of it, the isolation of it, the chill of it."

Yet they also urge us towards the light. After all, Lucas reminds us, "… it is love that we are destined for. To love in this life, more than we fear. No matter our condition. That love—our greatest destiny—is not something we generate but something we transmit, that love is not to be held or kept, it is only to be given."

A sense of gratitude and compassion permeates these stories as Lucas seeks out and embraces the at times unobvious strength and wisdom of his subjects. "Most have a hard time digesting Brad's simplicity in the face of his experience," he says of the late Brad Gobright, who for years survived that most demanding of alpine pursuits—rock climbing alone, unencumbered by ropes or safety gear or partners—yet fell to his death in 2019 while descending an ordinary climb with friends on an ordinary day. "You want him to be brilliant. But he's happy. You want him to be multi-faceted, but he runs perfectly as is. He is not what you want him to be, nor is he trying not to be, he just is."

For others, work and play intertwine in a dance of infinite possibility.

Shanjean Lee strives to balance the demands of medical practice with a still-vivid life in the vertical, recognizing and acknowledging that where one ends isn't necessarily where the other begins. "Every so often, when you execute the perfect climb or the perfect surgery," says Shanjean, "When you know you are doing something as well as it can possibly be done, then yes, it feels like you are a part of something greater than yourself... That's what all the work is for. It is to be one hundred percent ready to have a moment like this when it presents itself."

///

The sun has left us. My friend shivers a little as she dons the sweater wrapped around her waist, and as we part she leaves me with a final question to consider: *And what have you learned?*

Not as much as I'd hoped, I think to myself. *Not as much as I need to.* Three years and counting since my son Hayden's death, his absence remains an unfathomable mystery, a hole that nothing seems to fill, his memory an ever-present shadow at the edge of my consciousness. In that time I've discovered, as Matt Blank does in the first pages of this book, "... that grief doesn't get an answer, it simply must be endured, that it is an experience to be had." Yet I've also come to understand that when we speak of loss we also speak of hope, and such hope resides within the friends we know and the ones we have yet to meet, all of us in communion with the wind, the water, the ground on which we stand. "Tomorrow, in that Canyon, what you'll experience is sacred for us," Shaun Martin tells the 150 runners gathered for the 55-kilometer ultra he organizes each year on the land of the Dine in Canyon De Chelly, Arizona. "The walls will sing if you listen, the sky and the earth will guide you, the Spirit People will hear your chants and see your effort, and they will commune with you."

And perhaps a fraction of the truth of these stories is simply that while there are no easy answers to the big questions, it is essential that we ask them of ourselves, and to act on this questioning each day with divine intention and gratitude. And love.

—Michael Kennedy, December 2020,
Carbondale, Colorado

///

INTRODUCTION

December 2020 —

Many years back, I took to writing as one takes to running at a local level. Purely for the promise of movement, and a new experience. It wasn't to get anywhere in particular, aside from out the front door, considering I carried no great speed. I had no intention toward any great distance, nor had I any intention to arrive at any mythic destination. Surely, it was more fundamental than that. Each time I 'put on the shoes', I did so only to embrace a simple truth: the notion that no matter how far I went or where it may lead, without any goal in mind, life was simply better for doing it than not. The reward was always in the practice itself.

Some years passed, and the works evolved, as the subject matter also evolved with them. Being drawn to the outside spaces, and the communities who filled them, I began only with what I knew. However, where much of mountain literature—or adventure journalism—had sensational stories to tell, my trails took me, almost without my own choosing, to inner landscapes. That I had never achieved any fantastic heights or striking feats of accomplishment in my own adventures, perhaps, forced me to look at the value of the outside experience with an adjusted scope.

In no specific place or point in time, the landscape I occupied in my writing began to shift, and while I still knew not where I was going, I was sure that at the least, I had gone some ways from that front door. Soon, I began looking for stories, for experiences, which would shape a larger perspective. Truth be told, my hunch is that these things chose and sought me, more than I chose them. And perhaps that is the great gift of the tales in this collection, for me alone; that from each experience came a new, or deeper relationship, to a person, a community, and a brighter world.

Before even half of the pieces in this collection were first drafted, I began to sense there might be something holding them together. That, while unique in their own arcs, they might all be plotting a common terrain. And so, for the sake of curiosity, perhaps even a grand failure, it was decided that I would run all the branches of the trail before me, to discover in just which ways they might indeed loop, braid, and frame the space we call the outside experience. There must, I thought, be more to all of this outside business that I've fallen slave to, than simple fun-hogging. It may not need be an entirely esoteric venture. It may, like Zen, not even be subject to transcription by the rational mind. But at the least, it deserves more than the notion of a privileged, passing whim.

It was at this same time, in the fall of 2019, that I self-published a piece online, which caught the attention of some folks in ways I would have never imagined. This led to an unexpected, and surely unplanned opportunity to go full steam, to write with a purpose. The offer was clear, full freedom, no pre-conditions applied. Just say whatever you have to say. Write the book.

It scared the shit out of me.

I may have begun the journey of writing without intending to arrive anywhere, but now, tasked with creating a book I was forced to consider, at the least, where to go, or minimally, something to aim for.

At a precipice, I had to ask what of these adventure experiences was most important, for me. And, if I could only focus on a few characters, a few themes, a few modes of storytelling even, what would they be? After a soul-search I concluded, that in the world we occupy, in 2020, there was no longer time for flare or panache alone, at least not my attempts at it. We've come too far to appeal only to sensationalism, senility, extravagance, or even fun-hogging. Our lives, and our time, ask more of us. More than cleverness, I understood, that I need at least try for something like truth.

And so, here is my submission. It is not designed to impress, I am not at last, here to dazzle with great spectacle or dizzying affectation. Having come through my own dark nights of the soul, and having been led to the light, by the unsuspecting saints who fill the rooms of recovery fellowships, I am here to share the only message I know: that life is flush with order among chaos, goodness among pain, a deep hope in the midst of all calamity, and incomprehensible holiness. That the sublime itself can exist just as fully as the darkness seems to, and that it may even be born of it. Above all, my description, the aperture I use to inform my vision of life, and the outside experience, is not conclusive. If anything, it is simply an invitation.

The outside life is extremely complex—nuanced, individual, sacred, hidden even—and because of this, thin-slicing segments of it in the form of small vignettes was my only reasonable approach. The result, are simply shutter-stops, apertures with varying forms of light. Transcribing the inner experience, one character at a time, proved elusive, but it is precisely the elusiveness of it that constitutes its beauty. Surely, the depth of the outside experience is fashioned uniquely, for each of us. And so, I make no effort to dictate what any one person's experience should be like, but within these stories, in moments of reflection, I do stand on certain concepts, and principles, for the sake of direction on the path.

My aim was to shine a light, at least metaphorically, on everyone. The characters compiled here, I believe, are a sufficiently rounded cast from whom we may find direction and our own likeness. Against all appearances, the stories are less about rock-climbing, B.A.S.E jumping, highlining, skydiving, or distance running as they are about the inner life of those who do such things. They are about the heart condition of humans, out in nature, looking for their own. As a friend of mine has said, they are cairns on a long and winding path. They are not intended to declare any arrival, but to assure you that you are not lost. A trail cairn asks that you continue, as these stories ask that we also continue, individually, and as communities, onward.

Additionally, it is my belief that the outside revelation exists for all, period. I could, in short time, not possibly showcase that experience from all people groups, or gender groups, but I have made the effort to at least showcase the experience at a variety of intersections. The premise of this work is that if there is a great truth in living the outside life, it must be available to all! And, that it must translate to life in the lowlands. If it cannot be integrated everywhere, it likely is an illusory revelation, at best.

For the purposes of disclosure, I will say that all stories here are true, in that all the events which are said to have happened, certainly happened. For privacy, some names of peripheral characters have been changed, but the augmentation of details begins and ends there. They are all matters of fact. But truth is also more than the superficial details, it is a tone, a resonance, and with that in mind I also believe that events 'as they happened' are but a first draft of history, as truth would have it told. When writing I do my best to elicit that interplay, between exact details and fuller, or even subtler tones. Each and every word in quotation may not have been said, precisely as is, but there is no conjecture or untruth spoken in this work either. Nothing has been fabricated. It is, non-fiction, but it is not without some measure of interpretation, and surely not without appeals to a great imagination.

And that leads to the order of these stories. It is not lost on me, the degree to which loneliness, isolation, and fear pervade the current human experience. It has indeed been the chief make-up of my own life. Additionally, for outside and adventure-sports communities, death, grief, and loss are common and often unconsolidated fragments of our experience. So, that is where we begin. Not just with death and loss, but with darkness, sadness, and unwanted burdens of illness.

The first half of this collection, generally, focuses on persons in pain, situations of loss, and a general disorientation of purpose and direction. The second half, by contrast, is designed to showcase moments of clarity. Sometimes found at the individual level, sometimes found for only an instant, sometimes found in communities. The orthopedic surgeon and climbing partner, Dave Wright, finds in a second story, a deeper fuel source and resolution for life that he had missed on first pass. Matt Blank, close friend and veteran sky flier, consolidates the loss of his dearest friend in a new approach to skydiving and B.A.S.E jumping, one which embraces the beauty and the calamity assigned him in the very first story of the series. The truly nomadic, somewhat controversial and at times even polemic figure, Sa`id Belhaj, goes past his character defects and offers a glimpse of a deep mysticism in his Gnawan roots. And, through the examples set by the matriarchal *Dine* (Navajo) tribe of distance runners, and two feminine heroes, Faith Dickey and Shanjean Lee, respectively, we are given a gentle nudge, a warm invitation, to a framework for life that embraces energies equally feminine as masculine.

In closing, I'll share that while some ideas, axioms, and institutions are challenged, it was never my aim to put anyone or anything on trial. Second, if there is any slant to this volume, entirely, if any agenda is being pushed, let it be stated that I intend only to skew toward what the *Dine* (Navajo) have called, The Beauty Way. There, and in schools of thought of shared ilk, I will plant a flag. Surely, chief among my few, simple aims, was to honor the indigenous peoples, upon whose ancient lands so many of these discoveries, these revelations, have been and will continue to be found. I hope I have done them no injustice, and better still, some level of celebration.

I have done my best with the time I was given to tell the stories of all of us. There are those who do it professionally, those who do it personally, and those who can barely do it at all. There are those who come of privilege and those who come only of pain. I hope you can find some of your own experience in each of them, as I have. An aperture is simply an opening, or a source, through which light passes. My hope, in the apertures provided by the subjects of these stories, is that you may find something shared, something beautiful, something true.

May the characters of these stories shine more than the words I employed to describe them. May you feel all the emotions herein, and may you feel all of them more than you expected to. May you take up your own journey, and may you meet many others along the way. May you put on your shoes and step outside, in whatever fashion, for whatever distance, to whatever measure, with the simple belief that your life will be better for having done so than not.

—Lucas Roman

THE STORIES

///

UNDER CANOPY

On Tuesday, July 21st, 2015, two of my longtime friends, Matt Blank and Ian Flanders, hiked a striking cliff line outside of the town of Kemaliye, Turkey, under a crescent light which mixed shards of moonbeam across a murex sky. Ungodly as the hour was early, it was also quiet, the kind of quiet that is only broken by footsteps cracking granules of soil apart, and by the sound of cool, sharp breath. On the edge, where they preferred to forge friendship, they stood at an unopened B.A.S.E. exit. Staring down the canyon at an abysmal chute, the kind which only deals in terms of life and death, they asked only a few simple questions of each other. Tension and axons strung to the wire, they did not wait for second guesses nor daylight. Gut check complete, they dove, one after the other, in a hair-raising, fell swoop, the likes of which only birds of prey craft and contrive. Screaming into the void faster than their nerve endings could conjugate, they sliced through the heart of that godforsaken canyon as a comet does into the earth, with complete disregard for the eons and forces which formed it. At something akin to the human speed of sound, a few thousand feet later, they cleared the hazards and the shadowlands which housed them, and pulled parachutes; Ian landing safely into the current of a gushing Karasu River, just meters away from a small watercraft. Whether by skill or fortune, Matt landed a moment later, on a Goddman dime, both feet on the boat without even getting his parachute wet.

A media celebration, something both of them were familiar with, ensued, as they'd just established one of, if not the most dangerous, B.A.S.E. jumps in the world. It was a heralding day, all before most of the old men in the sleepy town had even had their first cup of muddy Arabica coffee. This also was by design. Not only was the air density better for the morning jump, but the company they intended to keep was as well. Matt, Ian, and their friend Scotty Bob had decided to leave in haste that morning because a local physician and B.A.S.E. jumper had hard-pressed them to join. The fellow, it was said, could not see the extent of his limitations, and for that reason, was left in his sleeping bag in those early morning hours. Neither Matt, Ian, nor Scotty, wanted to have a fellow flier's death occur on their watch. Even midway through the season 2015 had been quite the year.

Hordes of jumpers and fliers, some of them among the most respected in the nascent sport itself, had gone in that summer. Their departures had not been foreseeable nor within reason. It was the guy or girl that you swore wouldn't go down that way. It was unjust, unfair, and impartial to skill, craft, or capability. With that momentum, and the scars it etched, the boys had not only called the local doctor off the jump, once they completed their new B.A.S.E. exit they nearly called off the rest of the trip entirely. If you asked Matt, they were about one beer away from packing-in the parachutes and raising pint glasses for the remainder of the itinerary. But you do not come across the globe, to the heart of the ancient world, for cheap swill.

Matt and Ian decided, in the quiet refrain of the afternoon, to have another go at an easier location. No need for antics, Ian asserted, just one more, easy ride downstream. Couldn't hurt to have just one more look at those rock-floored, emerald waters. It was an entirely different, and entirely more secure exit, after all.

Between a thousand-foot, shadow cast canyon known as the Karanlik, Matt and Ian sat on the loveseat, a refashioned concept of a rickshaw bench turned cable car—about the size of two ass cheeks—while the crank ratcheted them into free space. With a nod of pure satisfaction, Ian stood up first, sun glowing through his Leonidas-like beard, turning his hazel eyes alight. Sure as he'd ever been, he gave Matt a fist-bump and a high-five, took a half squat to load the knees at force, and then pitched off in a backflip. An exit that Matt and many others had seen no less than a thousand times.

It was among the safest possible jumps in the sport.

///

Halfway to Vegas, we're stuck in a pickle; traffic isn't moving an inch. Rubber tires droop like Dali clocks, melting off their wheel wells, and the 15 freeway feels like the underarm of humanity. It's a long road ahead and we're nowhere close to the midpoint, let alone the endpoint, which is Moab, with a stop in Salt Lake. Radiators overheat, cars pull-over, spectators sweat in the sunbaked heat of the afternoon. Staving off our own meltdown, I quickly shuffle through the music library, pulling out a set of Ghanaian Afro-soul and psychedelia circa 1974. The bass line steadies, the horns syncopate, a little disco synth glues it fast, the band drops the beat and it's off to the fucking races. Volume up, the reverberations bubble over the rear-view mirror just in time for me to look through it and see Matt. He's a caricature of cool in a moment of joy, as he pushes a can of "Whip-Its" into his lungs with a shit-grin on his face and a pair of diamonds etched on the soles of his feet. Moments later, traffic clears, and the poor souls whose car burned beside the fast lane stand and ponder the ashes. The evening sky paints brushstrokes over the bulging horizon. The gas pedal goes down, and voices of the Sub-Saharan world serenade us through the desert.

He got those tattoos ages ago—the diamonds on the soles of his feet —long before losing Ian and so many others in the game of life. And he's walked miles on them. Be it the ten or fifteen straight and narrow steps on the line for Johnny Law, the thousands of kilometers slogging toward a B.A.S.E. exit, or in the handful of picturesque highlines he's walked in the canyons of the Utah desert. But nothing has put Matt or his ink to the test quite like the pain he's had since losing Ian. Once a bright, ambitious army green, Matt's diamonds now look more like a dimly lit OPEN sign over a seedy bar. They may not be the mission statement on life they once were, but they still shine. So does Matt, even now, as the shit-grin turns perma-smile while the nitrous oxide tickles his brain and the music hits him just right.

I've been sober for some time now, so I know Matt's trip is only temporary, but then again, so does he. Hell, it wasn't all that long ago I was the one shaking off the delirium tremens on his couch, while homeless and trying to shuffle out a new hand at life. He and I both have seen what a real dose of abuse can do. For now, I'm not worried, he's nowhere close to passing a recreational level with this stuff, even if there is a flood of grief behind it. Besides, Matt is good, deeply good, and he's always had life skills. Many of them have been collected on the fringe, but they have proven their worth in spades.

Deeper in the twilight, the desert sparkles with life. Stars shoot across the sky while indigo pours over the silhouettes of yuccas and Joshua Trees. It's a welcome overlay to the somber notes of our current mission. We're headed to Salt Lake to meet with Matt's friend, and film producer, Anson, who's making a short piece not just about who, but also what, was lost on that fateful day in Kemaliye. A film about friendship, about brotherhood.

It's been nearly four months since Ian passed. He and I shared our own escapades; long days out climbing, lucid nights chasing a good buzz and the perfect story to tell. We had our own stitches holding up our fabric. But Matt and Ian, Jesus, that was it; the real deal. They'd been inseparable for years, taken to each other's side, through thick and thin for the better part of a decade and across an uncountable number of climbs, jumps, and flights.

So here we are in Ian's van, which was infamously named the Rape Van Winkle (perhaps better known as the Love Bus), returning to old haunts. The same van Matt and Ian used to revel in, wildly, across the states and back again—while flying by the seat of their pants on all types of carnal missions and mind-bending drunkalogues—is now the vehicle of choice to get us both back into desert.

It's been just short of four months, but our schedules haven't allowed for any purposeful time together until now. Memories of Ian, bold, belligerent and petulant in nearly every circumstance, pass as mile markers on the highway. His absence, and the grief Matt rides in its wake, is also there, but tonight those bits mostly remain unspoken.

Passing Mesquite, Nevada, we laughed, remembering that first trip we'd taken out to the desert nearly a decade before. In 2008, Matt and I had nothing to our names but oversized ambition, a short stack of cash, and a junker pick-up truck with 220k miles on it. We laughed because back then we honestly thought that living, at its best, had only to do with vagrant behavior and long-term irresponsibility. A lifestyle of short-cuts, half measures, and con jobs to get whatever gear, goods, or stories we wanted. Back then, death was something we glorified. Matt always expressed, explicitly, that he'd be amazed if he made it past the age of thirty. Surely it would be the requisite cost for a life lived by such radical fashion, and of course, what other life was there? Back then it was all a hypothetical, and death was just an idea we measured ourselves and our egos by. We hadn't tasted a lick of it, and lord knows we hadn't walked through fire, but we damn well thought we'd be suited for the task.

Just past Beaver, Matt got a call from Anson. Schedules had changed, as it seemed the puzzle pieces in Anson's life had flipped, which meant the rendezvous was off for now. At Cove Fort, we turned off the road to the last gas station in town, making new tracks over fresh carpets of snow. Coffee mugs full, and steadied by the sound of Toumani Diabete's *New Ancient Strings,* we trudged under a new moon across the Interstate 70, the Fishlake Forest, and Green River, until our eyes burned out and we started seeing shadows come to life at Crescent Junction. Stammering into the rest stop, we crawled behind the driver seats and into our sleeping bags at 3 a.m.

"Thought about Ian a lot tonight, I imagine?" I asked after a few minutes of quiet.

Shaking his head, Matt responded in his trademark calm, "Dude, all the time."

Silent again in the dark of night, Matt later asked, "Did you hear from your brother? Any news?"

"Sounds like they're in labor tonight," I began, "Odds are by the time we wake up I'll have a new nephew."

"Damn," Matt shook his head again, "Wild how it all moves beneath our feet."

///

At 7:00 a.m. we shackled out of the van, stretched out the cobwebs, and made a round of light roast. Well below freezing, a fresh coat of snow on the ground padded the auburn soil, which stretched along with a bluebird sky to a sharp horizon. The satisfaction on Matt's face, back under wide open spaces, and back in touch with Ian, shone with a subtle smirk as we saddled in for the final trek to Moab.

Tradition, in the desert community, builds one story at a time, and always begins humbly. What started as the raucous dance of a few friends years ago quickly evolved into a cult phenomenon. Each year, in growing numbers, those of the tribe make a dusty bed in the Ute desert during late November in a co-celebration of B.A.S.E. and Highlining festivities, respectively called the Turkey Boogie and the GGBY (Gobble Gobble Bitches, Yeah!). While it seems like only yesterday that Matt and Ian took their first leap off the bridge in Twin Falls, Idaho, that pack job was time-stamped way back in 2009. And, in the B.A.S.E. world, six years practically adds up to a lifetime. It was no surprise that Matt and Ian both came into their own in the sport since those early days, not just in terms of their own piloting skills, but also into their found families. The ragtag tribe of wayward saints that make up the B.A.S.E. community became a foundation to Matt. The community was as much of a reference point for his sense of direction as the pitch of a slope off a cliff, or the atmospheric pressure at the time of flight. Matt found that solid relationships were the key to creativity—that togetherness was the starting point of progression.

But where there's progression, there's also the fanfare. In B.A.S.E., it's been no different. Matt has seen this small festival of friends explode in scale, from an occasion that could be handled with a few cases of beer and leftover MDMA, to a raging assault on neurological activity as expressed in cultish feedback loops of group-level, psychoactive mind-melts. Something like the Burning Man of the Southwest. As we crossed the Colorado, officially arriving in town, Matt said, "I'm fairly certain there's something in the range of a 50 percent chance that some kid is going to show up here in the next two weeks ready to rage his dick off, looking to become the next YouTube sensation, and get himself killed in the process."

There is a draw, especially it seems for the young lads, to rub shoulders with the greats and swing for the fences. Anybody can be a legend in some fashion—take a wrong jump and you'll see. As one of those on the tip of the spear, Matt was no stranger to the gravity that pulls in the drifting type. At this point he had been sponsored, flying fast and setting the bar. What he was doing was being watched by those kids in just the same way that he and Ian spent hours watching the old-school jumpers, way back when, before he cut his own teeth.

"You've got a whole system now," he started, "And I'm a part of it, too, so I've got to ask some questions as to my own complicity. People click and share these shots of us flying through the Alps and jumping out of space nets, and kids out there in suburbia or people looking for an escape-—just like I did—have no clue. They go and get an AFF license at the local drop zone, buy a B.A.S.E. rig, and then go, 'fuck it, I want to do that, too!'"

Matt's statistical analysis might not be perfectly in order, but his point is well taken. You might not know it on the first impression, but the lion's share of the exits and landing zones in the Moab area require more than an amateur attention to detail. These canyons, and the exits they house, are not for the uninitiated. There is some measure of craft, and one must be good—baseline competent—with piloting technique to have a shot at longevity, let alone legendry. Any local will tell you that you ought not simply arrive with fingers crossed and a blind faith in the learning curve, not in Moab.

"That's it, you know," Matt continued, "The people who only watch this stuff from the couch misunderstand the complexity. They have a notion of B.A.S.E. that's not fully with it, and which is probably just driven by a social media fantasy they want to live out, but it's not like that at all. You do not just pick up your shit one day and start jumping these canyons. Nobody who is doing this shit well, or for the long term, is doing it for those reasons. B.A.S.E. goes much deeper than that."

The conversation he's alluding to might be subject to each individual jumper, but at least he was having it. He was not the only one either. Based on what I had seen, the conversation needed to continue, for days, perhaps years, even. On the surface it was about people's perception of B.A.S.E. from the outside looking in, but according to Matt, that conversation was happening from the inside as well. It was high time for most in the sport to really look at themselves and ask what B.A.S.E.-jumping was for them, and what the hell they were actually doing out there in those tiny slivers of physical space we call the margin for error. For Matt, it was no longer cheap thrills he was after, it was something like purpose—as backasswards as it may sound, that purpose was looking more and more like the safety and longevity of others, like keeping people alive, like progress tempered by reason. It would come, with time, but just then, what was more apparent than the direction of the sport, was Matt's need for fellowship.

After Ian went-in, and once back home, Matt was charged with handling Ian's last wishes. Among them, to be cremated and scattered in his favorite mountain landscape. While the wishes were clear, Matt was also in no rush to pull chute for Ian's final flight. Ian was extremely plugged-in, with friends and loved ones seemingly everywhere. When Matt hosted a memorial in Ian's honor, and found that many of his closest friends couldn't make it to Southern California, he changed course. In a rush of insight, Matt came up with the only apparent solution: The Flanders Tour. Putting the sum of Ian's remains inside an empty coffee tin, just like the movies, Matt packed his chutes and his outdoor gear and set off on one of the last great American road trips. It was an interstate journey, covering almost everything west of the Continental Divide.

From Colorado to Utah, up to Idaho where they'd had their first B.A.S.E. jump together, and of course, to the Playa, at Burning Man, where Matt convinced a local skipper to let him board, and then skydive out of a plane with Ian's remains strapped to him. Ian may, it turns out, have his own record still, for logging the most time in the sky, post-mortem. Pretty badass.

The Flanders Tour was its own traveling road show. A dozen years' worth of friends and faces, shedding tears, grieving, and celebrating, their vices akin to sex, drugs, and rock n' roll—in this case just subbing out the rock for techno, trance, and dance. By the time all was said and done, and Matt found himself alone for that last pack job at the foot of Ian's final flight, it had been nearly a month of non-stop, communal expansion. The sudden quiet, in that final hike-in and twilight jump, and in the space following it, struck a different darkness. With no chapters left to close for his dear friend, Matt appeared to be facing a sudden, unwanted solitude.

Back in Moab, Matt drove us to the apartment of his good friend, Brian, for the first stop in town. When Matt got out of the van, walked down the basement stairs, and opened the door, he immediately hugged Brian. Not like you hug a friend either, more like you hug a survivor. It took a few minutes, the better part of an hour really, but Matt finally found the comfort he needed in that basement, perhaps a comfort even I couldn't give him. For the first time in a long time, he looked ready to deal with himself and his lot in life without the chaotic persona or the cans of "Whip-It's."

///

Established in 2008 by a local barista and a bike mechanic, The Love Muffin quickly turned from a humble breakfast spot to the kind of joint the outdoor kids like to call home. Just a block ahead of the trendy Main Street strip, it feels like one of the last vestiges of an eclectic small town, and for that reason, combined with the fact that it hires local adventure athletes, is considered the go-to place if you're making plans or breaking bread before noon.

From Brian's place, we'd immediately come in to rally with another counterpart in the local band, Mr. John (or Johnny) Verbeck. The Verb, as he's also known, is a blue-eyed, Appalachian stallion, with something of the happy-go-lucky attitude that you'd expect from the way his long, unkempt dirty-blonde locks sway around in front of his every move. He's another legend, in his own way, and has known Matt and Brian both for the better part of his time in the skies, a connection which was apparent from the moment he sat down next to us. Apart from being strikingly engaged in conversation, he's also exceptionally humble about his own accomplishments.

In the time it took for the coffee to hit a drinkable temperature I learned he'd just come back from Yosemite, usual by his calendar, where he'd done something of a speed ascent of Lurking Fear, on To-tok-ah-noo-lah, just to help get a friend of his up his first big-wall. John had an immediate shine, the kind that comes from his organic, no bullshit connection to other people—a forward, engaging trait I'd imagine would be a surprise to those not familiar with the B.A.S.E. community.

Next to John, was a friend of his, Glen, who happened to be passing through town. Being new to the outside culture altogether, especially to the inner workings of the B.A.S.E. community, he had some direct questions for Johnny, Matt, and Brian to chew on with our breakfast.

"If I was to just go right out there and ask the basic questions of you guys, you know, like, why do people B.A.S.E. jump? What is it that you're looking for in it? Is there a consensus for you guys?" It may have been predictable, but it was not a bad question, at all. Everyone wants to peel the skin off and get at the fruit on that one.

If we're honest, most B.A.S.E. practitioners aren't too thrown off by those questions, either, because in a lot of ways they've each got their surface-level answers at the ready. Answers that they've rehearsed to themselves as many times as they've pulled chute behind their backs.

What was interesting was how Matt, in particular, took the conversation. Typical for Matt's take on life, answers are less in words as they are in experiences.

To start, Matt replied, "Well it's clear to me that you are going to get as many answers to that question as you have jumpers. Some you might like, and others, you might not. But let's explore it."

He took Glen on a personal tour of narrative, connecting dots by allegory, and asked Glen about the practice-and-fulfillment process of his own personal pursuits. It couldn't have taken more than two minutes, but Matt had managed to tie two knots between them, as humans, without appealing to any form of rhetoric or his own scripted response.

To close, Matt looked at Glen and asked, "So, here's a question for you. Lord knows it's a terrible movie, but bear with me. Have you seen Point Break?"

"It's been a long time," Glen replied with surprise.

"Well, let me set it up for you," Matt started, spinning yarn with his trademark grin. "You've got these two sets of characters, right. These adrenaline junkies, extreme dudes, straight out of the nineties paradigm, who surf big waves just like they live life, and then you've got this main character, a master, soul surfer, okay."

"Sure," Glen agreed.

"So, at one point, there's a comparison made, right. The soul surfer looks at his new apprentice, and says, 'Look, man, those two guys, their brains are wired wrong.' The new guy looks up at him and says, 'What do you mean?' 'Well,' says the master, 'they only live to get radical, man, they don't understand the sea, and because of that they'll never get the spiritual side of it.'"

At this point, Matt is grinning ear to ear, literally overjoyed as he takes a drumroll on the coffee table, looks over at Glen, then looks over to Johnny and proclaims, "Now you see this guy, your friend John, our friend John, he's all about the spiritual side of this shit. What the soul surfer gets from the sea, before he even rides a wave, Johnny gets from the sky. So if you really want answers, you've gotta' have experiences, and they should start with him. He's all about the spiritual side of this."

To see Matt back into his own skin, riding on the high-side of the wave and perfectly in trim, was a joy. There was a magic in his just being here, closer to others who'd lost Ian, and other loved ones in the sport over the past year. And, while scoring complete points for panache, progression, and execution in his dialogue—its own level of mastery—I had to consider, still, why the table went quiet to explore the concepts like loss, grief, and death. But as Matt was quick to point out, discussions are good, and answers exist, but experience serves far better than words.

///

The next morning, after a standard weeknight whirlwind at Johnny McStiff's Pub, I walked with my climbing pack back down to the Love Muffin to meet up with Mr. Johnny Verbeck. McStiff's, at high-season, is an easy landscape for the local folk to rally around. On an average night, upstairs, between a circle of high-top tables and a billiards set, the veritable who's who in local action sports make a habit to rub shoulders and chase down the bottom ends of beer pitchers. Among the high personalities and decadent slosh of suds, where all the best plans for adventures are made, the Verb had asked if I wanted to get a deeper clue in on a B.A.S.E. jump.

"The bad news is that you'll potentially have to rappel that thing solo, which isn't super fun," he admitted, between a mouthwash of ale. "But it is Castleton, and if you've never been on it, I'm happy to hand you all the leads."

Verbeck laid it out there simple as; we'd go have a romp up the North Chimney, get to the summit, and spend an afternoon at idle until conditions were fit enough for him to have a leap. And as for the leads, well, it was clear he wasn't deferring. Like I said, he's humble. Last time he went up that side of Castleton he summitted in under an hour and had just three pieces of gear for protection on each pitch.

It's worth noting, even these days, that where Moab can feel a bit like the adult theme park, and just as crowded, if you've got a new set of eyes on it, it can still blow out your senses. Take that first turn into Castle Valley, under morning light, and ponder just what forces those fingerlings have danced with—and for God only knows how long—and you'll have one of those moments of wonder all over again.

Johnny and I took our time hiking up that gorgeous, cinnamon salted Moenkopi-Chinle talus cone, arriving at the cold, almost frozen base of the North Chimney sometime closer to lunch. It didn't take more than a handful of moves off the ground, however, to realize that the bloodsucking chill of the finger-cracks was no place to bide your time, and for that reason, we accelerated pace rapidly. Quick enough to top out just ahead of our friend Sa`id, and his partner Daniel. Elated, on summit time, we sat on the precipice of the southeastern exit point under those needed, sharp, winter sunbeams, waxing tales, and working down a shared pack of American Spirits.

"So," Johnny stood up and pointed, an hour later, "If you look at that smoke-line off that chimney from the house down there, see that? Right there! It's getting really still. A couple more minutes and it'll be perfect to jump!"

Johnny was pointing at the only visible house, down the road on a bucolic patch of ranchland, about five clicks out. The sun had turned axis toward the west and was beginning to cast rigid, hallowed shadows over the earth and its wayward snow patches, which glowed under a deep, Toureg-blue. Looking at the behavior of the smoke from that distant chimney, Johnny could gauge the wind conditions nearer to ground, where he'd hoped to be landing. Daniel, Sa'id, and I sat there, biting our nails off in earnest while Johnny walked us through his internal process. Neither of us had been witness to this stuff, and because of that we just sat on our ass-pads like dummies. A perfect day, a dreamy set up of gents on an ancient tower out in the vast lands, light like you can't imagine, and one of us was about to just walk the edge of Tierra Firma. We had no idea how to participate.

In a handful of near-gos, just when the moment would come clean, John would stand up, ready and steady himself, double-check the rig, shadowbox the pull cord sequence, and step right up to the edge. Just then, every time, the wind would shift, spin in circles, and flurry in a tantrum for minutes on end. This carried on for two hours.

"You know what I've learned?" Johnny shared as the afternoon drug down. "You've just got to love these moments in B.A.S.E., because they are a part of the richness of it. It's the whole process. And part of that is learning how to be still, how to listen."

He wasn't bullshitting. The spiritual one was having no problem with the conditions. Wearing a B.A.S.E. rig on his back no more made him want to jump, on an impulsive level, as wearing an umpire's get-up would make him want to call a game. That was Johnny, the image of stillness. He'd stand up every few minutes, spit into the wind, watch it fly, and then just come back into the conversation. What was apparent to me, was that surviving, thriving even, in B.A.S.E. has everything to do with a million decisions that are made ages before that pilot chute flutters out the canopy. You could watch a mash-up of B.A.S.E. flights in a two-minute montage on YouTube and have absolutely no idea that behind each 15-second ride was something on the order of hours of patient, steady mindfulness.

We had to listen, deeply, to the wind, and not like Cat Stevens either. You had to listen for real, like a line cook on that grill station, with twenty steaks all going for different temperatures and knowing, just by the sound of sizzle on flame, each stage of sear and exactly when action was or was not indicated. That's the kind of skill John was showing. We'd be deep in dialogue, running the gamut—from Sa`id and John's ten-year friendship across the continents to dark periods of life they'd experienced after failed relationships with women, from history lessons of West African music and Islamic tradition to the practices of griots and marabouts in preserving history and shamanic practice—when Johnny would get up, analyze setting, and peacefully make way back into the fold.

Nearing twilight, Johnny looked over, "How about we share one more cigarette?"

Reaching into my chest pouch, I softened the stick with a roll of my fingers and handed it to him. "Pack's nearing empty."

Johnny laughed, "It's almost five, already. Damn. I guess if the wind doesn't tame now, it's not going to."

He checked his watch once more, flecking another spit-wad off the top of Castleton, and started tilting back and forth, cradling, to keep the muscle memory of the exit sequence fresh. Once more the wind stilled, perking everyone's attention, only to lift in a rabid rush. Still, it didn't phase Johnny, at all. Anybody could have jumped there, according to Johnny, it probably wouldn't have qualified as rash or unsafe to do so. If someone else really needed it, if they had something to prove, if they had more anxiety at the edge and needed action more than acceptance, we could've been halfway down the trail. But Johnny was as balanced as a rock garden. The moment he wanted to dance with, to fly with, was his own to define; the fact that it never came, that he didn't force it, was a better demonstration of his craft than any actual jump would've been.

"Another thing I've learned is that you never want to be in a situation where you have to jump," he shared in the early-evening glow. "If you are in a place where you've forced yourself to jump or where there is no other option, you've already clouded your mind, and you're probably going to lose clarity on the situation."

Staying true, for the Verb, is just as much in the actions you don't take as the ones you do. With that carefree smile and the wind at our backs, we packed it in, all four us rappelling together back down the North Face, ecstatic to watch twilight work magic on the long spires at the golden hour. No jump, but completely stand out all the same. We'd gotten a proper view, a full-frame in the mental space of someone at practice in B.A.S.E.. We'd gotten a summit for the ages, hours of conversation, the real kind, up there on the high plane where you're supposed to have it. We'd gotten a long afternoon, and depleted what little snacks and water we'd had, hours ago, but none of that was of consequence. Out there, with the magic of the full moon rising, with chards of a lilac and purple skyline cooled by a hallowed winter chill, out there it was all-time. Out there, there is no hunger and there is no thirst.

///

At Brian's apartment, downstairs, just an hour later, Johnny and I unloaded gear and walked ourselves into the heart of a dinner party that was already bordering on debauchery. The crew in Moab, at least at that time, circa 2015—2017, reveled. Men, women, any permutation of them in any fluid state on the spectrum; if there was one thing they'd made a practice of aside from their outdoor pursuits, it was the regular, substance-fueled practice of freeform, human expression.

After spending the afternoon weaving the famed "space-net"—the main attraction of the GGBY, which gets hung across the stadium-size chasm of the Fruit Bowl, just outside of town—a dozen close friends gathered at Brian's for drinks and dinner. A simple gathering which turned mind-melting quickly, as noted by the lazy smiles, easy postures, and perma-stares for long periods at vacant spots on the polyethylene flooring.

While this was in play, Brian and Matt were at the other end of the spectrum, and the other side of the room, having a hard conversation with a friend, and flier, named Rio. Rio's recent journey in B.A.S.E. may have paralleled that of the sport altogether, and for that reason her position was compelling. She was new, enamored with it, but new. New enough to be pulled along quicker than she should've in its progression, like many. In fact, she'd recently leveled-up, far too soon and with no real mentorship, to a new wingsuit. In one of those first flights with the new rig, she'd lost it completely and nearly spun out of control. Flying hard like a bat out of hell and losing control is not just something one can sweep under the rug. It shook her, violently, alert and awake in a way she'd probably wished she wasn't.

"I'm telling you, Matt," she said, "I can't stop thinking, what the fuck am I doing this for?"

Nodding with his eyelids down, Matt understood by memory.

"I mean, I love these feelings up there," she began, "but I never really stopped and asked myself what they were, and why I was after them, let alone if they can be explored some other way. And who knows, maybe I should. But, of course, we've tangled this stuff up completely and when I think about walking away from B.A.S.E. it feels like I'm walking away from all these friendships, too. I mean, some people in this tribe will probably love you forever, but I get a feeling you can't keep all of them if you don't take the whole package."

"You're probably right," Matt started, "It's not an easy choice, but I do think it's good to ask yourself these questions. It's the beginning of a real soul search, and something like an inventory, you know? You'll always end up better for taking those steps, whatever the outcome. That's something you must know completely."

Rio, like the community, was at an identity crisis. The fact that many were also in this position but chose instead to stick their heads in the sand, left her feeling isolated, just by asking questions. She had damn good reasons to love it up there, no question. There's more than fool's gold in flying your cheeks off your face, I know it. Out there you're on the edge, and like it or not, being on that edge is both the essence of human nature and the place where you learn the most about your own. But, with an edge, comes a line. Whether you want it or not. It was time for Rio to define hers, and, it seemed pretty obvious that for her, this was an either-or scenario.

"I mean, at some point, you have to look around and see what it's doing to us," Rio shared. "You've got to face what and who it's taking from us. And after everything, I've got to ask myself if I can keep doing it. Not just taking risk, personally, but staying quiet to the risks of others. I'm not sure I can handle losing anyone else. It's crushing."

Rio could no longer just suit-up and chase a simple high off a cliff; if she was going to continue, there were deeper ways she'd have to process her actions and those of her friends—including the consequences. Perhaps that's where the most tension came; getting involved in a lot of these lifestyles is a carefree endeavor for most, staying in them, requires more from us.

"Haven't you had your own set of close calls?" Rio asked Matt.

"Absolutely," he shared, "I can show you them on video if you like. I think it's a good tool. At first, a couple of years ago, it was hard to watch the footage of that stuff. It would put me in a dark place to watch and relive the near misses. But I find it's really important now."

"What about you?" she asked Brian.

"Yeah, I mean, I think we've all had moments closer to the edge than we want. I had to be honest with myself early, I knew sooner than others, I think, that tracking and wing-suiting wasn't going to be for me. I've been relatively cautious in my progression, but it's ultimately kept me in it long enough to have a grounding."

Continuing, Matt added his own inventory process. He guided Rio through the steps he takes in preparation for an extended period of B.A.S.E. jumping, and the process before each jump. He demonstrated a network of data points, and emotional points he uses to plot a map of where he is, completely, within himself, his risk capacity, and his concrete skill level.

"Don't get me wrong, Rio. I've been in some darkness, especially lately on this topic. But it's also imperative for me to understand the painful experiences as growth experiences. Regardless of what their outcome for me is in the sport. I'd sit for weeks with the curtains closed after bad shit happened, and eventually, I had to interpret this stuff in a healthier way. Before I could get back to the higher performance flights, I had to start simple. I had to ask the questions you're asking, and be patient for the answers. You're at a crossroads, I know it. I think it's good to own that. You've got to weigh everything and take an honest appraisal of its value to you. If it's something you think you need to put down, even if it's just for a while, it's important to be honest with yourself."

Matt, showing his own vulnerability, did his classic gentle grin and head tilt, the one he does just as he opens his arms for a hug. He gave Rio real assurance and a human touch. In that hug, you could see he didn't have all of his own answers yet, not in the least. But he did have some of those tools we mentioned. Matt is an exceptional model. When he's on, its style to the max—it's full throttle, pop rocks and persona, he knows how to rage—but when life requires more than mojo, he can square right up to it and connect with such empathy, with such humanity, he'll draw the tears right out of you.

It was an important conversation on many levels. Rio's pain about the sport and her place within it wasn't unique. In the coming years, slowly, the tribe as a whole would navigate what some might call a culture shift, at least a little. What Matt demonstrated was a need for greater inside awareness, a recipe he'd only recently found for the long play. For him, as he shared it, it was about looking inside, taking a full inventory, and always acting with honesty, because that is the only way to live without an internal conflict in operating systems.

Matt was still grieving, of course. He had been since July. He knew that grief doesn't get an answer, it simply must be endured, that it is an experience to be had. And he wasn't the only one in that room full of grief, for Ian, and for others who'd recently gone in.

"So how do you feel when you're out there now?' Rio asked Matt after their hug.

"Well," Matt exhaled, "It's not all figured out. But, I know if I use the same tools I can approach any jump safely. For me. Ian and I were brothers, still are. He's never leaving my side. But I also know that what we built together were skills to jump and fly well. And, I've still got those skills. What I don't have is him, but I think, in doing the things we love and going to the places he loved, we keep him with us. I don't know if that'll last forever, but I believe it honors him now. He'd want us to be free, whatever that means for us. Every time I take a jump, there's a part of me that embraces that freedom, but I'd be lying if I said there wasn't also a part of me that goes back to Kemaliye."

///

On the official record, Ian's accident begins and ends with a bridal entanglement. A functional piece of the average rig that connects the pilot chute to the main canopy, which when entangled, compromises the ability of the pilot chute to sufficiently pull out the mainsail at full force and full inflation. How he ended up in an unwanted tug of war between the pilot chute behind him and the bridle stuck in his feet is still unknown. According to everybody familiar with it, he did everything right.

A nanosecond after Ian jumped backward, in that classic curling arch, Matt looked away without concern, prepping, as it were, for his own dismount. He knew when Ian did a backflip, it usually meant a double. He knew the time it would take, he even knew the sound the wind would make while tracing Ian's orbit, swooshing, as if an audible hour-hand itself. Matt knew exactly when the second rotation was finished, without even looking. He was completely sure. Not paying mind, given there was no reason to, he continued, assured the cracking whip—that particular, popping flutter—of Ian's canopy was soon to strike pitch. But it didn't.

That there was no scream, no raging, vocal assault against the sudden fury of gravity and impartiality of time, kept Matt distracted. Ian did not bellow in complete abandon. He was, one can imagine, using his last seconds of life completely in the effort to sustain it. It's not clear from the surviving footage of his helmet camera, but every indication is that he was trying to correct course till the bitter end. There simply isn't the time, from 1,000 feet to floor—roughly 7 seconds—to beg, plea, or cry out against the workings of those forces. Time, and gravity. What got Matt's attention wasn't anything that Ian did or didn't say, it was that parachute. Matt had listened to tens of thousands of chutes rip open in his lifetime; never before had the absence of it meant so much.

"It was the most horrifying sound I've heard," he said. "A deafeningly quiet, struggling shutter of airwaves." The parachute itself, gasping in Cheyne-Stokes, was all the death rattle Matt needed for a cue.

Plunging out of the sunlight and into the shadow, Matt lost sight of Ian, only getting eyes on him by the discolored wake of whitewater where he made impact. From 1,000 feet up, the blurred sight below suggested something of a water entry. Because of that, when Matt pitched off into that same abyss to find his dear friend, he truly thought there might be, somehow, a chance for them to meet eyes just one more time. Ian had, after all, walked away from one accident already. Goddamn it if lightning didn't strike twice.

"Immediately, I looked at the nearest watercraft down the canyon, against the current, and I knew I had a better shot to get to him first." He continued. "I pulled relatively high for the sake of safety, but I navigated down there as fast as I could. Even when I got in the water, just next to his rig, I still thought there was a chance."

What Matt couldn't have seen while Ian was lost in the shadows, was that he actually impacted about 20 yards in from shore, against a jagged rockpile which had rag-dolled him into oblivion, and then into that Kara-Su. Matt landed on the dime, for the second time of the day, and immediately dove under. It took three attempts and his entire lung capacity, but he found Ian under those rushing waters. Finally, desperately, at the surface, everything went quiet and Matt understood that Ian's final flight had not been survivable.

"He was barely himself," Matt said of Ian's state, "it was gruesome. He was so torn apart, pieces of him barely attached by ligaments alone. I had no idea he had hit the rocks first until I brought him to surface and saw what was left of him."

As with any trauma situation, our instincts have networks in place to override the shock. Because of this, Matt will tell you that the deepest emotional components of that loss were quickly put away, deep inside. No time for emotion, he and Ian were still in a high-flow Kara-su river, weighed down by the B.A.S.E. rigs and hardly afloat. Matt reached up to the rescue boat in a flurry, taking on whatever strength was needed to board both Ian and his own body into safety. Overwhelmed by each ensuing step, from getting to shore, to transport to the clinic, to eventually getting Ian's remains in the hands of the State Department, Matt spent the next 48 hours in a mired, hollow bubble of disbelief and autonomic takeover.

Among the more surreal of those moments, just an hour later, Matt was given entry to the morgue with the help of a local jumper, for twenty minutes only, before local authorities took over for forensics. In what Matt described as the most haunting, bare-bones hospital, with flickering old green halogens and equipment staged from the dark ages, Matt disrobed Ian himself. He took care to preserve as much of Ian's equipment as possible, because the two of them had always agreed that as a part of those last wishes, their equipment should fly free long after they did. Twenty minutes may not sound like much. In that haunted, flickering light, that morbid quiet, it was enough, more than enough. Matt had to trace every inch of Ian's mangled, partially dismembered corpse, holding for the last time the physical, anatomical being that no longer housed the mighty spirit of his adopted brother.

///

Friday morning, weaving on foot through trails and slot corridors which glittered from the night's frost, we turned a bend and entered from shade to sunlight, just as Brian pointed over our shoulders at a spring of petroglyphs tattooed into the earth. Mankind, forever, has been right here in full expression. Just under and behind what we now call the Tombstone formation, which no doubt has a deeper, older name, we hiked with fervor. Having just driven in alongside the oil-smooth Colorado River at sunrise, life was aglow. After Matt's talk last night, aware of his inner state, only one action could follow. Now was the time to witness human flight.

Trudging the final slopes above Pritchett Canyon, along the exposed shoulders of mammoth sandstone fortresses, we made summit just as daylight began feeding into the canyon. The mixture of breaking dawn against the dark, shadowy contrasts of the canyons, framed by the iridescent blue reflections of the snow patches above them, was all-time. Highlight-reel glory. Matt, Brian, and a young spring chicken named Chris, who'd just taken his first jump off the Tombstone the day before, took the time they needed to prepare themselves and gauge the wind after ascending the final calf burner—a natural staircase of sedimentary rock—to the exit point.

Where the day before, with Johnny, there was a tension about what I might witness, it surprised me to find those elements had all been dissolved. I had known Matt long before his first jump, but I'd still not seen it, not in person. Up there something was right, purposeful. To finally see all sides of a guy I'd walked through so much of life with seemed a great honor. Just as our friendship had been forged stronger when he'd hosted me on the couch, riding out those waves of withdrawal to come out the other end, I knew we'd be the better for this experience as well.

To some degree, a climb, a B.A.S.E. jump, anything we do outside is a statement we are making about what we value in life. Sometimes, though, those statements are just a little more concentrated. This was one of them. I'd say every jump Matt took after watching Ian go in was one of them. Just before the boys did their final gear checks, we spent another five minutes, remembering Ian and the flights he'd had in his illustrious chapters around Moab. We laughed, ached, and smiled through it, knowing he was as close as the Colorado, running to eternity just beneath our perch.

According to Matt, "With nothing left to do but shadowbox the pull sequence and swallow that last lump in your throat if you've got it, up there you take the time you need to wait patiently, but you don't wait too long. You've got to take the moment, you've got to consider it all, and you've got to engage."

As a bystander, bearing witness to such emotional, profound statements in human behavior, I can tell you that up there, you begin to clue in on the magic. Talk is cheap in moments of truth, just as armchair living and conjecture are also. Up there you realize quickly that whatever you felt about it, about B.A.S.E. jumping, is irrelevant. It is a supremely emotional experience to watch mankind willingly disobey the laws of nature, and even if you wouldn't do it yourself, there's a notion that strikes you, that this may verge upon excellence after all.

Brian first. Completely within himself, comfortable and measured, he strode with a calculated pace, almost verbalizing the final one, two, three, and four steps to the brink. He charted off the deck with a proud, confident posture and caught a rising thermal. He rode steady for a second to establish freefall, and then by muscle memory operation, reached back to the pull-cord. One pregnant pause—the time between him ripping the pin open and the chute unfurling—and then it was that thunderous roar echoing across the canyons. The gallery of newly arrived jumpers, all parked and packing chutes below, erupted in a raucous affirmation while Brain navigated steadily to the landing zone.

Chris next, the young friend they'd just met down below; relatively new to the sport but seemingly with all his gears in place. Stepping up from their exit point to a higher platform, I took in a better view while Chris approached the exit with a cool, rhythmic momentum, almost skipping with a kangaroo's undulation. Striding gracefully to the very edge, Chris sprung out in one last full-body kip. No surprises, no antics, just smooth sailing until the chute ripped open, again, in a cacophonous roar that you felt more than you heard.

And finally, Matt. After Chris cleared the landing Matt joined me up on the highest summit shelf, above the exit point the others had taken. Looking at him, backlit, struck by beams of morning light, glowing with his neon yellow jacket and a shit-grin I hadn't seen since the rearview mirror, I knew he was ready. Fixated on his approach, I was fascinated to see how his energy met the moment, under what seemed like a new light. I had known the man for ages, and for just a second, in a pulse of neural fluttering, that emotion swelled in my heart and got the better of me. He's the guy I've seen through thick and thin, entangled together on big-wall missions, on hundreds of slacklines, out in the surf, and on land, waxing large on life. But I had never seen him like that. That was something of his deeper energy. Perhaps a deeper fragility, too. I saw at once a human being fully alight and a person whose safety I cared the world for. I saw a man, arguably at his best.

Taken out of my attachment to Matt as he fit in my box, in my narrative, I saw him gather a baseline set of steps, purposefully moving in only one direction. Within meters, and at full sprint, Matt's steps echoed out the hollow center of the sandstone beneath him, vibrating into the balls of my feet as he rushed past me with his final stride. Exit, full sequence, Matt jumped with his entire being. That bastard leapt like he was going for the Olympic record, gaining at least a few feet in vertical, and then, just at the apex—at that zero point neither rising nor falling —the morning sun grabbed him, fully wrapped, in a rapturous light shining all the way to the snow-capped mountains on the horizon. At a million frames per second, Matt stamped a slideshow on my highlight reel, falling at last into flight like a comet blasting for earth. He pulled exactly right, unfurling the chute with a righteous crank on the cord, and as quickly as he'd disobeyed the earth, he'd found his way safely back to it. The pride I felt right then and there, to simply be a living creature with waking consciousness, upon this earth where both petroglyphs and modern man express the same great fascination, to the very power and wildness of life, was indescribable.

///

Hours later, in the Love Bus, seated recliner style while Brian and Matt handled the steering and music selection, there was overwhelming ease. After the Tombstone we'd gone back to Brian's for a lunch hour, mostly hearing tales from Brian about what a grounded life in Moab actually looks like. How on any given day he'll explore one new canyon after another, never on repeat for something like two years now. The only redundancies: his favorite climbs, jumps, sunsets, and the once-a-year hike deep into desert land to an ancient meditation outcrop of petroglyphs during the summer solstice.

As we pulled off Highway 128, along the dust patches that lead to the Fischer Towers, Matt suddenly looked back through the rearview. This time it was him in the driver seat, as he did his trademark "Uhmmm!" It's an affirmation of his, wherein he honey-smacks his lips while simultaneously taking his pointer finger out from an otherwise closed fist, which he scoops, bottom to top, in a J-shaped arch just like the damned Nike swoosh.

"Roman," he laughed in my direction, "this is the shit!"

I won't forget it, no way. Just like so, under a carefree sky, against all apparent stress of life, a gang of boys just freewheelin' out to climb. It was an easy choice as well. Brian had been in his own trials for the past month—coming home from a long trip in the Himalayas where he was a part of a humanitarian project, he learned his partner wanted to explore her own freedoms outside of their relationship. In what he might later call something of a codependency, coming out of that separation took him into rare darkness. Brian hadn't climbed in months, not since Spring, and any time he attempted he just couldn't find the will. Matt, of course, had mostly been jumping for a few years now, and with all the madness, all the despair ensuing after Ian's loss, he had barely been outside since the Lebowski-inspired Flanders Tour, in September. If you asked him the last time he roped up, even for a casual multi-pitch, he'd have been hard-pressed to recall. There was always, only, going to be one right way to spend that afternoon. It had to be something classic, something magical, something purely for the human spirit. For us, that day, it was Ancient Art, an all-time, highlight route on the Fischer Towers.

For Matt and I, it was our first venture out there, period. So when Matt turned south on that dust-track, saw the Fischer Towers for the first time, and looked back at me with that righteous grin, I was right there with him. After the morning B.A.S.E. jump, and all the landscapes we'd traversed, mentally, and physically in the past few months, that setting was an act of God.

Hiking in, Brian spoke about his relationship loss, I spoke on rock-bottom and themes of a recovered life, and Matt spoke about Ian.

Somehow, they all connected, easily, one footstep after another until we reached the base, where, to our surprise, Matt offered first lead. Halfway up, in disbelief of the mud conglomerate holding an entire monolith together, Matt shouted, "Jesus, it's like a lazy pour of concrete and a half-ass mixing job. How incredible!"

"That there is geologic wonder stone, buddy." I replied, "Roper and Steck said it's due to the rain coming off the La Sal's."

"Whatever it is, it's both terrifying and beautiful." Matt laughed while taking off a chunk of loose stone.

Matt continued up the entire pitch in geologic fascination until he made anchor, where Brian followed first, and I tagged on last. I led up the second pitch, right to the shoulder of the famous, mushroom tipped tower, and the boys quickly followed. There, protected from a gale of afternoon winds, we sheltered among the stone and spoke on those larger pieces in life, on all that movement under our feet.

"You know," Brian started, "I may not have a grip on detachment just yet—if that's something you even hold. When life moves big and all at once, I don't know about you, but for me, that's all pain. But that's exactly why I keep coming back to this desert, to these towers even. There's an understanding up here, a force, and I swear it's blocked by something in the atmosphere, the elevation, who knows, man. Whatever it is, things click up here, in ways I'll never fully understand and often don't at ground level."

Matt looked over at him, as if to place a bookmarker on the page so he could read it again, and snapped a portrait shot, up-close, with all the snow-capped glory behind him.

"Damn right, Brian." He smiled. "Man, am I glad to be here with you guys. No better way to settle in for the next chapter, that's for sure."

And Matt was right. It was as good as it gets. I got on board first, but we each took turns walking the final plank to the summit ledge— a meager foot-and-a-half wide floorboard cut on both sides by a 400-foot sheer panel break. Ancient Art is good like that, it requires something from you, it moves you in a way that other formations don't, short as it may be. Up there on the summit block, that toffee-stained lava lamp frozen in a funk dance, things happen to you. The exposure, all 360 degrees of it, that tiny perch you stand on—barely big enough to balance both heels and the balls of both feet on—really is something. It's a tiny ledge, but it's got room for all your needs. All that emotional stuff, those shifting plates, the baggage. The weight you and I and all of us have. The expectations, the things you have or have not done which you somehow always measure yourself against, all that you carry but isn't packed in your rucksack. There is room. It's old, sure, a bit hollow and unnerving, and you can hear it moan when you give weight to it. It requires something on the order of faith, even, but I suppose the fantastic always has. Up there, you, and only you, take one long look around; you gaze the sky, hoping to zoom past the blue into the outer reaches. You scan the kaleidoscope of earth, the layers of time folded into amber, charcoal, and burgundy canyons, arches, and cliff bands. You take that one hallowed breath, and you get whatever it is that is meant for you to have.

B.A.S.E. jumping or climbing rocks, they aren't so different, depending on how they're practiced. Might even have the same targets. A community for starters, and contact with the greater forces. Once you make a habit of stepping into that next dimension, whatever it may be for you, you're branded. You can no more go back to something behind you, you can no more operate as it was, as you can turn the earth suddenly clockwise. At least not for long. Not without things calling you back. It doesn't have to be extreme, or even much on an edge, it just needs to be authentic. That's what all this getting outside business was about in the first place, having moments of truth, in the great wide ocean of life. Because what these guys—Brian and Matt, Johnny even—are after, isn't a feeling, it's the source. It's about exploration, not about arrival. Whether it be B.A.S.E. jumping, climbing, or highlining, whatever the permutation, what it comes back to is the movement.

I could see it in Brian, unsure how to handle new horizons he hadn't even asked for, seemingly alone. He stood up there on that summit, but he was on a precipice of life itself. A position which he'd practiced, because of B.A.S.E.. He knew what it meant to fly when there was longer earth beneath your feet. He knew that the movement of life comes whether we ask for it or not. It does not care what we had or have in mind for ourselves, or for others we care for. It moves, regardless. Brian didn't know what was next, and he didn't much like having to go at it solo, but up there he got both the detachment and the clarity he'd spoken about.

And I could see it in Matt, behind that caricature of cool, the shit-grin and that giant smile, he was moving. He had no choice. That's the thing about life, it forces us. It weighs anchor without permission, and usually away from things which, for better or worse, we are fully attached to. But just as it can be devastating, it can be giving. The timeline for such disasters to turn into blessings is different for everybody and is not guaranteed, but the possibility is always there.

Nobody envied the loss Matt experienced with Ian's passing, but it was obvious, to me, that he was now on a track that not even he could comprehend. The fullness of it, like the stars in that damned twilight, was just beginning to reveal itself. Matt stood on the tiny, tip-top of that tower in complete abandon. With total disregard to the eons of genetic programming that birthed in us a check on our equilibrium, he lifted his hands and his head completely upwards and backward into that great sky, and where many would have fallen, was held up in a perfect balance—a weightless suspension.

It was a balance he was familiar with, just as he had found on that last flight with Ian, where it all came clean. With that same great force that got him through the heart-breaking, final pack job, where he poured Ian's ashes into the fold of the main canopy and hiked to the top of that sacred cliff, surrounded by endless peaks painted in the everlasting spectrum of sunset; Matt jumped. He dove, as those birds of prey, screaming into that void, blasting, celebrating, mourning—human speed of sound—until he was ready. With Ian, for the last time, Matt pulled chute, immediately freeing all the million and one pieces of him to scatter with those light rays into the horizon. And right then, held up in that perfect suspension, in the glide of life—with no separation between himself, Ian, and that endless twilight, Matt understood both the necessity and the illusion of it all. There is ultimately no separation, only connection. But for us to live, things must move; to grow, some bonds must be broken.

On top of that mud-cast, frail old tower out in there in far reaches of the ancient lands, Matt found that truth once again, a reminder, that even without Ian, without a plan, even in all the grief, there was simply no place he could go in this universe where he would not just the same be held up, cradled, and sustained in his flight. And that is all we ever wanted. All of us. Whether on our own volition or by the force of shifting plates beneath our feet—no matter how hard, fast, safe, or abandoned we fly in life, what we really want, what we're really after isn't just the ride, it's not only where we are going, it is the experience of being held up exactly in our moment of greatest exposure. It's being under the canopy. It's coming back.

///
THE GREATER FOOL

Brad Gobright is pure of heart. So pure in fact, that he may never have faced a dilemma in all his life. That's not exactly serving him well right now, as he's stuck in a pickle of his own making, at the top of the first pitch of Southern California's gem climb, "The Vampire." He's never taken a whipper like he's about to, and Lord knows I've never caught one. But forget about what the Lord knows for a moment and focus on what Brad does. With his last piece of protection 15-feet beneath him and an impossible move above him, he knows there are those who take caution, and there are those who take whippers, and by no choice of his own he's compelled toward the latter, pre-programmed to it even. Knowing full well that I've got no clue what a "soft-catch" is or how to feed it out, he's up high looking like a hot mess.

"Okay, okay! Fuck!" he shouts above the clanking sound of gear rattling from his quivering leg.

Down below, I'm nearly out of sight at the belay. Perched above a few hundred feet worth of slab, making a quick sling around a feeble tree as an anchor while Brad flushes out his options. My fear, no doubt, is that once he takes that whip, his house-of-cards excuse for protection will zip out cleaner than a surgeon's scalpel on white flesh and send us both on a stone-skipping path toward the Bone-collector. He's got the reputation for it after all, and even though we've only climbed a few times I've already seen plenty of his gear go south.

"Okay. On the count of three! Three, Two, One!" Brad shouted.

I clinched the brakes and gnashed half the enamel off my teeth, but nothing happened. Brad just couldn't let go.

"Fuck," he stammered. "Fuck me."

Sweat beaded from his white brow under an uncaring California sun. Uncaring rock, and uncaring world it seemed, especially when measured face to face with the grandeur of his dreams. He was just a kid, after all, not far out of high school even.

By this time, the local hardmen who were on neighboring routes had worked up into a frenzy, laughing and heckling at the poor bastard. Aware of the bitter circumstance, I don't know whether it was peer-pressure or fatigue which led to Brad finally taking the ride. But, come to think of it, he's never had a need to be accepted by others. At least not primarily. And what's important in this case isn't what made him take the ride, it's that he took it. Because most don't.

On the next attempt, Brad started at three, then counted two, and as if to surprise himself, he never made it to the one. All I heard was the long, upward "u" following the hard "t" and then he was off. Brad flew through the sky and crashed into the wall with a hard thud, provided by my helpless belay. And that was it. According to him, it was his first real whipper. This would turn out to be just one of many repeating moments in his now infamous ride on this orbit. Brad Gobright, by all measures the fool. But for just a moment in flight, between heaven and earth, wrapped up in a gorgeous flicker of light that most in their short time on this blue spinner simply will not know, he might have been the ideal man.

An honest conclusion I wasn't ready to reach about him.

I wanted a double-take on the revelation, but real moments in life are only lived once; they violently stir us awake, and then quickly pass. Enough time has passed between then and now to realize that in a lot of ways, it's the brevity of the highlight reel we spin that makes it so bright. Our fortune is that these moments do burn, deep, like a sunspot into countless frames after the fact. You see it even when you aren't trying to. That was back in 2007.

///

Brad was my first climbing partner. As a person, he astounded me. His capacity was so specific to just one dimension, to climbing alone, that it moved me. Not in the way one is moved by a demonstration of love or sacrifice from one human to another, not in the way one wants to emulate on merit of its grace, nor in the way in which we come to fashion heroes and heroines—it was much less traditional, and in that sense, more profound. Brad lives almost exclusively on the surface. His walking narrative, his energy, is and was simply of the now. One suspects with his type there is not so much an arc of character—or if there were, that he wouldn't concern himself with his place on it—as there is simply character. Didn't matter what came before or what lay ahead. It is not a knock to that character but an appreciation of it, to note that with Brad there is a complete lack of guile, of architecture, design, or even noticeable levels of depth in his quieter moments of reflection, and it is exactly that simple purity of heart and his inability to engage in anything but the present moment, which is his greatest asset.

He spent more nights in Yosemite hiding from rangers, bivying alone under scrummy boulders, hitching rides, and shivering without fire, than most of us ever did. For years, he'd eat anything he could, from the left-over plates of the tourists he so loathed at the Yosemite Village cafeteria to campfire-cooked roadkill in the Creek. He'd stomach expiration dates for calories, steal any gear necessary, work any bum job, and take any ride to get wherever it was that he needed to go. He'd do anything. He had that contagious swagger of someone with nothing to lose, whether he realized it or not, and it both got him into and out of every cluster he could fuck.

Shit, I even remember getting pulled over by a Valley Ranger with Brad in the back of the open cab of my old pick-up truck, in 2008, when he'd first put his five articles of clothing in the car with his climbing gear and "moved" to the Valley. There was already three of us in a two-seatbelt cockpit upfront, but Brad didn't care, he jumped in the back and gophered under some gear, "Hey, throw that crash-pad on top of me, would you? That'll be perfect."

Down the road a few miles later, pulled over without a working brake-light, when the Ranger peeled back the onion layer and Brad was right there like a deer in his flashlights, the Ranger was so shit-scared by it he actually dropped his flashlight.

"Jesus Christ," he sputtered while picking up the Mag-Lite, "Do I know you, son?"

"Maybe, uhm, officer. I work at the Ahwahnee."

"I need you to exit the vehicle now, young man."

More pissed about Brad's surprise appearance than our brake light and overstocked cabin—and naïve to our open containers—the Ranger shooed us off on down the road but kept Brad hostage. All we heard on our way out were the beginnings of his plea deal.

"Hey sir, could you not tell my boss about this? Please? She thinks I'm sick today and if I get busted AND I lose my job, that's gonna kill my climbing."

A confounding riddle, completely untouchable by the fabric of reality.

Society never had a chance with Brad, and neither did the Ranger. It couldn't make him want to be someone or something else any more than the Ranger could. You couldn't punish it out of him any more than you could sell him on an alternative. Brad was exactly himself, and the only person seemingly not concerned about that was him. No dilemma, just Brad. He simply couldn't fathom any other way to live.

///

Brad climbed while he still had baby teeth. If that wasn't enough to set his life course, he fell into it just after the free-climbing revolution of the early nineties. He didn't grow up with a smartphone or a streaming service, but that didn't matter. Content was out there, and whether it was Dano's locks or Lynn's cutoff jean-shorts and purple cotton top, when he saw human beings way up on that stone with their hair flying in ballads of splendor, he knew it, immediately. He was only ever going to go in one direction.

He once told me that as a kid he used to stay up in his room watching climbing movies, and that carried over into adulthood. The first night he and I stayed illegally in Camp 4, on our first trip to the Valley, while sleeping open-bivy on the floor with a cardboard buffer cause a Thermarest was too high a price, Brad played a Masters of Stone DVD on his handheld while other kids smoked pot around a fire and chugged down a good Valley blackout.

A month later, on our way home from the Needles, after just spending a full weekend on the yellow spires, he watched the entire series while riding co-pilot in the pick-up. He literally couldn't get enough. At that point, society couldn't sell or give Brad anything, but if it was in a climbing film that he'd seen, you can bet your ass he'd beg, borrow, cheat or steal for it. And he did.

For most of us, those first few seasons of dirt-bagging offer an inspiration, a drunken freedom for transient souls, you might say. But, generally speaking, if you do it for long enough, there's often another cost involved. At some point, each one of us meets a deeper calling out there. Somewhere, we all gotta answer to something. And it's not a question that society asks of us, it's something we do. When it all comes clean and the ropes are pulled from the chains, will all the sunsets from all the summits ever actually be enough? And if not, what, in the end, will be the cost? What of all the relationships we've left in our wake as we've been chasing shadows?

For many, the greatest climber is the one who rides the ultimate line—not that of danger and absolutes—but that of a holistic life. He or she whose balance is as much in life altogether as it is weighted upon the smallest smear of the smallest crystal. That is the finest line, one which most of us who venture outside only ride on the lop-side or in a state of perpetual conflict. But where others sink, Brad soars. Climbing, the real thing, out there on the big stuff, has always been his fullest expression. With a featherweight conscience impervious to even the most compelling gravitas, he soars. That he has a program which runs without dilemma is his gift, for sure. It has enabled him to go so big and so far without the need or the compulsion to even once look back. And yet still, beyond the gift, how he runs the operations, what he's done from the close of that gas-cap in 2008, until now, that will always be his art.

///

In 2008, five of us including Brad rigged our first high-line above the Rostrum, spanning 70 feet in length and fluttering 1,000 feet above the valley floor. It was gangbusters. Four of us spent the whole of a perfect Fall day trying to walk that thing, romanced by the notion of expanding ourselves in the process. But not Brad, he didn't try it once. Not out of fear, but because it wasn't even in his register. He was there to climb, as always. Climb. Execute. Repeat. Ad Infinitum. It's the only function that runs in his programming. Like any other drive it doesn't even require a qualifier, it's just a core drive. It operates on condition of consciousness.

Having spread the word on our highline earlier in the day, our new acquaintances, Mason, Nico, and a strapping Belgian-Irishman named Sean, arrived. These guys were the type who took on everything with an air of impeccability. They countered Brad in the fullest. Their entire style lay on an impossible line where an ungodly ethic, and the level of suffering it prescribed, was met with premiere abilities and a carefree attitude. Highlights of their climbing achievements included first-ascents of big-wall free-climbs, including a route on To-tok-ah-noo-lah (El Capitan), all established completely ground-up. To the average among us, theirs was an impossible bar.

Highlights of Brad's accomplishments, to that point, had been nearly dying on a rope-solo top-rope on the Cookie Cliff, killing a squirrel in a bloody Tarantino stand-off while cleaning rooms in the Ahwahnee Hotel, and being known locally in Southern California as having been 'The Guy' to use an actual construction ladder to aid in the ascent of Intersection Rock's Left Ski Track, in Joshua Tree National Park. If Sean and Nico had taken wind in their sails from Royal Robbins, Brad had surely blown down from a Harding howl.

In the afternoon, while Sean was walking the high-line and playing his mountain flute, we cracked beers and took it all in, because, conditionally, you couldn't have asked for anything more. Unless you were Brad. After asking each of us, and even a party of Germans who'd just topped out via the standard finish to climb with him, Brad set up his rope for a rappel into the final pitch, alone. Just before yanking the Gri-Gri brake release, he looked up to Sean in a last effort.

"Hey man, any chance you want to rap in here with me and top-rope the Alien-finish? It's supposed to be classic!"

I swear the gust of wind that had been blowing steady for hours suddenly came to a pause. One single strand of Sean's beaten hair lifted in the last of the wind with a spiraled flutter, while Brad, young as he'd ever be and pure of heart, waited out the pregnant pause.

"Haha," Sean started, with his marbled Irish accent, "No chance, my friend. I bet it's a great pitch, indeed." Smiling through his warlord's beard, he finished, "But, that shit's just not in my ethics, man."

The four of us had to double-take. Jaws dropped down to the floor.

Not. In. My. Ethics. Are you kidding?

He'd pulled it off better than Jesus. We didn't know whether to laugh or cry. Surely, Brad looked the fool for even asking such heresy. At the same time, it was obvious that Sean hadn't intended to scorn the poor kid either; there wasn't a bad fiber in him for that kind of shit.

It was just so profound, so clear. Sean had identified an ethic and made an informed choice to follow it. And not only to follow it, but to do it joyfully. Forget climbing for a moment, in life at large, we'd never seen anything like it. Sean's ethic emphasized how you got somewhere, not where you were going to end up.

Digesting it, Brad turned to a dumbfounded gaze. It was as if someone had asked him if he wanted to go to college or if he had a life plan. Deep shit for him, maybe too deep. But, with Brad what is incredible is his ability, his unwitting ability, to rise back to the surface. There's nearly no amount of gravity in a situation that can override his operations in the present.

He doesn't have a lot of the same questions as the average among us, and if he does on occasion, for the most part, he doesn't need answers on one condition before he can proceed to the next. In a world where we often feel like something is not right if we don't understand it, if it's not going our way, or if we don't' feel quite right or ready for the situation; Brad is a refreshing spring of water. Always at the source, and the destination. Now. Here. Always. In action.

He went ahead and rope-soloed the Alien anyway.

If you don't have to ask why your programming runs, you also don't have to navigate the how of it. You don't have to navigate the ethics.

Brad was always honest in reporting how and by what means he did something, but it was never really as important to him as the fact that he was doing. Doing was being.

There's a lot that seemed to fly over Brad's head, and it's easy to want to write him off in some ignoramus script. But pay heed. On land, the common point of view is that he's not doing much good for society, but you put him on the rocks and it's magic. The fucker will glide across planes and depths of the human experience that most will surely sink in. Make no mistake, his lights are on, perhaps on a different circuit; but the longer you spend with Brad the more you sense that it is unwise to write off what you do not understand.

Here was Sean, the valiant, Sean the heroic. And then Brad, the anomaly. He didn't serve an ethic, he just was, and that level of being is impenetrable. You almost call it foolish until you see just how it has served him over the years.

Since then Brad has done all of it. Nearly. Speed record on El Cap. Big-wall Free Climbing. First-ascents. Hard climbs in almost every discipline of the sport. Free soloist of a generation. Including more than a handful of times rope-less on the Rostrum and an uncountable number of laps on the Naked Edge, in Eldorado Canyon. Back in 2008, that same group of the four of us voted him off an El-cap team, because his climbing had gotten so frenetic and dangerous. As fortune would have it, we didn't summit. He's now climbed it more than 50 times.

Ian and I had a good laugh about it when we considered that not only did we not summit on that go, we suffered. We dropped climbing shoes off the Ear pitch, a tag line off a backpack, a sleeping bag off the Alcove, and got pissed on by the Aussies under the Monster Offwidth, and that was all just on day three. When Brad did climb El Cap for the first time, it was in a single day. I can remember Ian's characteristic laugh, the maniacal kind, jolting till his ribs hurt when we considered the irony. Ian later left us in his own accident a few years ago, B.A.S.E. jumping in the remote parts of Turkey with a bridle entanglement. There are fewer of us left these days, but there's also a comfort in knowing we can spin that reel anytime and see the mark of their sunspots.

///

Fast forward a handful of years and a lifetime of memorable ascents later, and Brad is home in Southern California for the summer to earn a few extra bucks while the weather is hot. I catch up with him at the local climbing gym, where on this day—as opposed to ten years ago when he'd be heckled by his peers—the entire place goes quiet when he climbs. There's even a kid who asks for his autograph when I lower him off his first climb. He can't be more than 10 years-old and is as shy as you could possibly imagine. Timid on the ask, his father nudges him to say a few words, but the youngster rolls his shoulder into an inflated ball and hides under his dad's wing. Having worked with kids at the gym for years, Brad eases the anxiety with a brief hug and poses for a photo. It's a brave new world. Brad Gobright is the stuff of dreams.

A moment later, after he wrestled with a harder climb, I ask, "You ever think about route-setting yourself, while you are home?"

"No way, dude," Brad replies. "I'd be absolutely terrible at it. For a fact. I'm definitely more in my element with kids, goofing around."

Which is true. Compared to my experience with other high-level athletes across the disciplines, Brad has a really-low register for his own biomechanics. Keeping track of his movement patterns, let alone constructing them for others, is admittedly out of his league.

For all the things he's done, especially in the realm of soloing, where mistakes wager in life sentences, he's not exactly tuned in. He has as hard of a time describing the experiences of his body as much as

Lucas Roman

experiences of his mind. If you ask him about the tension in his body while navigating a crux, he can tell you what he did with each limb from points A through C, but he can't necessarily tell you how. The experience gets away from him. Which isn't to say he doesn't have it. I'm sure that he does. In fact, when he gets to a crux, you see it. When he isn't getting as much back from a rest as he'd like, you see him move into a new position. He does make adjustments; he makes mental connections in the moment to physical positions and takes the appropriate actions. It's just that he doesn't necessarily catalog them. The nature of his programming is to run the functions, not to run analytics.

///

When Brad and I last spent time in Squamish, he'd just recovered from the first of his career detours, a broken back. He'd come by for dinner, and we discussed his thoughts on soloing after his injury.

"I had a freak-out the other day, and I'm really not sure what caused it," he began. "I was completely fine on the route, but I dunno what happened. I've never had any feelings like that, you know, real nerves."

He later described it as a response to the exposure. Even though he was fit for the climb, just the idea of another backbreaker and the recovery process, caused his body to shut down. Still, as he reflected, it wasn't as much a fear of dying, but a reaction to the sudden exposure. A flashback. A surprising reminder that he was a little human, after all.

Now that it's been a few years, and we were back on the topic at the climbing gym, I asked him if he's had any similar experiences since then. Because, I think most people are curious about the process of fear management, altogether.

"No way," he quickly responded.

"What about fear in general? How often do you feel afraid up there when you climb? Not afraid to fail cause' you aren't sending, but afraid, like actually scared to be just where you are?" I asked.

"Not at all," he offered.

"Never while soloing?"

"I don't think so," he shrugged.

Brad is honest, so it was obvious he wasn't saying this to sound bold. In fact, if you asked him, he's not that bold at all. His core drive is to climb, so in his mind, he's always on the right side of the risk and reward curve. Others might hesitate to do something in the sport because it could mean losing family, or functionality in some other part of life deemed more valuable. But for Brad, climbing is the function, and he doesn't want to do anything that would risk not being able to continue doing it. Even at what appears to us as his most extreme.

"Yeah, I just never really get gripped up there. Never have when soloing. I mean, I've been nervous and had some anxiety before doing something, but once I'm off and moving, I don't think it's fear I feel. That would be bad," he concludes.

He must have some internal bearing, though, like the rest of us do. That feeling that talks us off certain climbs and away from certain risks. We've all got climbs we haven't done, for reasons which are usually more a mystery to us than they are apparent. Times when it just didn't feel right.

"What about last year?" I ask, "What about that day when you bailed on the Half Dome solo?"

He'd planned an all-means solo, free-climbing most of it but also clipping bolts at a few crux points and common pendulums.

"Oh, that day," Brad's cheeks putter with his exhale. "That day, I don't know."

He struggles for a moment, going deep to explain, then comes right back to the surface. "I don't really know what happened that day, but I'll tell you what. It's a really good thing I didn't go solo it 'cause I would've had to call some friends for a rescue. You know, after that big rockfall a few years ago, some guys went up there and put up a new bolt ladder, but I guess those things are sketch, at best," he says with a look of fright. "I mean, it's only been a couple of years and rumor has it those bolts are already sticking out a quarter-inch and ready to pop. No way I would've trusted my life to one of those things!" Brad pauses, "So yeah, it would've been a pretty epic bail."

"Come on Brad," I press further. "You're telling me that was it? I've got tons of climbs I haven't done, and we both know guys who have them, too. Stuff that just didn't feel right for one reason or another. Stuff where you wanted to do it, you really did. But when you woke up that morning or when you hiked into it you just had a deeper feeling that took you away from it. You don't think you had something like that happen that day? You don't think you had something deeper protecting you from going into that situation?"

Brad paused for a moment and finally conceded. "I guess you're right. I did have a really good Spring and I wanted to end it with a bang last year. But every time I was going to do it, something just wasn't right. I'm not sure what that was, exactly, but I can see what you are saying. It could've been a deeper voice."

Maybe that's as good as he needs it to be. And I shouldn't insist otherwise. Most climbers I've known who have that deeper voice, or compass, really make it a priority to look for it before each climb. Most of us want to find that voice and get practiced in how to hear it as often as possible. Brad, to no surprise, might just feel that it's there when it needs to be, and beyond that, he doesn't need to figure it out—beyond that, nothing needs explanation. And that is his remarkable Zen.

He is aware of danger all the same. Not too long ago, he repeated Indian Creek's "Carbondale Short Bus"—first climbed free by Hayden Kennedy—with the use of pre-placed gear on the critical opening sequence. A perfect example of why, to him, he's not that bold, nor does he take risks that would disable him from that core drive to climb free.

He'll free solo terrain that would make most of us quiver, but on the same coin, he'll insist to pre-place gear if a ground-fall looks possible.

A moment later, as we look over to the bouldering area, Brad notes the position of a crash-pad and shakes his head with worry. "Dude, that pad-placement, that's super-dangerous. Total ankle breaker." It's a funny outlook considering his total sense-of-cool after having just discussed nearly a decade of soloing in the death zone.

A lot of what he's done in climbing has that feel of paradox. When you ask him about speed climbing El Cap, he'll just tell you that it sprung from his first experience on it. Recall the first time he ever climbed it, it was in a day; and it wasn't because he read Largo's article about the 1974 excursion with Bridwell and Westbay, and felt inspired, but because he hates hauling systems and haul bags. Admittedly, he's terrible at rigging. And for Brad, any big-wall which takes days, is, to him, much harder than a climb which takes only one. That simple. It's not the history books he's after when it all comes clean, it's simply climbing.

///

For some, the greatest experiences found in climbing come down to partnerships; to who you are with regardless of what you are doing. The powerful moments of exposure on physical and emotional heights can bring out an expanded capacity to work for a greater good, for something more corporate, above the individual.

Admittedly, Brad's never been great with relationships, and that's not a fault, it just is. Lately, though, he's moved the needle, a little. In his hardest ascents and fastest climbs, near his limitations, he's understood that he needs others. It's not a strong suit, yet, but it's certainly in process.

"What about friendships, mate?" I propose. "Any blooming friendships up there on the wall? People who you just want to experience any climb with, no matter the grade. Any relationships that are made richer simply by sharing the rope?"

Brad ruffles his cheeks with an exhale while stalling. "I guess so. But I mean, there's always an objective, too. So maybe the climbing is always coming first." Then just a moment later, "I guess I've got some friendships that are cool, though."

"So, when you talk about moving back to Boulder next summer, is that cause there are people you want to see? Friends you miss and want to get closer to?" I question.

After another pause, he comes clean and states, "Not really. I think I'd just want to go back for the summer to climb stuff."

It's understandable. I don't think he's in tension about it, but I think he's also learning that there's a part of the human experience that he can access, a level of interaction with others that isn't based on doing things together as much as just being with each other. Growing up, the lack of articulation skills made it hard to navigate social endeavors, and, for all his strength as a kid in the climbing gym, he never really came into an outfit. He didn't gel on a youth team, and he wasn't all too interested in competitions, sport-climbing, or bouldering as an end unto itself either. You wouldn't call it hazing, but in a lot of ways the flimsy swings and bad footwork that got him up climbs in the early days made him more jester than knight. People laughed at him, but they loved him too.

"Fair enough," I continue. "And what about romance? Do find yourself longing for anything more committed these days?"

"Not really. I don't think it's a good time for something like that, because I'm just way too into climbing. I think I learned that from the last relationship." He briefly struggles to find his words and continues, "She wanted to plug into society and still climb and stuff, you know, but her focus was more wholesome than mine. I think we both realized it wasn't going to be a good thing for us to do long term. The good is news is we're still friends and everything."

Brad might not need intimacy as we've just discussed it, and if he's honest he probably doesn't get how the whole thing is supposed to work. Few do. But, what he does get, suddenly, is an inspired look on his face, which leads him to open up further. He's got a sinister grin and the look of a kid about to share his favorite secret on the hush.

"I'll tell you what. I did briefly get on that Tinder thing lately. And man, that's a weird way to meet people if you ask me. Girls these days are pretty forward out there." He smirks like he's living in a flickered memory on repeat, then continues, "Wanna know something even weirder? In Yosemite Valley, right now, a lot of people are using it and it's kinda wild. Climbers and tourists."

"Wait a minute, Brad, you're telling me that on any given day during the high-season in the Valley, when thousands of tourists are in bumper to bumper traffic, that a whole flock of them are on Tinder, parking at the nearest spot off the road and just running into the meadows or the forest for a fucking shag?"

"Bro," he laughs out loud, "You can't even imagine the stuff I've seen out there lately. It's everywhere!"

Let's not forget we began this discussion looking for intimacy and connection, and now we're buck-naked in Yosemite having unprotected sex. But, that's Brad. Right on the surface, exactly where he's best designed.

///

Most have a hard time digesting Brad's simplicity in the face of his experience. For all his efforts, especially in soloing, where his level of execution must be finer than a Michelin-star kitchen, popular belief is that he must operate—not only on a wall but on the everyday activity—from a plane of excellence. We demand that it be so. When we come to find that he floats lighter than a newborn, and in similar streams of consciousness, it is we who find ourselves confounded, not Brad.

Among other feats, he's arguably most famed for his soloing efforts on Eldorado Canyon's "Hairstyles and Attitudes." The nature of the climbing style, the insecurity of it, the sequential detail of the crux moves, the near impossibility of reversing any of them, has made it a solo for the ages. Even in the wake of Honnold's Freerider solo, the sheer improbability of Hairstyles as a solo climb will probably keep it in the annals of western rock ascent.

It was profound enough, that when Hayden Kennedy remarked about it in a B-side cut of Cedar Wright's "Safety Third" film, he spoke of it with reverence, and likened the entire experience to enlightenment.

"Whatever was meant for Brad to have in that moment, was meant for Brad alone," Hayden said.

It's not even that anyone can have that experience, but that that experience may have only ever been meant for Brad, alone. It's not as tall or sustained as El Cap, sure, but it's quite possibly just as singular as a human experience. For no one else, perhaps ever. That profound.

"Hayden said that your experience up there might have been meant only for you and that whatever it is that you got up there, that it must have been special." I looked at Brad and asked, "So, what was the experience like for you? What did you find?"

In a most typical, short, and inspired fashion, Brad probed into the recesses of his mind looking to read from the teleprompter. When it ran blank and without text, he just smiled for a moment, almost as if he'd taken flight again, unhampered by the weight of such an achievement or the need to explain anything about it. Whatever the *Hairstyles* experience had provided him, had long since left, if it was ever anything he'd attempted to hang onto anyway.

"Uhm, you know.... I'm really not sure. I just knew I could do it, and I always wanted to."

He didn't do it just to say he'd done it. He just did it. The only qualifier: a certain knowledge he could. He didn't want what was on top. He wasn't after a revelation and he wasn't running away from anything. It wasn't going to solve a life problem or make anything better. He didn't want to be known as the guy who did it. It was literally just a thought that came into his radar without any check against it. No voice telling him otherwise. Nothing to analyze. It doesn't matter in the feedback loop of Brad's programming, because after all, there is no origin, only operation.

You want it to be so much more, you want a feat like this to traverse the infinite plane and lead to the divine. You want to look inside the formula and find the perfect expression. But the simplicity, the honesty, the perfect, unaffected level of naivety, that comes through his blue eyes when he looks at you, is just as good.

///

Brad Gobright is pure of heart. So pure in fact, that he may never have faced a dilemma in all his life. What to do, and when to do it? Who to become and how to go about it? What are the designs needed to construct the life you want to live, and how do you even draw them? If anything, it is we who have suffered his decisions, more than he has. That he's never been in any form of tension with his course in life, begs explanation. That we can't seem to carry on with ours until he qualifies his, begs our own. He is a Zen koan, placed in this world to reframe our concepts completely. Indeed, just how we see Brad seems to say more about who we are than who he is.

You want him to be brilliant. But he's happy. You want him to be multi-faceted, but he runs perfectly as is. He is not what you want him to be, nor is he trying not to be, he just is. Zazen.

Of all the characters in the lore of Western Climbing history, of all the heroes and the heroines, the maniacs and misfits, one could hardly script Brad's character. The madman and the obsessed we've seen, in our tradition they are in-fact, a dime a dozen. The willingness to sacrifice anything and any relationship, those who quarrel about ethics, those who burn bridges and craft a life so self-centered it will abandon all for glory. Those who are coded by a pure obsession for a summit, for notoriety, for achievement or even a feeling of peace in an otherwise chaotic world, we can understand. We've seen the type. Even if they fail to ride that most fine line, even if they fail as fathers or sons or daughters, for the places they take us, for how they lift the human spirit, we are willing to call them heroes of some kind.

Even when they face a tragic end, we consolidate their memory, as one would with an addict of any type, suggesting to ourselves that our heroes were indeed good people, making the best of a condition not of their choosing. We think that when they knowingly pursued summits over simpler obligations, they did so not because they wanted to, but because they were compelled to. We say it made them the happiest, to be doing X, Y, or Z, and how could we ever ask of them to be otherwise. But momentary happiness is not our entire expression. That happiness, the kind that is attached to achievements, is always unsustainable. Usually, nobody knows that more than the hero who finds, at last, more emptiness after the fanfare of each ascent. But ask any recovered person about real happiness, and they'll tell you it only ever came when it was given away.

Brad, really is different. Same look. But different. He's never had that dilemma. He's never tried to juggle capacities. He's never run counter-intuitive functions. At first, that can seem basic, almost one dimensional, but looking closer, temper the judgment and you'll see that his character is, in a most eastern aspect, perfect. Fully reduced, nothing to add, and nothing more to possibly subtract. Pure. Realized, not with prose and pomp, but with action. He flashes before your eyes and if you are too busy looking at the incident—which is his manner of living itself—you'll miss that flicker of brilliance

If it's hard to close a box around, if his humanity seems just too far to grab, hold to this. He does believe in beauty, and all that it promises us. It might be the one thing which supersedes his whole drive. The one thing that can put a pause on the feedback loop. The one thing that will freeze action. As he described it to me, the one thing that can make him stop what he's doing and just look around with total wonder. In the middle of a 24-hour day on the stone, somewhere deep on a trail after some ungodly link-up, even if he's going for a speed record or is trying to rush out of the tent at daybreak, even if he's got an agenda for something which seems pressing—when a beam of nature is suddenly lighting up the empty corridors of that unconflicted mind, beauty will overwhelm him. He'll stop, he'll be raptured with the same rush of love and incomprehensible glory as you will.

"I definitely think that climbing El Cap, just being on it at sunrise or sunset, is the most beautiful thing I can do in my life. It's the most beautiful rock out there. And there have been times on it, where the sky is so perfect, I can't imagine anything else. For me, that's it. I've had it happen all over in nature when I get completely frozen by something beautiful, but it happens to me the most on the Captain. I can climb all over the world, but I don't think anything will beat it. It's just the most beautiful thing I've ever seen."

That's it. That's what's up there. Beauty. There isn't so much a "why" to his action. There never was with Brad. It's not in his nature to ask why he has the drive. Beauty is up on that rock, and so is Brad. He's not going to take our aspirations up there with him, Lord knows he's not carrying any form of science or philosophy into that experience each time he goes. He is taking the only thing he has and the only thing he's ever needed, that pure heart.

///

As hard as it was, at times, to watch him live, it's much harder to know he's gone. It is terrible on context, terrible on condition of how it happened, and terrible on timing, as it always seems to be with loss. Brad was on an arc after all. He'd grown and was growing, in a lot of new capacities, and we could all see it. Some of us had been on that arc with him longer than others, but the truth is it doesn't matter where we were on it, it just matters that we were there. It matters that we can keep him and all his indelible, robust, comical, and even gentle aspects, alive in memory.

He'll be missed for so many things—the million or more quirky details, the mimes and the sarcasm, the infamous chicken bock at the tourons, and for the jokes and the laughs he provided. He'll be missed for all the superlative measures we kept a record of him by. Those blanks, those frames are scripts we all get to fill in, with our own stories of him. But he'll be missed for so much more than his lightness and his amusement. He'll be missed for his singleness of heart, for his honesty, his authenticity. For all the things we struggled to consolidate about him, for all the things that made him, him. That's what we'll miss the most.

We're all going to have that last text, that last phone call, that last hug, that last beer, or that last climb that we shared with him. Those painfully close will have that last 'I love you', too. Painful as they may be, those are priceless memories, and we should nurture them. Grief is a force of nature, a part of the cycle we must submit ourselves to. It does not get solved, it is not a matter of logic, and there's nothing pretty on face value with it. Grief simply must be had. But, grief is of nature, too, and for that it is good. It is good because it keeps us together. Let's remember all those sunspots Brad burned on our reels when he was flying through the frames. Let us play them back, honor them, celebrate them. They were real, they were special, they were once in a lifetime.

To me, he had it. When you are known as much for your failures as your success, as much for the falls you take as the summits you make, you're onto something. That's my image of him. Brad Gobright, up there looking the fool; could be an epic fail or his greatest ascent, it doesn't matter because he's shining just the same. That same light we're all shielding our eyes from as we find ourselves looking on from below is the one he's wrapped in. Radiant, fleeting, glorious. Light.

///

WESTERN MEDICINE

Dave bellowed in his sleep. Just beside me in the passenger seat, the hapless sounds of his strange Doctor-moans rang out, as bass notes of a man who sleeps too little and dreams in neurology. Behind his barely-shut eyelids, were years-worth of study—rotations, roll-calls and winces at rectangular screens for hours on end. Nearly a decade of post-graduate focus. In-fact, just under that flap of skin covering his eyes, he was REM-ing his way through EKG's, X-Rays, Electron Microscope Slides, and Magnetic Resonance Images, for days. I could see it. They were all housed in a high-speed rolodex which was flying in circles behind his eyelids. An entire lexicon rolled out of him, involuntarily, in shunted syllables and slurs of unfinished medical terminology.

"Peripheral systemium...," then a snore.

"Arachnoid motor-mid-uhm-vascular...." Cut off by a brief apnea, he came right back on the inhale, "Sequard's syndrome!" Momentarily awakened, he looked more disturbed by it than I was. With yuccas flying by the window at 80 mph, he sulked into a fetal curl. Desperate to find sleep, Dave hummed back into the deep.

On the northern artery of Interstate 15, just past Baker, I was at the wheel as a shard of Mojave sunlight burst through a cloud and pierced the windshield into our cabin. Dave rejected it immediately. Wincing from the unconscious void of mind he rolled his shoulder into a nook and began the moaning pattern all over. He passed out mid-conversation and had been nearly catatonic since. Somehow, while explaining the tactile sensation of sticking a hypodermic past the subarachnoid space and straight into the CNS, this guy just knocked right out in the passenger seat. Zonked for miles on end.

Dave was rubbing up against the road of life much the same way our tires were; endless revolutions per minute, per hour, per day— cycling through a blur of rounds and cases and operations—scrubbing in, scrubbing out, the sight of his two hands lathered over the sink, seemingly the only mile markers between what were reported to be moments of consciousness. Something like 90-110 hours of work each week, and 4-5 hours of sleep each night, at best. If Hippocrates were still in him, somewhere, surely, he must have been strung between the tensioned clefts of Dave's brow.

Still, we had ambitions. Somehow a handful of days lined up for us and we were taking that Interstate for a good measure of what it was worth, all the way into Utah. Red earth, robust skies, and a rich Indigenous backbone. Utah, just the kind of healing we needed. A fantastic canvas of wide, open, space. The kind of space where you could walk back, a bit, into what it is to be human. Just beyond the rolodex, past the optic nerve and the into the mainframe, I had a hunch that a little more humanity is exactly what Dave, and I, both needed.

Having just watched each of our significant others disappear into the blur of the rear-view mirror, we didn't leave on our road trip with all the same joy we might have in our youth. This wasn't just about cutting class and trying to get away with it anymore. Life was too real to spend on cheap thrills, and we weren't trying to fashion stories that only served the space between the campfire and the icebox. So, when I leaned over to kiss my lady in the dark at the 4 a.m. hour, as I departed and left her to a lonesome bed, I was well aware of the part of me which has to go against my instincts. Time away had a cost.

What we were looking for out there was a sense of place. And that place wasn't just a spot on a Trucker's Map, it was just as much a point in time as it was somewhere you might put your feet. We were looking for our place, as human beings, at this time. Side-by-side with the petroglyphs on the Wingate Walls, ours is this unique window in collective human history. Somewhere, it seems, between mankind's mystic antiquity and the current era of environmental and cultural collapse. Humanity is what we were after, between the locking carabiners and knots tied to nylon cord. Who we are, who we've been, where we've come, and at what cost? What have we missed in the process? And, what of all this mess we've made?

What of mankind in a land like this, once upon a time, not so long ago? What of the stories which came of us then, and the stories that come of us now? In the years of climbing we've sewn together, in those special places up in the vertical realm, I had seen Dave ask his own questions of life. What of all the disease he would treat, and all the disruption we humans have woven into the environment? What of that notion that all chemical equations must be balanced, after all?

Even when busied by life, when torn between its many obligations and the lack of time to serve them, there has always been something outside, something under the surface that mandates we go and pull at it. Something of promise and revelation, a solution for things we may not even realize we need. Subatomic and sublime, the primordial jazz of life vibrates from the earth. Often, it's more concentrated on the tops of those desert towers. Wide, open, for all who seek.

We were up the highway, passing yuccas at more than 80mph because what was clear to Dave in all the sickness he had treated, was that mankind, you and I, have a chronic condition. In fact, the consensus in the field is that it's fully of our own making. Hell, Dave's even got it, too. We are all beyond and outside of our capacities. As he fell asleep once more, somewhere behind his flickering eyelids I could see what he was really looking for was to get some of his life back. There was something on the order of 70 trillion cells in Dave's body just then, just like there is now, and each one them was in that car for one thing. Healing. To find it, and to draw a perfectly deep breath out there, to know it, completely, from the membranous single layers of our alveolar tissue, down to the capillary exchange on the arterial end of the little toe itself, that's what we were after.

Dave loved the desert, always had, both for its magic and its great emptiness. But he was yet to spend any time on a desert tower. No question, of all the spires to top-out, Castleton was not the most remote; but it was sacred. Always has been, and always will be. Something of an institutional must, a rite of passage, a spiritual classic. It was historic and ageless on merit of its aesthetic alone, even after all the years. And, while it was going to take a few days for us to reorient ourselves to the rock after months away from it, Dave and I both kept space for our own moment of truth upon that skyline.

For that reason, 730 miles passed in a flicker.

///

"I just can't believe this place is here, just like it is, all the time." Dave proclaimed with half a sandwich stuffed in his mouth. "Seriously!"

At the Donnelly Canyon parking lot, just after the drive-in from Moab and the morning rope session, life on earth was shining. Our good fortunes started well before sunrise, having driven in before dawn, after a night of sleep on the banks of the Colorado River and the company of a billion sparkling stars. And, further down the 211, bearing south, it continued as the entirety of the landscape, from the peaks of the San Juan's to the pastel canyons undulating into the horizon, bewildered the both of us.

Castleton was still on the top of the to-do list, but as mentioned, the busy lives we'd both been leading had taken us down a few levels in fitness, which we had hoped to reboot with a quick turnover spent cragging. Besides, in Bear's Ears National Monument, on the borders of Dineh Bikeyah, there is no better place to be than exactly where you are. Planted firmly in the middle of a desert canyon, lush with the spring bloom of Cottonwoods and the pale shoots of morning grass, we both agreed. The fact that such beauty exists out there, in perfect serenity, at every single moment of Dave's day-to-day life in the hospital, was beyond him. All that revelation, with or without witness, just constantly happening, perfect expression whether or not you plug into it—it was almost maddening. It probably would be, were he not so damned tired.

"What is this music we're listening to, oh man, wait a minute, what's in this sandwich? Wow!" Out of nowhere, a particular bite of arugula or spicy mustard or something in a bite he just took distracted him, mid-sentence.

"This sandwich, Jesus!" Dave shook in disbelief. "I might not have actually eaten food made with caring hands for a long time."

Picture a wrongfully accused man having his first meal after serving time. Picture the crumb he's willing to pick up off the floor because it's so good. Picture the satisfaction in every wrinkled fold of his face. This was Dave's gratitude.

"And the music, wow, what is this? I bet you've got a whole story about it, yeah?"

"Sure man, this is Mahmoud Guinia, a legend, and some of that Gnawa I was telling you about. They've got this whole system and history over there, generations of tradition and healing all wrapped up in this amazing music and culture. Predates Islam even. There are these Maalem's and ceremonies called Lila's and..." Before I could even finish the trailer, Dave was passed out, again; asleep on his climbing pack under borrowed shade from a parked car. It was a lights-out, complete parasympathetic takeover.

A moment earlier Dave was firing, though. Spiking on the opposite end of the autonomic nervous system, Dave was in paradise going hand-over-hand between perfectly uniform panels of clay-colored drywall.

"Goddammit, it's good to be here again," he proclaimed from on high. Considering the guy never curses, it was an obvious tell. Leading the 3 a.m. Crack, it was a pleasure to watch Dave go large, fully thumbs-up, with hands-to-heart lock-offs; perfect, big reaches from one sinker to another. Climbing language for restoration.

The fact that neither Dave nor his high lasted long up there was no surprise, though. Not considering what he was coming in from. One look at him, any point when he's wasn't on the wall itself, and you got a sense of his deprivation. He had a bug, a weariness, born from being neck-deep in his crux year of residency; a residency which bred both a deep gratitude when he climbed, but also a palpable urgency. You could see him racing against it, almost like he was crawling out of some creeping shadow, trying to beat the inevitable, whole system body failure from rushing in. The interplay between those states gave a hint to just how hard his internal operating system was working. Which, if we're honest, is not so different from the rest of us. One thing the doctor had noted, in the short reality checks we made to one another via the phone, on a weekly basis, was that nearly all his patients were just as overwhelmed by life as the resident surgery staff was. Everyone, indiscriminately, seemed just a little too pressed for their own good out there. Something he, and his fiancé, Kate, struggled to facilitate.

Dave and Kate both rode a thin line of health, even as physicians, a line that was also strung 300 miles and one State-line apart. To hear their tales was to get a special peek into the level of sacrifice our medical professionals made. Both Dave and Kate worked nearly 18 hours a day, at an average of 28 days a month. Both saw things in the operating room you might wish you hadn't. Both slept far too little and communicated with each other even less. And both would tell you that more than passing with flying colors, becoming physicians felt more like flying in the dark. It was pure, fucking, instinct.

But, beyond what they'd both tell you about their workload and all the forms of acute trauma they'd seen in the clinic, beyond losing friendships during residency, beyond all the stress and deadlines and consequences and commitment; what took the most out of them was absorbing the statement about humanity that came together, piece by piece, in all the high-stakes and morally bankrupt cases they saw between the admission and discharge of a patient. That was the heaviest truth: how to swallow, and at the same time effectively treat the beast that is our human condition.

Often, the undigested fragments of Dave and Kate's medical practice erupted out of them like Dave's neurology lexicon did back in the car; just completely out of nowhere and in random bursts. They would just spout out some batshit crazy factoids about a case they once had, as complete non-sequiturs, like war stories that just need to be expelled from whatever cavern they had been bubbling in.

///

When he awoke, the first thing Dave did was apologize. "I'm sorry man, I guess I've got some catching up to do. I really want to just go-hard out here. These five days may be the longest time out I get all year, you know, but my body is kinda workin' against that aim at the moment."

"It isn't just your body that needs the rest, buddy." I replied. "Don't worry about it, at all. This is going to take a few days for us both. Good thing we've got all this to look at in the meantime."

Walking up the scattered path of the talus trail after his nap, we approached another buttress, and both sweat hard under the arid midday sky. Along the base of the sheer, dark-cherry walls, and among the oxidized-green of copper soil, Dave gazed in wonder at the walls around us. Ancient glory in the utmost spread out between us and the horizon, golden beams of Ute, Pueblo, Hopi, Zuni and Dineh majesty.

Pausing on the precipice of the talus cone, with a perfect overlook on the Bridger Jack Basin and the west-facing canyons, I shouted in his direction, "Take a little bit of that view in with your next breath, buddy!"

Almost with burden, Dave replied, "I still just can't believe all of this is out here, you know?"

"You and I both, mate."

Panting his way further in conversation, he continued, "No man, I mean, I know you're busy too, but it's different in the hospital. I live in unnatural light; my shifts tend to start before sunrise and end after sundown. I'm around illness constantly, and it's probably a good thing doctors only get six weeks of nutrition, cause what I end up eating in there isn't exactly health food. I'm basically detached from nature from the tight junctions to the stratum corneum."

"From what?" I laughed.

"From the gut to the skin, man. From the inside out," Dave confirmed. "I'm not complaining, but it's another world, man, and not a natural one." Turning his gaze again to the earth below he shrugged out, "It's certainly not this one."

As we sifted the gear from the packs, Dave continued, "I'll tell you what, sometimes it feels like we (physicians) are just topical, you know, even in chronic disease, in a lot of ways our system in the West is just designed to treat symptoms and handle critical moments. I can reduce a fracture, or someone else can open an airway, we can stent a closed cardiac vessel, but it seems like we're just fixing the short-term. It doesn't take a doctor to realize what we need is more total health, and that only comes from having more of this."

This, was a live postcard the State of Utah would love to have hanging from a souvenir shop, an image shining brightly behind Dave's outstretched arms.

In fact, in every conversation we'd had in the medical parameter, Dave's always kept a humble approach to his expertise. Western medicine was never going to be a savior on its own. Human health always depended on more than physicians and healers.

"I mean, I know this, that science does not currently, and may never, have all the answers. There's definitely limits of medicine for the West. I think it's important for more doctors to understand that, but for people to also. Physicians may get defensive over this kind of stuff because we've committed so much of ourselves to this lifestyle and science, but we don't have the market cornered on all the tools that lead to health."

It is exactly health, real well-being, and not just disease management that Dave was thinking of when he looked out there at the red canvas.

"Yeah man, we don't seem to be getting any healthier in the chronic scope," I suggested. "It's not even that medicine is failing as much as the system is. There's a greater distance between people and nature than there should be, and not just nature in the hiking sense, I mean it in every sense. We're just as distant from our own nature, as we are from the nature of something like food production, as if the two are even different. The whole thing, man. It's all on overload."

"You are not wrong, my friend," Dave replied. "I guess what I get from being out here, what I'm honing-in on is just that notion of a better connection. The benefits of the connection and the consequences of living continuously at a distance from it."

Under one of the ubiquitous, five-star routes of the desert sandstone, we racked up with these thoughts and carried them with us as much as we carried our gear. Dave tied one of the thousands of figure-eights he's woven and joyfully went vertical.

Halfway up the first pitch, he blurted out, "You know, this one time, at the end of my shift, I was walking out of the hospital around midnight or something. And right as I exit the glass door, I walked straight into a cloud of this dude's cigarette smoke. Mind you it's a non-smoking campus, and when I looked up who do I see but the same patient me and my Attending were just lecturing twenty minutes ago. He's strapped to his oxygen tank, hacking the only small bits of lobes his lungs have left, having just been educated on the severity of his COPD, and the fucker is going pale face taking the whole stick down in a single drag."

As my grin opened in absolute splendor, Dave locked-off a move and finished, "What the fuck is that about!"

///

At the Creek Pasture campground, a few pitches later, we sang serenades to the Four Cardinal Directions above a humble fire.

Dave hadn't played the guitar in years, and while it was a pleasure watching him, tactically, refamiliarizing himself with the neck and strings like the arc of an old friendship, what was more fascinating was watching him recollect all the moments behind the songs he was singing, like The Girl From the North Country.

"Yeah man, I learned that one early in our relationship, you know, cause Kate's from Minnesota, way up there, so for me, she's the girl from the North Country." After a moment of pause, he shared, "Damn, you know what? I fucking miss her, man."

"Oh, I get it, buddy. What I wouldn't give to have the two of them sitting right here with us."

Dave looked into the white glow of the fire and mused, "I can't believe how bad I needed this. Residency has taken a lot from me. I gotta' be honest, sometimes it even feels like those things are gone for good, even if I know they aren't. Looking back, there's a lot I didn't realize that I was signing up for."

"Well, man," I suggested, "you're a real champion of the cause, to me. Watching what you are going through in this residency path has been pretty eye-opening."

"Yeah, for the both of us," he offered.

"Looking back, like a lot of things in life, I guess I had no idea what I was really signing up for. I mean, you can see the 8-year plan or whatever in front of you on a piece of paper, but you don't know anything about it until you commit to it. And in this case, in medicine, you definitely can't know what it means until you get in and start learning all the other stuff that comes with it. You know, things about yourself, your strengths, and your barriers. There are much deeper parts of who you are, inside, and what your motivations are, that has to be checked as you go along. A lot of times, if I'm honest, it's actually pretty hard for me to marry the guy I was at the beginning of this to where I am today, it's hard to touch that initial spark and inspiration."

"I suspect the part where you check your deepest motivations can be one of the most frightening parts of it, depending on what you find?" I replied.

Dave responded with an unexpected laugh, "I mean, there's gotta be quicker and better ways to make money, right!"

"Hah! Lord knows you didn't sign up for that," I replied.

"Well, yeah man, call me a romantic but I felt like there was something more important than money behind this life," he mused.

"You wanted to help people. That's why."

"Well," Dave considered, "I guess that's a part of that hand I was dealt. You know, I got so much more than I deserved, it'd be criminal not to plug into something like this, right?"

When Dave talked about that hand he was dealt, what he was referring to was a stellar childhood. He the elder brother to a younger sister, the two of them the caring focus of two loving, well-educated, and professionally accomplished parents. A quality home, a good upbringing, model parents who lived well and didn't take anything in life for granted.

The thing is, this wasn't Dave's original script. Dave was adopted into that home. What his life could've looked like, we'll never fully know. What we do know is that on his biological father's end there were scares with substance issues. Issues enough that when he came to term, his biological mother understood that Dave's parents today could offer him a life that every young being deserves; love, a nurturing environment, and a bright future without restriction.

That he is the living end-result of two people's voluntary, unconditional grace and care, is a truth that has never been lost on Dave. He's always desired to give of himself however he can. He's got all the ethics of a good man, and a compass directed to live for more than his own ends and means. When he eventually decided on medical school, it wasn't so that he could live the life of a hot-shot in a Ferrari, or for the ego-stroking notion that he belonged to any class of born excellence. It wasn't to rub shoulders with icons at cocktail parties, and it wasn't to have a house on a hill and a perfect white family framed on canvas above the mantle; it was to balance the equation.

There was an entire road trip, once upon a longtime ago, particularly between Fresno and the Tunnel View of the Yosemite Valley, where Dave and I went deep on the exact notion—that for a physician-in-training to take the Hippocratic oath was tantamount to a monastic taking an oath of silence or a clergyman taking an oath of celibacy. To truly live by a code which premises that above all, you shall not do harm to others, is to live an inward life. It's not just about having a steady hand with the scalpel, it's not about avoiding a wrong diagnosis, and it's not about the wherewithal to choose against operations just as often as you move toward them. At the deepest level, the Hippocratic Oath compels the surgeon to live well. The true skills a physician must craft lay well beyond his or her surgical kit, well beyond the textbook, and are much deeper than the focal capacity of a microscope; the pursuit of them beckons a man or woman of the doctoral tribe to summon their very best, at an interior level, into the fabric of all their life.

A moment later Dave added, "I'll share this. If you really want to help people or make a change, it's gotta be in a process like this. You've gotta get in deep, you've gotta commit beyond your dreams, you've gotta see multitudes of cases, man, multitudes, to get a sense of something. Something bigger than just the condition of a patient; it's the condition of people. And it's tough, and you've gotta be without all the answers at times, and just be willing to experience the entire thing as it is. The thing that often kicks-in and powers me through hour 18 or 20 on the floor, is that each one of my experiences, whether good or bad, will come to be of use later in the practice of medicine, and my life."

Ending his run of thoughts, Dave closed, "But, being out here, it also hits me just how vital this stuff is. In a lot of ways, I'm just as disconnected to the heart of life as my patients. What I need is what they need, a life with more of this!"

When he said, *this*, he was looking up at a half-moon fingerling perched in Van Gogh, ala *The Starry Night*, over the Six Shooter formations, a million stars, and silhouettes of ancient lands that were still warm on the inside. When he said, *more*, it wasn't a van-life or an endless road-trip he was entertaining, it was not peak-bagging, and it was not grade-chasing either. For Dave, it has always been more about what passes through your hands when you're out there than what they are grabbing. And it's always been more about who you're standing with than what you are standing on.

With a little more hope in his eye than he'd had a day before, that sense of urgency he was carrying seemed to be dissolving, if only a little.

///

"There was this one time when Kate and I both had the ass end of the stick. Somehow, we both got the on-call shift during a holiday, Memorial weekend I think, and it all went down the tubes from there."

Dave started the morning with another processing error, probably something from his half-finished dream state, as he had just crawled out of the tent.

"We're sending each other our case photos and we just couldn't believe it—because she's out in Vegas, and I'm stuck in Orange, at the hospital, you know. There were a couple of amps [amputations], a bowel obstruction, a super-amphetamine case, a lady who was near full-term and didn't even know she was pregnant while coming off opiates, just one after another, man. We couldn't believe, like 72 hours straight, every case a product of a lifestyle choice."

Not wanting to be a downer, Dave looked up with his boy scout smile and chuckled, "It's like the old man said. Sometimes, you just gotta eat crow!"

"Yeah, but not today, buddy!" I offered.

That's because this day was fucking aces. It was our second and last day in the Monument before we jumped up to Castle Valley. Our bodies were broken, already, but as the old-timers like Robinson would say, that's just the process of the mind, the spirit, coming-to. The Climber, as Visionary, stirred within. That requisite breakdown of the body, that essential brokenness which comes when you distance yourself from the comforts of life, was stirring. I felt it, and I could see it in Dave, too. We decided to take the morning easy, as we had some new company joining us for the day, and thus kept time to chew the fat and take in an extra round of coffee. Our mutual friend, Taylor, joined us the night before, for the tail end of that guitar and campfire session. He, more than Dave or I, had recently spent much more time in nature. And so, for both his genuine companionship and his incredible climbing skills, Taylor was a very welcomed partner for the day. Yirgacheffe and oatmeal in the gullet, we quickly got on in conversation.

"So," Taylor began, "What's it like now that you are well past medical school? You getting some of your life back yet?"

"Ha ha," Dave cracked back in surprise, "Quite the opposite, my friend. Just what we've been talking about actually. Things are probably more out of balance now than ever before. But I'll tell you, on day three in a row of climbing, I can honestly say that these moments, however short, are so much more enjoyable than they ever were for me when I had more time. Something about being plugged in, in there, makes everything shine and connect better out here."

Up at the cliff, an hour later, we were still on that thread, on that seemingly needed dichotomy Dave had just referenced. There was something honest about it, that struck Taylor and I both, not just in the words but in the way that Dave had shared it. How, while he could recognize a need to reconnect to the pathways of nature, he just as deeply had to connect to society and a purpose, and how his health was just as contingent on that connection as it was to the outside variety. It resonated, especially with Taylor.

Taylor, among many things, was and still is a master class rock-man. A freeform, handsome, chiseled sculpture of vertical accomplishment, he was the real deal. He was always out somewhere, always doing it, colored tan and carefree by sunbeams and the metabolites of constant, fresh air, he was living the closest thing to the Great American Road Trip. Mostly satisfied by high-end climbing goals in high places, as often as possible, Taylor was still trying to figure out what it was exactly that drove him—whether he was running toward something, tangibly, or only away. Because of that, he was always on the road, looking for it, detached from the mainframe of society to connect to the only thing he knew how to grasp: open spaces. It sure made him a fantastic climber, though perhaps his distance from the world had left him with fewer answers than he'd have hoped for at that stage.

As we traded leads for the better part of the day with Taylor, we were also stuck right there on the contrast between his lifestyle and Dave's. Within which, we were exploring what value there was to a pursuit like climbing, period. While Taylor might have been the opposite of Dave, committed only minimally to society or a long-term process like a surgical residency, he had an expression of the same divide you saw in Dave. On a rope, he was a magician, but in fellowship, there was a certain unease. He left society a thousand miles and a thousand pitches ago, for what seemed like good reasons. But if you asked him about happiness, if you asked him about long-term purpose and the peace which came with it, if you asked him what it was like standing on what must have been the greenest grass out there—the perpetual road trip—you'd slip right between that dreamy exterior.

"I know three things today. Like right now after we've just climbed, from this talk we've been on in the last few pitches," Taylor summarized. "One, instincts are a guide and they are totally undervalued. That's what got us here, as humans. That's what got me here, outdoors, and they work from the smallest foot-chip you choose to step on, to the next place you pitch a tent. Not enough people get outside, man, no way, not enough people are in touch with the human instinct for constant exposure, there aren't enough people tapping into the raw side of life. We're all domesticated and that's not what we're born from."

Tally a strong affirmation on point one.

"Two, I don't want to end up like the legend of Alf."

"Alf?" Dave asked with intrigue.

"Yeah man, Alf Randell. The dude's got a route named after him in the Park at J-Tree. This might be all hearsay, but legend has it that he's been out here around Moab for decades now, looking for his glory and first ascents, always trying to make history. But the fucker is completely alone. Rumor has it he goes around town and campfires begging for belay partners. Like he's just been out of touch for so long that's all he's got, he's climbed himself into a cell out there. Like we all dream of climbing all the time, but no matter what you climb, it's empty if that's all you have. That's not the life I'm gunning for."

Point number two conceded that point number one should not put us at a distance from others.

"And that leads me to number three. Three is simple. Sometimes you gotta go against the instincts. That's what makes us human, right? The ability to go against our instincts. If I'm going to do anything soon, anything that starts to bring a purpose that climbing can't provide, I've got to start going against some of these. I'm selfish as fuck, man. I'm scared to commit to this long-term relationship thing, which means I'm scared of partnership and all that. I'm scared to plug into people if I'm being real about it. If I'm ever going to get anywhere besides a climbing grade or a good story to tell, I've gotta start doing something else. I gotta change the course." To finish, he shared, "At this stage, having climbed in so many special places, I'd rather have the luxury of a purpose and good people to share life with, without the luxury of time, than I would have it be the other way around and be stuck without a purpose."

Clearly, Taylor was at a turning point. He was a savage, born for the wild, but he was more than just that—whether he liked it or not. More than his instincts as a man to get into something wild, more than the instinct to make an effort as a warrior or fight for a cause, more than the pursuit of a prey, his deepest instincts were in the connection he sought to others. It was just as much in the sharing of the meal as it was in the kill. A reminder that in life, it is not just the instincts of the masculine, but also those of the feminine which fulfill our humanity.

Taylor's interplay with instincts left Dave and I both in contemplation. Operating on instincts can produce deep good, or a lack thereof. Here was Taylor, unwilling to buy into a standard life, like many, looking for truth in free and open spaces, in bold deeds and achievements of will— seemingly a righteous rebellion. But somewhere, an invisible line for us all, there is a threshold where our tools become vices. That Taylor found it hard to connect with a purpose; that reintegration threatened the structures he had built; that it was easier, less threatening for him remain apart from, rather than a part of, told all. And he was not unique in that.

There's a missed target in complete abandonment. Because, what's the point of restoring the wild within us, as Taylor would suggest, if we are not tethered to others? What's the point of the big kill, or the big cottage, if there is none to share it with? The beast spoils, the house withers, as do our adventures and achievements in life. The primary self must be threatened, it must be stomped, and that is the deepest, or perhaps highest instinct; the one which allows us to act in spite of the others.

///

"You know what, man," Dave began. "Here's a wild one. This one time at the V.A. Hospital I was on rounds and this Vet who's probably struggled since Vietnam is coming in off the street, almost totally wet-brain. I mean, I've seen a lot of the derelict and the withdrawal, but this guy was by far the worst. Absolutely. The Worst. Shot with ascites and a liver that must have already burst, this guy was barely human." Dave zones into hyperbole. "He was dropping into seizures from withdrawal, and when we finally got him down to take a blood sample, it fucking came back at a point four. A point four. Not point-zero four, fucking point four. Dude, that's like five times the legal driving limit, that would tranquilize a horse. For that guy to be in withdrawal at that state, holy fuck, man. Fuck.

"I mean, just consider what that guy's condition says about his environment, where the only way through it is to live like that. What does it say about how we're managing our society with that shit happening to people?" Dave sympathizes.

It was one of those moments, again. Dave had just gotten off the phone with Kate for the first time in a couple of days, as we laid back at our camp for the night and looked at the Milky Way over the Colorado River. Kate was on his mind, but somehow the withdrawal story came out, too. When I asked him how it went, he didn't look too happy about it.

"She's going through a really hard time right now, you know, and she's the one who moved. She's basically alone. Residency is tough enough, you know, it's really hard to be a friend to people when you're under the gun. Life is still happening for people we care about, and lots of times we can't be there for them. It honestly feels like you're losing things in residency, and friendships are a part of that. I think she feels exposed without friends right now, and on top of that, I'm away."

Dave took a deep breath. "I just feel like I should be there with her, right now."

"Yeah, but when you're not climbing, you feel bad about missing that part of yourself. And then when you're at the hospital you feel bad about that 'cause you aren't being a support system for your friends or family. Of course, then, when you're with your friends or your family, you probably feel like you should be working or studying. Fuck that man, you're always feeling bad about something. Probably from the moment you wake up if you're like me," I interject.

"Total stress response, almost all the time," Dave replied.

Stargazing, just moments later, we pondered the magic under

the microscope as we also contemplated how it had fashioned the constellations in the skies. Quickly, we turned the discussion to the chemical make-up of all life, and how humans shared many of the same elements as the fixtures in the Great Beyond. In no time, Dave and I were unraveling DNA and weaving it all the way to Pleiades.

From the hunter's bow of A]tse a]ts'oosi, to the smallest particle spinning revolutions of electrons in otherwise empty space, Dave and I both agreed, there was a perfect design to life, everywhere. The same elements up there, fixed in eternal legend, in constellation, were and are inside of us, inside of you, right now. The same laws of physics that held them in place and filled us with wonder— as we laid looking across light-years of spacetime—are working right now, inside of you and me, keeping every one of the trillions of biological and chemical events which define us, in operating order. Without that conservation of mass, or energy, without gravity, there's not only no planet or constellation. There's no cell, no enzyme, no electron transport chain on the mitochondrial border that allows you to maintain all that is you.

That, we realized, was connection in the utmost. Under those stars and serenaded by the gentle wash of the Colorado River, we considered the opposite as well. The end manifestations of all that disconnection we'd been circling recently—what of all that?

What many chronic illnesses, including perhaps the most feared medical diagnosis, certain cancers, have in common, can generally be reduced to is a dysfunction as a result of stress overload. An isolation not unlike what we've seen in Dave's case sequiturs. In a state of constant damage-control, due to environmental strain, the body loses the perfect unity of its communication pathways and the network from cells to organs, and organs to organ systems, is compromised. By the time a cancerous cell emerges, often, it has lost communication completely. And, in a sense, it has also lost its own cellular identity. No longer plugged into the system, no longer a part of, but apart from, the cell cannot integrate.

It will not see the rest of the network as co-operative, but rather as a threat. This microcosm, when applied to Dave, to his patients, to all of us, is eerily mirrored in our lives.

That total stress response, the one that's got Mr. COPD sucking tar from tip-to-filter in a single drag, the one that's coursing a point-four through a Vet's veins, that one on top of you and me both, does the same to us on a larger application. It puts us at a distance from each other. It's the unease Taylor feels out on the road in glory land, still unable to connect with the greatness the ancient man and woman did. It's the divided interpretation of the present moment Dave has on his leads; and it's the isolation and fear written on the eyes of every patient in his entire practice. It's all tied together just as our core elements are tied to those in the stars above our heads on the banks of the Colorado River.

///

When morning came Dave was slow to rise with it. There was no sudden war story or outburst, no case study, no look of joy even. As he first limped out of the tent, all I could see of Dave was his exhaustion, surely earned by three—-going on four —successive days climbing. That, and the internal tension of being both demolished by life and yearning to be present for it. At the least, to be present for Kate. The coffee was strong, and the music was right, but neither mattered much. Dave was haggard.

However undone he may have been, as we skirted the bends of Castle Valley and Castleton Tower finally came into Dave's view, the mood did shift, if only just a little. The smallest spark, the most unsuspecting note of willingness connected the line-of-sight between his eyes and that tower out there, and for that, I was suddenly hopeful.

The bastard was beat, no doubt, but maybe he was beat just enough. Maybe that's exactly how it should have been. Maybe the brokenness in his bones was finally akin to that of his spirit, and maybe that was the best place to enter communion with it all.

Hiking up the softly lit, maroon-colored behemoth of a talus cone, I had set a firm pace for Dave to follow. In no time he was behind me and then altogether lost from sight behind the many cornered switchbacks, seen only by the dust plumes he kicked up on his way; signs that his feet were dragging as low as his energy was. He might have looked like shit and the hike-in might have been savage considering the context, but what I've seen by experience tells me that that slog he was doing was exactly where the magic happens. Right there, in the muck, Dave was coming into contact with billions of bacteria and microbes and a wondrous cornucopia of primitive life particles, all things the ancients knew about. The exact kind of stuff people talk about when they say that getting outside is good for you.

As we rounded the saddle with the Rectory coming into view to our left, and Castleton and its mythic white calcite bands on our right, I offered Dave the choice.

"It's not too late to decide on something else today, my friend. Considering we're probably not going to be doing any link-ups based on our energy levels, the question is, if you could only stand on one summit today, if you could have only one experience, what's it gonna be?"

Covered in sweat, Dave's boy-scout smile snuck up from his fatigued face, "No question, man. It's gotta be that North Face on Castleton."

"Just what I'd hoped you'd say."

With Dave beat to hell, I offered first lead on the crux pitch. Feeling connected to earth and the elements, I kissed the rock face in my usual ritual and went all in. Halfway up the pitch, however, and short on gear, I suddenly faced an unwanted choice; conservative action or full abandon. Knowing that Dave was below, weighed down by all his emotions, even with his pack off his shoulders, I went against my better instincts of security, and reached forward looking for that moment of truth. A conservative approach to the pitch—not being willing to take a fall or plugging more protection than necessary—wouldn't have done anything for his morale or mine. What both of us needed was an inspiration, and while I could see quickly just what it might cost, in a rare form and connection, I was somehow willing. Navigating the crux and a pump from hell, I managed to tap into something beyond the climbable holds, and just didn't let go..

With the red earth as a witness while I climbed past my comfort zones and above protection, I thought of Taylor. Particularly, the notion that to be human, fully, one must rise above certain instincts. When the fear came over me, more than any paralysis, I felt equipped by it. Able to use it to step into another gear. In a pickle and out of a comfort zone, without a skillset for the job and no way to eliminate the necessity of it, something began to feel gut-level okay. To my surprise, that's when it all came clean. Suddenly, I was overcome with a deep peace, and awareness. With all the tremens and all the fear experience still in my veins, I'd managed to connect on a parallel frequency. It was duplicitous, nearly out of body even.

I found myself almost frozen in each move, mystified by the complex structures of the white calcite on the red stone; looking at the details of each mineral and each grain of solidified sand, as if into a new dimension. Still moving, the entire experience happened on a separate bandwidth. It wasn't as much the speed of it as the depth of it. It was not profound on virtue of it being like slow-motion, as much as it was on a different plane of motion. It was a space I could not believe, nor did I have to. I had only to experience it. Still, the fact that I, the hesitant one, was moving through it, mystified me all the more. With the hand of some other grace and fortitude, I passed through the threshold and came to the anchor with every hair standing on end.

"On belay, brother!" I shouted down to Dave from the top of the pitch.

"Climbing, I think," he registered back softly.

He started out alright, but by the time he got into up to the second piece of gear, Dave moved like a man defeated.

About a hundred feet up and at the crux, he slid out of the flake system from muscle failure, with a firm whip away from the wall. Swinging out over the Castle Valley, he couldn't even put up his legs or arms out to pad his rebound into the wall. When the tension came on the rope, he just limp-fished back and forth against the stone in a lackadaisical pendulum. Defeated, finally, he sat there for a minute until he was overtaken by an unexpected fit of laughter.

"This," he began with his arms out, slightly delirious. "This is it, man. This is what we came for."

Dave laughed at a joke only he seemed to get, before consolidating his mental state and sharing, "It's just so good."

The Visionary, it seemed, had arrived.

Admitting defeat, broken in mind and body, perfectly okay with all his emotions and all the baggage—willing to just sit in it, as he'd mentioned by the campfire a few nights ago, without the answers—he found peace. Dave got back on the line and climbed up to me at the anchor. To my surprise he even asked for the rest of the gear when he arrived, so he could lead the next pitch.

Where there had been a slog, there was now a dance. Like Mohammad Ali, he danced. Halfway up the second pitch he even began to smile again, looking down, joyfully, and sharing. "Dude, look at where we are man!"

At the second anchor, when I caught up to him, he smiled again while we sorted our gear, saying "I don't know what really happened just now, man. Something clicked, something just started to make sense. Being on lead helped, too. A lot. You see it all better."

"Well, then" I proposed. "If you recall, I had the pleasure of topping out our last big climb together, so if you're still in the mood, this one's all yours."

Dave took the bits of gear I had gathered and re-racked his harness, double-checking his stations one gear loop at a time, and then re-cinched his laces. With a smile like I hadn't seen since he started his residency, he dipped his hands into the bag of chalk at his backside and smattered his palms together like a boy scout trying to start a wood fire with a tinder stick.

"Enjoy, my friend!" I said to him to confirm the belay. "You're going to love what you find up there."

It's a beautiful thing holding the line for someone who's having a genuine moment on the stone. About halfway up the pitch, Dave ventured into some committed sections of climbing, situated around a series of off-width angles. Here, at the last defense of the North Face, Dave's movement came alive. From down below I could even see the makings of a shit-grin on his face as it all clicked. He paused above a large flake, at the midpoint, and stretched out one hand in the wind to capture it all—from the snow-capped peaks to the dizzying landscape below.

Dave climbed through the wide sections and finally passed the last 50 feet, through a gulley, like a rising tide—slow and steady. He'd adjusted his pace notably, not because it was difficult but more-so because, at this point, he was just taking it all in.

At the summit, he let out a kingly howl, from the depths of his being, from every fiber meant to express joy. True exultation. But then it went silent. Five minutes, maybe more. Nothing to report but a line of climbing-rope that hung over the lip of the summit, and the quiet of the empty Utah air. He'd later say that he was looking for an anchor to build, but I knew when he topped out that it was a special one for him. It was a culmination. Just for a few moments, on top of that tower, he was alone; just him and the hallowed things meant for him to hear and to see, and to feel. As if everything he needed to continue in his residency lay before him in his quiet moment up there alone.

I followed the pitch and when I got up there, I'll tell you, Dave had changed in that 150 feet since I'd last seen him. We often think it's just in the tough spots of life, or trauma situations, that we immediately age; but there's a mark of the beautiful just as there's a mark of the mortal. Enough light adds more than wrinkles. Dave had a shine, from the inside out.

After a robust, gargantuan hug, I found the nearest nook to lay my feet flat and dwell on the occasion. Pensive and satisfied, I lit a cigarette and took in a good pull, only on the exhale speaking softly.

"Magnanimous, my brother."

Dave had to lean in to hear what I was saying, so I repeated, "Mag-nan-i-mous."

Unsure what I meant, Dave gave a curious stare while coiling the rope, as I continued off the next drag. "I mean, it's just so good up here, it's so generous, right! Life, it's so fucking rich, and it always is. It's always this good, we just don't see it till we get to places like this. But when we do, we realize it's beautiful, all the time; perfect, all the time; a privilege, always. It's just on us to make the space to connect to it."

"That's it." Dave nodded. "That's it exactly. The reason all of this comes down to contact is because that's exactly where the grace happens. It's the only place it can happen."

"Is that what happened to you down there just now? You got some healing?" I asked.

"Indeed, my friend." Dave nodded in agreement, content to have found something of a new understanding. He stood there, as did I, quiet for the better part of minutes, contemplating all that had occurred within him since we'd left the ground in favor of the vertical.

We stayed still up there, just like so, wanderlusting on planet earth and its Castle Valley the way young kids stargaze at the cosmos. In no rush to get down or go home, time stood on end, as if we were on the very tip of the hour-hand which had stopped at high-noon. When the moment felt right, we traded stories of whatever came to mind, whatever was rich or valuable at the time; whatever felt good for the moment and its grandeur; the only thing bigger than the skyline up there, was the smile on Dave's face, lit up in all directions by the turmeric glow reflecting from the great state of Utah, from Dineh Bikeyah herself. We sat on that summit like it was a champagne bath and swam in the luxury of life at its finest.

///

By the time we got down, Dave and I had tapped into the soil so deep you couldn't shake the stillness out us if you tried. Every footstep was an emotional experience with the earth, and it was no short hike back.

"Pretty amazing summit registry up there," Dave shared. "Pretty special to have a page in there with all the others, too."

"Ah man, exactly what I was thinking," I started. "That feeling you had up there with it, connected to everyone in that book, connected to all those moments of clarity and what it must have looked like for them, that's how the sunsets have been for me. Especially at the reservoir the other day, it was a feeling like I was watching a sunset that had already been experienced before. A part of a realization that had already happened."

"Yeah man, up there, it's like you are living in touch with more than just a singular moment, and more of a reality." Dave suddenly narrated.

And he was exactly right. The reality, the one he was blown away with on day one, with that sandwich in hand, is that there is a universe of constant, perfect revelation. It happens, all the time, because it is, all the time. Because it is deeper than time. And, it occurs with or without a witness. It does not depend on you, or me, or Dave and all his best intentions to make Hippocrates proud. It just is. Mountains, summits, wild spaces, they too live in deep time. And, to be with them requires us to summon something fundamentally wild within us, something deep within us, as well. When we do, and when we make contact, we enter that space they inhabit, or as Dave would say, we live in touch with more than just a single moment, and more of a reality.

That, what he was describing, was being in touch with something deeper than time on the clock's ticker.

It is where grace occurs. It is what gives the healing Dave wanted to prescribe and the purpose Taylor was chasing.

It is where we find our place, as humans, in this time. But we can also go deeper than that. If we look to our past, to the petroglyph and the ancient man and woman, if we connect to them in a sunset or landscape or something vast, surely we see them looking further; we see them creating a life and a lifestyle that holds to the truth, that it's less about our place in a particular time as it is about our place among and in a particular reality. A reality of mystery, and healing. One of overwhelming beauty, harmony, and grace.

That is what life is to be modeled after, just as that, is where health begins. Because connection, contact to source, has always been the deepest medicine.

We were lucky up there, fortunate. And we knew it. We also knew the best thing to do with anything so freely given, was to give it away. I'm sure that when Dave re-entered his practice, just a day after our long drive home, his approach, like that of his climbing, was completely different. When a physician has themselves been in touch with grace, when they have felt the light, they have a deeper capacity to heal.

Lucky are we, blessed rather, to be able to stand on the shoulders of giants and feel the universe flow through time, space, history, and heartbeat alike; lucky are we who howl like schoolboys at the moon and the stars, unshackled and alight; lucky are those who glow in that secret energy whom few but the pregnant, the sober, and the healed ever experience on this earth. From the membranous single layers of our alveolar tissue, down to the capillary exchange on the arterial end of the little toe itself.

رْظُّلاَ ةالَصَ

ṢALĀT AL-ẒUHR

In 2015, at the Al Masjid Al-Haram, in Mecca, Kingdom of Saudi Arabia, somewhere between the first and the seventh, counterclockwise holy circles of Tawaf, an unassuming friend, Ghazaly, carried a secret burden.   Nearly lost among the millions of devout acolytes, who penitently circled the Kaaba in a haze of trampled, shaken earth and sand, Ghazaly carried something holy. It wasn't a relic, it was not even a religious article. It wasn't something to be held at all. It was inside of him, where all our holiest parts are, right next to the fears. Surrounded by millions of others from all corners of the globe, shuffled between those countless varieties of foreign tongues, Ghazaly quietly carried a sickness, a brokenness, within. He wouldn't know it yet, but his walk for freedom and for truth would not end soon. It might, he thought, not be the type to ever get lighter. The kind of secret, he feared, which could not be walked away—not with the thousands of steps and host of kilometers around the Kaaba, nor those up and around hills of Safa and Marwah.

It couldn't be reversed by the waters of the Zamzam Well, not by the throwing of stones at the Devil, not by any stomping of feet. Not by a petition of prayer, by will, by deed, by a song, nor by any other rite of Hajj in the holy month of Dhu'l-Hijjah. But, that didn't stop him from trying.

He didn't know what was wrong, only that something wasn't right. He and his wife, Naureen, were newlyweds on their first Hajj together. The two had, in many ways, waited their entire lives to meet one another, to find partnership; to marry in a most traditional sense, the beautiful sense. But just as they'd have hoped to embark on a romance together for the ages, Ghazaly's problems began. Honeymooning, as a phase, would have to take a back seat to the sober trek of reality.

In the few years that he and Naureen had known each other, Ghazaly had gone from a renaissance practitioner of the faith—a woke and conscientious Muslim in a modern world—to a man in defeat. His focus and his energy, not just in physical activity but in all his activity, had dissolved; he was threadbare. Ghazaly was a joy in a simpler time, always a deep thinker, sure, but always a joy first. A proud Brown man, an Indian man, an educated man with just enough imagination to flavor the life of the rational mind. The kind of guy who'd find a way to genuinely smile over a bowl of cereal and milk in the morning, before the office job. Because that's where gratitude shows up when your parents came from a different time and country. He could weave the concepts of his faith and tie them to the web of events in the modern world, with a panache that made you believe it just on virtue of seeing it. He could blend the sleeplessness of his legal profession with his restless activities in the outdoors, no seams showing. But the best parts about him were those simple, humble smiles at the seemingly most mundane parts of a day. The cereal being one of them. We're talking about elevated states of being as a direct result of plain milk and a khaki-colored grains. That's where he found joy, and, I assume, God.

All that caved, however. Boarding the plane to Riyadh, Ghazaly was sick, strangely sick, and strangely alone. These twilight days, and his physical dysfunction, quickly piled up as recurring dreams. Relationships, once fertile, were quickly overrun by a hidden isolation. Emotionally, spiritually, physiologically, he digested the symptoms and the confusion which came with them, mostly alone.

When the wheels touched down on American soil, and Ghazaly and Naureen were back in Georgia, they'd had a spiritual experience enough to sustain their faith, but they hadn't yet found what they were looking for. They'd neither received clarity on Ghazaly's condition nor the miracle of freedom from it. That diagnosis, however, wouldn't remain in secret for long. Many phone calls, a few doctors' visits, and a handful of months later, they finally received their diagnosis. Ghazaly had a robust case of Early Onset Parkinson's. And doubling down on the stakes, in the months following their Hajj, Naureen was diagnosed with ovarian cancer.

That quick. How's that cereal, now?

In the span of a single breath, before the doctor could finish that sentence, Ghazaly felt something deeper than his own DNA. True fear. Fear that hollows the core. Fear which makes you the fool, that terrifies the mind, that shrivels the spirit, that suggests only pain rather than an opportunity. The kind that takes you fully out of body, and yet traps you from within.

Fear, no doubt, is a most human trait. It can be overwhelmed by the capacity to love, but at its core, love is more divine than it is human. We only transmit love. Fear, we can hold. Fear, we can generate. Fear is human. It leads to the dark night, to the shadowlands, to the long space of time that must be endured until it simply cannot be. Ghazaly would sit in that fear, as many do, for the better part of a few dark years. Deeper than a black hole, yet holy just the same.

Truth is, to get anywhere in this life, we all have to crack. If the constructs don't fold, we simply won't.

III

We met again on a warm day, bright blue, at high noon. Stitched together by sincere, but only occasional, messages, our friendship had idled at the surface for years, and unfortunately, that's where it stayed with the distance between us. And for a time, for a few years really, Ghazaly would've preferred it this way. But as the distance shrunk, with Ghazaly and Naureen moving back to California just a few years ago, so too did the gaps in our conversations. It had been eight years exactly since we had shared an apartment, and I wanted the chance to be touched by his simple, humble charisma—even if he felt like he'd lost it long ago.

Like many who struggle to manage a chronic condition, when you're deep in the labyrinth, navigating the first steps of a new life and all the disease which comes with it, it's easier to keep the bubble small. How many times and to how many friends had Ghazaly had to explain his condition? How many times has he had to retell and curate his story? In the last five years, he's watched himself have an out-of-body experience every day, in slow motion. How much easier, how much simpler it is, to seek healing in a pocket rather than a community? How hard is it to reach out to others when the sickness tells you that you have nothing of value to give?

We sat for lunch and three hours later, we'd barely scratched the surface. Three hours, just kneading out the tight spots of his experiences, stretching them into something we could share. What I knew was that while slightly better of late—due to a change in meds—Ghazaly needed something of an outdoor reckoning.

My ambition, contingent on his willingness, was to go and abide with the natural order—the raw, the grizzled, the unkind—so that we might find a parcel of its grace. To break him, a little further and in a different way, to crack that small seed of imagination still left within his rational mind. And to get at it before it's too late.

Ghazaly may have been managing his condition on the surface, but there was an obvious passivity about him. A sense of just sliding by. As if his only request was that his life simply not get too much worse and not all too rapidly. Degeneration was imminent. His hope was that the things he will have to let go of not be taken from him too soon, nor all at once.

"You're telling me in all this time since your diagnosis, you've basically not been outside, at all? No hikes, climbs, water sources, nothing?" I asked.

"Not that I can think of," he answered.

"A park, at least?" I probed.

"Well, I guess not."

"You understand that we've got to lay this all out over a piece of rock, right? All of it, the shit you've been through. That shit you're wrestling with in your faith. We're gonna take all of it and move over some stone and scatter it to the wilderness."

"Okay, my man, if you say so," he said, resigned.

///

Two weeks later, driving up to the Eastern Sierra, we traded war stories on living with disease as we shot up the freeway and out of Los Angeles. Not that he ever wanted to be an expert on the subject matter, but in the last year things had progressed faster than expected. Unable to focus for long periods and unable to produce to his firm's standards, Ghazaly was fired. To be taken from his career was a devastating blow. For Ghazaly, as an Indian man and as a practicing Muslim, work is not just a thing, it's an ethic.

He comes from a family, and a generation, which is defined by academic and career focus. And beyond that, he's simply passionate about law. He loves it. At a core level, he lives and breathes the legal field like he lives and breathes the spiritual. Because, for Ghazaly, they are one and the same. To him, laws as a whole carry a fundamental notion that humans thrive by creating order, structure, work, and routine. That we manifest our best when we have targets to shoot for.

Parkinson's has been an anomaly to that order. For Ghazaly, losing touch with the workforce was more than losing a job, it was another example of him losing touch altogether.

"You know, it really started to spiral in a new way this year," said Ghazaly, "And I with it."

"You mean the symptoms of Parkinson's?" I asked.

"Yeah. Since Naureen went into remission and started school, she has been away from time to time, studying for her Physical Therapy program, even out of state occasionally, for a month or more sometimes. Which has left me with more time than I probably needed alone, just thinking. It's almost like I'm watching myself in a depression from the other side of the same room."

"Shit, man. That's a hard loop to get out of," I said.

"Well, yeah. It's tough to think about anything other than yourself when you are sick, and when you do it usually makes you feel like you're more alone," he shared.

"You suffer more," I offered.

"Exactly."

"You ever think about connecting to a care group, something like a community of Parkinson's patients? I bet you'd get so much out of that. You know, there's something to be said about a group of people held together by a common disease," I suggested.

After a scroll back in memory, Ghazaly replied, "Yeah, I thought about it. I even went to one meeting, a while back. But it put me in a dark place for weeks. I mean, the issue was definitely me, not them. I just didn't know how to deal with what I saw in there. Some guys progressed so far down they could barely function at all without full care. It scared the shit out of me."

"Why do you think that is?" I asked.

"Because all I could see was my future."

He wasn't wrong. The future which Ghazaly described is not clear. Parkinson's is not greatly understood at present. The best most people can hope for, today, is some level of disease management. What we do know, is that it is progressive and that the chief action, or lack thereof, is in the brain. Zoom deep into the cosmic stellar-sphere of the cortices, and you find that one of a handful of chief neurotransmitters in the human body's communication channels, is dopamine. With Parkinson's, it is the absence of dopamine which causes the greatest disruption. It's all chemical and electric charge in there, so if a message cannot transmit across the matrix, shit gets haywire quick.

When the brain orders an operation, dopamine carries the order through something called the nigrostriatal pathway, until the target cells carry out the order. Without the appropriate conditions for the message to carry, parts of it or all of it are lost and result in the classic motor dysfunctions which are trademarks of the disease. Tremor, rigidity, bradykinesia, and postural instability.

In the end stages, a complete loss of motor control occurs, forcing a need for permanent medical care and eventually, a slow, bedridden shuttle out of this body and into the next frame. The decline in mental health including loss of memory, language skills, hallucinations, and dementia, awaits further. While the bedridden nature of the late stages may cause infections and organ insufficiencies, this end-stage of Parkinson's is not, in-and-of-itself, terminal. It will not cause death. Which means, that while losing all autonomy and enduring perpetual sick cycles, a person will weave involuntarily between states of consciousness and hallucination. The later stages of Parkinson's, it seems, are more suited toward torture, than toward the kill.

That's a rough sketch at the future Ghazaly took a long look at, face to face with elders in that recovery group. As he put it, an entire room filled with it.

///

An hour past Inyokern, just as we came into the first real view of the Sierra's, I broke what was almost an hour of silence. When we left the conversation, Ghazaly had continued painting that dark future, and had also included his fears about how his condition might affect Naureen— afraid that she'd be suffering, too.

"Hey, Ghazaly. Now that we're coming into some better views, I'll say this. It's no doubt that what you are looking at is terrifying. When you saw that old fella' at the support group and you freaked out, I get it. The physical prognosis, the fear of losing the primary components of what makes you, you— that's terrifying. But let me share something, a parable from a guy I heard recently."

"Sure," he replied, "I'm all ears."

"A decade ago, this guy was trying to get sober. Being a proper alcoholic, he had years-worth of darkness. Finally, one day, it happens, and like it does for a lot of people he's all washed up. No job, and he hasn't done anything he or society would care to score as valuable. The guy has lied and cheated as a lifestyle, for decades, so you can imagine the self-esteem.

"Now sober, he's also broke as shit, and even though he's ashamed of all the wreckage he's caused, he realizes he's got to move back in with his folks. But, praise Allah, he's broken enough, so he's got some willingness. The good news, it's the first time in his life he can do something to help his parents, 'cause now they're pretty old and dad is actually sick, like

Lucas Roman

really sick. Six or nine months to live kind of sick. The bad news is, all he can see is the impossibility of trying not to drink or use for the rest of his life, all his shortcomings, and the fact that he's living at home with the parents. Still, he's willing to follow what the other sober guys tell him. So, he does it one day at a time. Sober, but kinda suffering, right?"

"Yeah," Ghazaly replied, "sounds rough."

"This goes on for almost a year. Eventually, his dad dies, and even through all that, he stays sober and keeps at it. Just as he's getting on his feet with a new job, he's speaking with his mom one day. They're talking about his dad, those final years, and the whole time he can't shake this feeling that he's always been a piece of shit son.

"That is, until his mom just looks at him and says, 'Son, those last few years, that last year with your father, those were the best years of our lives. Your dad and I both were so happy to have you home. We were so thankful to see you in the world in a new way. Every single day that you were sober, and we were there to see it, every day you were back under our roof, those were some of the happiest times of our lives. It didn't matter that he was dying, it only mattered that we were all connected. Out of nowhere, this guy is staggered, right? Just cracked over the head because it hits him. That his feelings, his experiences, all the shit in his head is not the full reality, at all! His perceptions, how he felt about the situation was completely out of touch with the deeper truth of what was happening."

When I stopped and looked over to my side at Ghazaly, I saw a reaction I had not intended. Ghazaly had a thousand-yard stare over the dashboard, flooded with tears that were rolling off his cheeks. The beauty of Tumanguya (Mount Whitney) itself, was barely visible behind the blur of his lacrimals.

"I know you are scared as shit, man," I continued. " But just consider, that when you say, 'that' is your future. What you saw in that support group when you think about all the suffering ahead. When you think about Naureen and how you think it'll be the worst time of her life,

APERTURE ALIKE   117

caring for you when you get to where you are going. I say this humbly my friend, but you might want to pause, 'cause what you see, or what you think is happening, might be all wrong. Her caring for you might be the closest she ever gets to God, and it might be the same for you."

Stammering, Ghazaly replied, "Damn, dude. Inshallah."

///

Walking across the shore on the south end of Lake George, in Mammoth Lakes, we approached the Dyke Wall for an afternoon acclimation exercise. Ghazaly had only climbed with traditional gear a few times, ever, and no more recently than six to seven years ago, so a refresher felt in order. As we hiked in, though, just watching him engage with the land was fascinating. Even the simple tasks, things most of us would overlook, like taking on the short rise of a steepening bank or the aggressive sway of an acute switchback, was special to behold. Short on practice he quickly realized that it was not a set of steps he was on, it was a hill, each pass of a foot required a different power output and a different balance. You and I might not take that into account, but he does.

"It's magical out right now," he shared halfway up the approach and with a heavy breath.

As I smiled back at him, I had to acknowledge he was right. Afternoon light was in, and it was in good. The trees were taking on that extra glow, and light columns were piercing to the floor in the way they do in those old-world, alabaster cathedrals. The holy forces were at play, no doubt, as Ghazaly shook his pack off his shoulders in a full tremble.

The Parkinsonian drum-roll is the signature move of the resting tremor, and like Elvin Jones or Art Blakey, Ghazaly has his own beat. Of course, it's not jazz he's playing, but if you didn't associate it with a disease, I bargain it'd be considered just as cool. For Ghazaly, it's a constant reminder that he's managing an illness. For me, it's holy. An ever-present visual demonstration of an uncountable number of atomic and electric combinations, a microscopic mass exodus of electrolytes in each sliding filament; a revelation that in our very own make-up, there are always forces both beyond our measure and beyond our control.

Considering that drum-roll, and the fact that Ghazaly was out of practice to climbing—the idea that I would be taking a good lead fall from the top of a cliff, with him belaying, or even trusting his lowering skills, was something of a test of my convictions about said beauty. But, it was exactly the empowerment he and I both needed. I led, and he followed, as we spent the afternoon on the vertical.

My act of faith was submitting to him as belayer—empowering him to feel as needed and valuable as he is. And my only hope was that it was as beautiful as his submissions. Because when the alpenglow really got going, and we started settling in for the night, Ghazaly took a moment to face east and perform his rites toward Mecca. Seeing him touch base with that, with the afterglow of a California sundown on the Sierras, was medicinal, and not just for him.

The humble bastard rose from prayer, unashamed as he should be, and reconnected to our conversation after having closed his ceremony.

"Thank you, for this." he shared, in his intimate way, "It's really more than I could've expected already."

"I feel the same, my friend," I acknowledged. "But, there's still tomorrow, buddy. And I'll say this, too. You'll probably get pretty busted up out there at some point, but just remember that's exactly what we're looking for, okay? You might have to lean into that part. When it's less about the beauty than it is about the pain, don't be afraid to stay right there."

III

At 3:30 a.m. it was dark in all the right ways. Just below freezing, quiet, and lovely. After a stretch, we packed the car, hopped on the 395, and made our way toward the Tioga Pass while I chugged day-old coffee. Less than an hour later, at 4:30-ish, we arrived at the Cathedral Lakes Trailhead. Ghazaly isn't quick to do much, and that's not a fault, it's just a matter of fact. But if you can take some of the urgency out of the situations, even out of the alpine start, his pace breeds a level of peace.

At about 4:45 a.m. Ghazaly took his leave for Salat al-fajr his ritual prayer, just a few meters from the car and readied himself for the day ahead. After which, and with headlamps aglow, we set off. An hour later, pausing in a morning meadow, we took our first break.

"Hey brother," he shared, "I'm sorry if I'm not moving too fast. Are we still okay on time?"

"No worries at all, my friend. I bet we'll be making first tracks up there."

"Okay, that's good," he said. "I'm feeling the altitude already."

"Ah man, don't worry about our pace. We're exactly where we are supposed to be. It's cool being first on the wall, but honestly, it'll be perfect however we get it. Whatever the experience, you just gotta trust that's the one you were supposed to be having."

Looking up at Cockscomb Peak in morning rays, and glowing just above the hidden Budd Lake, Ghazaly took what appeared to be his first real, relaxed breath. His shoulders softened and just for a minute, just by the reflection held in his iris alone, it was as if he was staring at light which for the first time was shining out from some long darkness.

As we reestablished the pace of our trudge, I asked him. "Hey man, why don't you tell me more about that dark shadow you mentioned."

"Well, it's a lot like I told you yesterday," he began, "but it's funny you ask, 'cause now that the sun is coming up I realize it's something I'm starting to come out of after all. In life as a whole."

///

The darkness, or his cloud as he might call it, is his ride-along. Most people with a chronic illness have some form of it. The passenger. The co-pilot. That unending press on your chest that you can't shake at night. The feeling that gloom is not a phase but a sepia-tone overlaid on the slides of life. Ghazaly calls it his sadness. It's the grief of the things he's lost in life and the fear of things he'll miss out on later. He says it's a part of him, has been since this disease kicked in.

When he's having his best day, but still feels that shade of grey on the horizon. When he prays to Allah, but isn't sure if the concept of Allah he now has is acceptable. When there is an ellipses after God's name rather than a period. When it's all in suspension. When he isn't sure how to feel about the doubt. When faith in anything feels more the leanings of a fool than the tenets of the wise. All these moments are the outlines of that passenger, that shadow.

He's in been in the haunt for a while now. That's why he's got that passivity I mentioned. He's afraid of the impending change, afraid to wrestle with it all. And he's afraid that the deepest loneliness, the worst parts of the illness, may just come back at any time and without warning.

"Yeah man, I wrestled hard in that darkness. Took me years," he admitted.

"Well, where you are coming in from, you've probably always been told to interpret this kind of thing like it was a judgment on you. To feel like you did something wrong. And it must have been hard to take an honest stock and realize that it just is what it is. You are a good person and you've done nothing to deserve or not deserve this. It's just something that is happening."

"You said it, man," Ghazaly replied, "You know, I was in therapy for years, too, and it took me a long time to understand that I was struggling with my concept of God. That's not something you question as a Muslim, you know. It probably took me just as long to share that, because I was scared to say it. Personally, not concerning others, but even admitting it to myself. I didn't know what it said about me if I questioned God, so I blamed myself for the illness, for years, even though I was wrestling with God in the subtext of everything."

"I understand, brother. For whatever reason, there are just some things that feel impossible to question. Things we can't imagine altering or going away from. But even in the Abrahamic faiths, it's there, man."

Continuing, I added, "If you ask me, that's a part of who we are. It's deeply human. We live by doubt and fear. It's where many great faiths started and it's where each individual journey starts. When there's something on the line, you know? We all need a reckoning. Even Jacob, the guy they called Israel, was famous for that. He wrestled with God, man. And for me, that's not history, it's allegory. It's what humans do, we wrestle with our place, with our faith, and with our concepts. Because even in sickness, ultimately, living itself is a task of expansion, and we resist that kind of change."

"I guess so," Ghazaly conceded.

Passing a lightning-struck, centuries-old pine which was split clean down the middle, I continued, "Look at this pine, dude. This thing is absolutely beautiful, completely standout by virtue of the fact that it was smote by God. Probably didn't feel that way when it was being burned from the inside out but look at it now. Now there's a message for you!"

Ghazaly laughed but made a point to stop and scan that tree to the bones, losing himself for a moment in the mirror of memory.

"You know what that fool was doing anyway?" I carried on. "Everyone forgets the context of that story. Jacob was scared, man. One, he thought he was about to die. Two, he was scared to make amends to his brother. That's the point we all miss! He wrestled with God because he was at a crossroads and he didn't have the capacity to think on a new dimension. He struggled with God because he had a living problem, a life problem. God wasn't lost anywhere at any point in time during that narrative, and God wasn't struggling to wrestle the fucker either. In fact, God didn't wrestle, that not's the story, Jacob wrestled. God was Zen. What Jacob wrestled with, was how to interpret death and how to find harmony in this life. He wrestled with suffering. That's the jig, man. That's human."

"Ha ha. It always sounds better in nature, doesn't it?" Ghazaly proclaimed.

"Trust me, man. I only speak about this shit because I had to live it, too."

///

Another trademark of Parkinson's, that rigidity, can normally be tracked along the half-life of the current scrips he's on. When the dopamine and the blood sugar are low, Ghazaly robots more than he walks, and in the last hour of the approach, he and his feet faded, fast. Sliding like a B-boy in Houston, his hometown, Ghazaly quickly took on a wicked toe-drag that bordered on a ganster-lean, tracing dust plumes across the trail. Popping in a pill for a shot at homeostasis, he anted up for the final kilometer, one small stagger after the other. No hiding it at this point, the suffering had begun.

Sometimes, I did my best to remind him just how righteous he was. Looking back, catching his thousand-yard stare, his reservation, and the drops of sweat pooling at the lower scoop of his glasses. All of it inspired. "Dude, you're a badass."

"If only ten steps at a time," he replied, "I'm trying to be."

When we got to the base and confirmed our fortune to be the only duo in attendance, we took a good siesta. No rush now, all we had to do was sort gear, breathe deep, and get vertical.

"How you holding up, my friend?" I asked.

"A bit more rigid than I'd like to be," he admitted, "But I think I'm ready for this. I mean, look at this place. Pretty unbelievable stage for a rock climb."

"Welcome to the high country," I replied, "And to Cathedral Peak!"

Handing him the rope from my harness before setting off on lead, I checked the feed on our gri-gri, shook his hand strong, and set off with a smile. "Thanks for the willingness to be here, Ghazaly, may it be a revelation!"

What surprised me the most was the way it all came back to him so quickly. On dirt, he skipped like a record, but on the rock, Ghazaly found a cadence. It was like his joints loosened to the point of flow, and it wasn't for a lack of fear either. At the first and the second belay, he was decidedly terrified. At each belay station, he would look down but not lean out, he would stare at the anchor five times over, and then curl into a fetal feint. But dammit, the minute he started a new pitch, he just found a way to move, disease-free if you ask me.

At the top of the second pitch, though, the day started to get the better of him. His meds had kicked in, but other parts of his body and mind were beginning to crack. By the time he came up to the third belay, halfway up the route, there had been a palpable shift. Joy had left him completely and in its place was that beady look of pain management. Feeling self-conscious about his performance and his energy, Ghazaly quickly slid into an apologetic posture. A lot like he was during our lunch a few weeks back.

"Ah man, I'm sorry about the lag," he said while I pulled gear from this harness. "And, yeah sorry about the disorganization," he said a moment later, as he unclogged an alpine draw from its tangle.

"Not a problem at all, Ghazaly," I replied, "but, what's this carnage on the rope all about?"

"Uhm, sorry about that," he replied. "Not sure how I did that one."

During the third pitch, or while cleaning the anchor on the way out of the second belay, he'd somehow managed to tie the rope around himself in an overhand knot, about 10 feet ahead of his figure-eight tie-in point. Out of his wits and his comfort zones, he followed that entire pitch with it sliding through the carabiners on the gear and the cracks. It chewed the sheath right off the cord, but so long as the core was intact, so was our mission.

In an effort to get us further, faster, I strung the fourth and fifth pitch together. After a little more than 200 feet and with the rope pulling tight behind me, I was forced to make anchor on a slab between a pair of ledges; a position I knew he would not appreciate. Sure enough, moments later as Ghazaly shuffled into the fold and clipped the master point, he made it clear that he did not enjoy our real estate.

"Oh man, can we do something to change this up?" he asked.

"Shit," I replied, "I know this isn't your ideal setup. But, if you get out of the discomfort and have a look, it's pretty nice out." Pointing to Budd Lake behind us, royal blue with that turquoise liner, I continued, "Not a bad way to see Yosemite for the first time, right?"

Hoping the beauty moment would salve the pain of his body—pain and discomfort I can't pretend to understand—I noted that just to our left and down the Valley itself, Tis-se'-yak was in view. "Not a bad way to lay your eyes on Ahwah'ne and Half Dome for the first time either, eh?"

Sullen, Ghazaly tried his best to look at the place with wonder, but his eyes were no brighter and his heart no lighter from the gaze he gave it. "Brother," he very slowly pronounced, "you better get a move on it, cause right now I ain't looking at nothing."

Truth is, I won't know the pain, or the tension, or the fear that grips him. I can't know the exact discomfort either; my cells don't shake the way his do. But I do know there is a safety, both in the brokenness and in beauty. I jumped ahead and scurried up that last lead, confident that while he might have felt at his worst, he was in a good place, after all. At the first ledge, thirty feet up, I looked back at him and did my best to summon the morale booster. "That shit I said about leaning into the pain experience when it takes over the beauty. You're right there now, my friend. Sweetest spot on earth."

"You sure about that?" he replied.

"I'm sure it doesn't feel that way right now, but I bet if you have another look when you get up to this ledge in a little bit, give it some time, something will turn over."

At the top of Cathedral Peak, squatted on the tabernacle block of the summit moments later, I belayed Ghazaly up that last pitch. I couldn't see him and the wind was on it good, howling, so there was no point trying to holler down at him for a status update. Instead, as often happens on a climb, I got information solely by the rate of the rope I was taking in. I wasn't sure if it was a drop in his glycemic panel or a case of something worse, but Ghazaly was moving slower than he had all day. And from my end of the device he seemed to be broken, at last.

When he finally came around the headwall, standing under the ultimate 30-foot block, and I got a look at his mug, the fucker had a grimace mean enough to stop a deer in its tracks. And yet, with all suffering included, he took hold of the moment anyway. One, deep, deerga-swasam later, and with hands trembling to seismic levels, he ratcheted up the last 15 feet and achieved the goddamn summit proper. A feat well earned.

"Well done, my friend," I said with a pat on his shoulder.

"Not done yet," he began, "but thank you."

For a man at the summit, for all the context that brought him here, Ghazaly was surprisingly without emotion at first. In addition, he was surprisingly ready to be off the top, no sooner than he'd just arrived.

"You doing okay, man?" I asked. "Took you a while on that last pitch."

"Yeah," he started, "I just needed a few moments for something out there. Also, I think I'm just a little sick from this exposure. I'm not good at this part, you know."

That much I could see. His nerves, apart from being shot on the physiological level, were frayed just from the position. I don't know if he's ever taken well to vertical exposure, but my hunch was that in today's case, standing at the top of this thing was not making him feel any stronger. Hard-pressed for energy to safely exit the premises, the exposure was just that—exposing the fact that he was a frail man most days of the week, with no business taking risks like these just for kicks. I've been there, in my own trials, too. Sometimes, in the fragile moments of life, the outside experience can make us react with more fear.

"Look, brother, I know you aren't too comfortable up here, but it's still a hell of a view, even if you just keep your eyes on the horizon, eh?"

"Yeah, I think so, too. We can take it in a bit more," he admitted. "You know what, I need to take it in more. Jesus, look at me! I'm so ready for these things to be over I don't even look for the lessons in them. And man, it's beautiful up here."

Was it a turn of the wind? A protein channel opening up in a cell membrane? A surge of dopamine sent from the microbiome? God with a whisper? I have no idea. But right then and there Ghazaly had his realization. He understood the value of staying, of pausing, and of, at last accepting his brokenness.

His resting tremors were now whole-body palpitations, like sizzles out of a sauté pan, and his face was a moving target, but he kept on, saying, "I always run away from this stuff. Pain. Discomfort. But the truth is this is where I'm supposed to be, especially when I don't feel like it. It's what we came up here for."

With shakiness in his voice that acknowledged a real fear experience, still ongoing, he said, "Thank you for this."

We sat for a few more minutes until the perspective settled deeper than the pain, until the pride of being alive and the joy of participating in it came back. I even got him to forge a smile for the camera so he could keep that one and show it to the family. He looked haggard in the freeze-frame; but he looked damn good, too. It was one of those things you just need to capture. The day when he stood upright in the face of his disease and did something perfectly badass. Something perfectly audacious.

///

Ghazaly's suffering did not end at the summit. In fact, it got worse, as things do, before it got any better. Walking off Cathedral, especially for someone at their breaking point, is not an easy task. Especially in his condition, at exhaustion—with Parkinson's—forced to take big, off-balance steps down committing slabs, to make sharp turns on awkward boulders, teetering blocks, and slippery scree. Those are all high-performance mechanics that the average among us take completely for granted. With Parkinson's, and a fear of heights, it's a nightmare. He sputtered down hundreds of feet of third and fourth-class slab, having a terrorizing experience in place of the whimsical, freeform descent entertained by most of us. By the time he was halfway off the shoulder of the peak, his eyes had outgrown his glasses. Honestly, it felt like the scrambling off took longer than climbing up, maybe it did. But with a few resting stops staving off the moment of full breakdown, he kept at it—and may have been prouder to arrive at his pack than he had been to make it to the summit.

At the base, sometime later, Ghazaly collapsed under a branch of shade by our packs and moaned in an octave of gibberish.

"I don't know if I can make it back, man," he said with a shakiness. "I'm kind of scared to move, but also scared that I can't."

"Well, we're in no rush," I began. "And, we've got day old bahn-mi and a liter of water, buddy. Have at it."

Unwrapped and cracked at the crust, Ghazaly gulped down the day-old baguette more than he ate it. It took him a good half hour maybe more, quietly sitting, thinking, and waiting for the macro-molecules of food and water to sink in, but he came around slowly. When the sun finally crossed over him and the shade slipped away, he got up and reset his glasses.

"I think you're right," he started in an apparent epiphany.

"Right?" I said surprisingly, "Right about what?"

"About staying there. About embracing things when they don't seem to be working out. About being broken."

"How's that?" I asked.

"Well, you're right that being broken is a good thing. That situation depending, we probably shouldn't flee from it. If we would've just rushed off that summit, I would've missed a moment of truth, a truth I saw when we stayed on it. One of those realizations, that we're connected to everything out there."

"In ways you and I probably can't even imagine." I laughed.

"You know, when you are at Hajj, in Mecca, it's kind of the same thing. There are a million people there with you, everyone wearing the same outfit, people of all nations blending into one—you lose yourself. It's designed that way. When that happens, when you realize just how small but just how connected you really are to something way more beautiful, it's indescribable. I think that's the point of the spiritual game, man. It's all about the moments that make you drop the self."

"It always has been," I confirmed.

"Yeah, it's funny. I'm all about it in Mecca, on my terms. But up here, on steep rock, or down in life in my illness, I rebel. I reject it. I run away from life when it gets painful. Like you said, I wrestle, and then I drown in fear. Brokenness can be a real thing, I know it is. I've spent years in darkness thinking I couldn't connect to others, or to God. But it's not everything you think it is, being broken isn't a life sentence, it's what you need for a real connection to happen. Every spiritual experience I've had has required some form of it."

Just like that moment on the summit block. I'm not sure what hit him.

The network of his brain and body, of all of ours, is so incomprehensibly complex I cannot begin to trace it. I have no idea what triggered who and when and how and where. But an hour ago he was having one of the deeper pain and fear experiences of the day, thirty minutes ago he was nearly comatose, and just like that, with the right combination of molecular dance and spiritual awareness, all of a sudden he's speaking in proverbs.

///

Ghazaly's moments of glory ebb and flow like he does. What you learn, what he's learned, is to just be grateful when the good ones come. To count the blessings when the status quo is exactly that, in equilibrium. A minute after declaring the profundities of his experience and standing up in heroic posture, he shouldered his pack, made a handful of steps down the hill, got off-trail and slid down a patch of scree. Suddenly frail and scared all over again, I got the hunch that this was just one more of a million familiar moments in his path. Reset, reboot, try again.

Still, as we made way and dropped in elevation, the neurologic haze slowly lifted, and it was apparent just by measure of him being keen for conversation. At one point, nearly halfway back, he hollered out from about thirty yards behind me, with a boisterous giggle, bordering on delirium.

"Hey man, check it out. Do you see it?"

"See what?" I had to ask.

"Me!" he shouted with a smile. "I got my arm swivel back, man! I mean look at this mean machine!"

Sure enough, he did. The afternoon meds and drop in altitude must have been working because with that giant smile and my full attention on him, Ghazaly noodled those arms like Ali in the ring—with a swagger and zest you just can't imagine. At least ten paces, in pure freedom and self-expression, unbound, grateful and carefree down to the last neuron. He stood over his illness the way Ali stood over Liston after that phantom punch, if only for a moment.

Finally, back at the car an hour later, Ghazaly and I sat under the shade of a pine, looking out over the famed meadows of the high country.

"I gotta tell you, a year ago I wouldn't have thought any of this was possible," he shared.

"That sounds like a win to me, buddy," I started, "Like you might just be living again."

"Inshallah," he said coolly, "Inshallah."

"You know, that's one of my favorite terms in Arabic."

"Why is that?" Ghazaly probed.

"I'm not sure, but to me, it just has this undeniable fortitude. There's an acceptance baked into it, that a higher force is at the helm. For me, inshallah touches the reservoir, the same reservoir you touch in brokenness. Like all is well in the deep order of things. Like God ain't lost, and She ain't wrestlin'."

Quickly processing, Ghazaly shared, "Yeah man, I think I know what you mean. We say it a lot, to apply to something we want to see happen, but what's really said with it, is that whatever will be, should be. Because it's kind of saying that everything that is, is good. Even for someone like me, especially for me, that's an important thing to acknowledge. That even if things don't work out like I would have them, the peace about life is just as available, because God is, too."

"That's the stuff right there, buddy" I acknowledged, "And speaking of the good stuff, did you end up having the midday prayer up there by yourself at some point?"

Ghazaly nodded, breaking an almost secret smile. "I did. And it was a hell of a moment."

"I thought as much," I laughed.

He wouldn't say what pitch, or at which anchor, but it must have been high on the route. My guess, it was at that ledge after the last belay, the one I'd told him to stop and look around at. It would explain the pause I felt when feeding his rope through the system at the summit.

The image of that man, stricken and all, up high and in sacrament, brought an indescribable joy. Especially considering how he looked a few weeks back. Ghazaly, the guy who'd been to Hajj and back looking for the Lord, to high and low places, through lonesome nights in the trials of his personal faith. To envision him humbly bending east and making rites on the Southeast Face of Cathedral Peak, exercising the four rakats with the whole of the Eastern Sierra, the domes of the high country, the shadows of Mount Dana, the plains of the Owen's Valley and the caps of the White Mountains in range of his offering. That is the image I choose of this man. That is the deep holy. Right there, in the ⬛alāt a⬛-⬛uhr.

We drove home like old highway bandits, joyous at our fortune, and with all intent to share the bounty.

///

In this life, there is no shortage of the beautiful, the hallowed, and the holy. Indeed, it pervades all reality, and often in the simplest forms. The organic make-up of a cell. The sacred bond of an enzyme. The dance of trillions of microbiota sweeping through us and our innards, as rivers do to enliven the earth itself. The tingling magic of oxygen binding to hemoglobin. A motor impulse carried out by a dopamine molecule. These events, and multitudes more, occur in-cycle every day, in each one of us, right under our noses. Life, its complexity, is an orchestra, orders of magnitude beyond our awareness or appreciation. It is by no accident that we stand on the precipice of that life, of those innumerable, minute, and holy iterations but for one purpose: so that we might look over our shoulder and see the other—the fellow human, the love of our life, the child, the parent, the stranger, the animal, the living tree, the entire system—and that we might acknowledge the beauty of it enough to love it.

The broken among us teach us how. They have the key. They know deeply what it is and what it feels like to be human. They know pain and loss, they know frailty, and darkness. They know fear. They know the paralysis of it, the isolation of it, the chill of it. But, when willing to reach out and beyond it, it was the broken who found the truth. As humans, it was always fear we would generate, but it is love that we are destined for. To love in this life, more than we fear. No matter our condition. That love—our greatest destiny—is not something we generate but something we transmit, that love is not to be held or kept, it is only to be given.

Two weeks later, early in the morning, Ghazaly texted:

Hey man, I went on a backcountry hiking trip into the sierras last weekend!

It was amazing and grueling, really pushed my limits.

Also found that in the suffering I came closer to God.

That when I was surrounded by beauty, by friends, and by pain, my prayers were prayers of joy.

I imagined he must have sent it while having that bowl of cereal again, thumbs shaking and all. An image that filled me with a quiet joy. To see him embrace his brokenness and his condition, not as his greatest liability but as the canvas where he and God toggle toward one another, is to see fruit sprout from a tree, to see a cell divide under a microscope, to see childbirth and first breath. It is all the stuff of life. I put the phone down, convinced that was only a matter of time before he'd send another one, telling of his new fellowship in a Parkinson's support group. Surely now, that freedom and many more lay just ahead for him as they do for us all.

Inshallah.

حزق سوق ة وشن

THE GNAWAN

Any given day, among the millions of particles of dust which scatter the rises of the Ute desert, a lucky few make flight across the canyon rims and land just like so, coating the sandy blocks at the summits of its towers with a saffron glow. In certain months of the year, and with a touch of wind, this alone is a goddammed revelation. For most of us, everyday life in technicolor is beyond our comprehension. The atomic level, we think, is far too small to ponder for our great lives. So, it floats along under our noses, perfectly; an undiscovered river in perpetual motion.

In the middle of a cold November afternoon, Sa`id Belhaj's right-hand rounds over the lip of the classic Kor-Ingalls route, smashing palm down on a million of those dust molecules, and then spreads open like it's making a snow angel in the Sahara. His five phalanges find traction, and like a kid at an ice cream stand, his head peers over the lip in a fit of uncontrollable curiosity. Einsteinian tufts shoot off from his unwashed black hair, as he gives the landscape a satisfied once over. He plays the part well, both of genius and child all at once, and makes the final move, placing his feet to the summit proper.

Freeze frame. I snap a photograph before he can get eyes on me behind the lens, just in time to save that perfect windswept look on his mug. It's as raw as he was. While he may or may not be comfortable with the title, Sa`id is a professional climber. On his resume, a climb like the Kor-Ingalls route is biscuit-crumbs, at best, from a performance point of view. His sponsors couldn't give a rat's ass where that one fits in his catalog. But, summits aren't into bullshit, and neither is Sa`id. He's into climbing, and climbing for Sa`id has always been damn near holy ritual. By that measure, today is historic, because it marks a transition. Whether he knows it yet, or not, Sa`id is up there looking for direction. Maybe that's why he is so in love with the wind.

The top of Castleton tower is where our friendship begins. Castleton, a spiritual tenet, an ancient spire, a fingertip of earth which reaches up in praise, toward God Herself, draped all around us in shades of Toureg blue.

A vagabond of another time, a xitano by trade, a seeker, Sa`id has been to more places than most. While each has left its own mark upon his character, there is perhaps no deeper substrate to Sa`id than his African roots. Everywhere Sa`id travels he brings a piece of the mainland with him. It could sprout out of him in any situation, in any color, indeed, even in any expression of energy. Like a speckle of sandstone grain, Africa spreads out from Sa`id and into the wind of everyday life.

The other day it was just a passerby on the street. "Did you see the way that woman walked," he stammered, in flash of Deja-vu, "Just like a Sudanese, my man, I swear! I saw her kind exactly as we drove in the bush toward the Hand of Fatima." The next day it was in his explanation after a stranger asked about the gri-gri on his wrist.

"These things are sacred to many people, you know. Some folks in the Congo believe them so powerful, they can even protect from bullets." He'll say it all with his trademark, curled brow. He'll even raise the wrinkles of his forehead into five distinct, pillowed folds, just to sell the point further.

But on today, Sa`id is African, beautifully, proudly African, by merit of his knowledge of the desert wind. "It's like the Harmattan across the Western-Sahel, yeah! Really spiritual stuff!" He notes with a sharp affirmation. "All across Mali, in the North, they have songs for this stuff, man. You'd love it up there, your beat for sure!"

Sa`id's English spans the globe as much as he does, and before each sentence has even passed his teeth it's been channeled through lingual filters to become its own dialect; equal parts Scandinavian cordiality, and Pan-African street slang.

"I've seen people fall into a trance and move like this wind, man!" He sits with arms wide open, "Just righteous!"

A strong gust of wind agrees with his point, and bursts between us in spindrift.

Like his speech itself, Sa`id's cadence, in life, is all his own.

"Johnny, do you think you'll be jumping off this thing in the next twenty minutes?"

Johnny Verbeck and I had climbed up the North Chimney an hour earlier, with the keen ambition, for John at least, to B.A.S.E. off the western exit near sundown.

"Not anytime soon, Sa`id." John flecks a ball of spit out to check the wind. It ventures past the brim of the summit, over the 500 feet of fresh air, then curls and shoots straight back at him, grazing the cuffs of his cheesecloth-excuse for a pair of climbing pants.

"Well then," Sa`id musters with a heckle, "Let's talk about the rituals of the Donso-hunters and their hunter-harp. I felt this energy of the wild, in particular, at Johnny McStiff's last night, around all those girls you and your Moab friends keep company with!"

Sa`id is a gentleman at heart but an animal in instinct, just the human experience of people watching has always been enough to get the man going. The most exciting emotions, those which a poet could muse for hours, and that which a painter would fold into layers of oil on canvas, Sa`id could usually cut down into single-syllable explosions.

"Rrrrrraaggghhh!" the man growls at the thought.

///

Three weeks later, Sa`id and I are ten minutes removed from the 'Roman Road', a two-thousand-year-old foot-soldier's switchback trail, turned goat-path, a couple of hundred feet up the main west-facing wall of Tannourine, Lebanon. The aptly named Shawarma caves sit perched atop a 500-foot-tall cascading massif, dripping with tufas and stained in blue and bronze tones. Ageless as the villages which bed the canyons below, the walls themselves brim with life, still warm from the hands of the potter who cast them.

At the center of the cliff, on the lower tier, there's even a hermits lodge, as old as religion itself, where persecuted monks and seekers have gone for both revelation and protection. It's as humble as bread up there, held together by only a handful of molecules, and looks very similar to the Anasazi equivalent back near Moab where we've just come from. It calls back to an ancient time, a pulse just barely present, that underlies many of the places where Sa`id chooses to ground his feet.

Today it's just us, and a thicket of clouds riding up the breadbasket of the canyon. Steady and hallowed, those clouds tease the landscape as daylight teases the morning. It's hard to put your finger square on it, but there's something mystic out right now. I feel it, and I know he does, too.

"Kind of spiritual at this point, isn't it?" he points down at a rising band of clouds. "Like you want to reach out for it, taste it even. Eh!" You can feel his tongue scratch the back of his throat with that "Eh." Sharpness, like a short and compact left hook, is what you get with Sa`id's speech.

"Shit, you said it," I reply. "I haven't seen this place shine this way, ever."

Real-life, full technicolor, is profound for Sa`id, so profound it can take the climber right out of him.

"What can you do mate? When it gets like this, the weather, just bursting in perfect score. I mean, come on, with a cloud like that carved out from a sky like this. There's no way to match that, man, there's no need for climbing now."

We don't. Instead, we sit, the two of us, forearms pumped to all hell from our earlier efforts, climbing packs for ass cushions, and a cigarette, taken deep to the lungs and disbursed along the hemoglobin super-highway.

"I don't normally smoke man. But! In times like these, my will is no match for the occasion." He smiles like it's the first drag of his life and seizes the moment, "Give me one of those puppies would ya'?"

"Allah w'Salah," I smirk, handing one over to him.

Quiet for a few minutes, we settle into a nicotinic vibration until returning to a conversation we'd struck before the clouds came in. Sa`id's current moment of transition—-the one he was sailing with up on Castleton— is less a single moment as it is a phase. While it may be faint, elusive even, when it comes it brings a fair amount of retrospect. Today, he's sniffing again, putting out his feelers to catch a drift in the wind, looking for direction. Lately, he's been looking back just as much as ahead. Recalling a variety of experiences, past lives, and could've beens. That's where we were before those clouds came in. In the past, on a beach, in-fact, with a woman of his dreams and an open frontier.

"So there I am, traveling, as usual, for months on end, when I came to one day on a beach, with this girl. And realize I'm about to live like never before. What I choose right now, as she's tempting me, this is going to be it. Am I going to be a wild man, a fanatic, a real womanizer, a drug chaser? Or will I be someone else?"

Sa`id was a free man on that beach because for the first time in a long time, he was accountable to nothing. A very long-term relationship had just ended, and that can put a man in many directions. His time, to rage and ramp and fuck and all, to strike his unplayed notes, was now. The sudden awareness that right then and there, he truly could choose to be anybody, pierced him. On the road, accountable to nothing but the next sunset, thoughts of freewheeling crept in, thoughts of a fleshy, wild, psychedelic life and all its splendor glimmered. Sa`id faced a question. Who was he, after all?

At a jumping off point in life, where he would have suspected all impulse to leap, Sa`id paused. It is the last instinct you would expect from a man with such animalistic character, from someone whose best tuning is somewhere between the keys of hunter and shaman. But, that's what came to him.

"It was one of the greatest opportunities for freedom I'd ever had, mate," he paused, "Really open, wide open in life! No more relationship, no one to be held accountable to. At all! Just myself and this great God we see out there. Was she going to be a female, was she going to be all females, was she more rocks in countless lands, or was she going to be the mystery behind them all?"

Sa`id's stories always go Mariana-deep, without effort.

"And I'm on the Mediterranean Sea, man. On this beach. With the sunset, and God knows, the most beautiful woman, man. Beautiful! And she pulls out this spliff and offers it to me. All I can think is holy, shit! If ever, ever, there was a time to get high and be satisfied, it is now!"

But, to his and my surprise, he passed.

"Nah man, I paused, and I don't even know where that came from." Sa`id and I both put our cigarettes out in the barbequing pit that our local friends have carved out of the soil—where on a normal day they would be cooking that Shawarma—and pack the butts in a plastic bottle.

"For the first time in my life, I thought, what am I really doing this for? Not just the thought of a spliff, but the thought of it all."

Lucas Roman

"Sure, I can say it's the occasion. But I'm lost, man, I'm lost and deep down I know it. That's the whole reason I'm here, with this girl, in this place, looking at something transient and beautiful! I was completely lost. And that's when I realized, to start smoking dope, or drinking and drugging now, just because I felt I had some new kind of freedom or happened upon the perfect opportunity, God only knows where I might end up, man, no joke!"

He says it came to him, just like so. Unforeseen and out of nowhere. Sa`id had a moment of clarity that the average drunk only finds when half beat to shit, somewhere deep in the far reaches on desolation's road. What takes some men the better part of an ill-spent lifetime to realize, Sa`id found without so much as a contact high.

It's important because there are some things that Sa`id has done his whole life, without question; as a life lived purely on instinct. But the second dimension to his character is right there, in all the things he doesn't do. Those things are like the keys you don't play, which make the song just as good as the keys you do.

///

Born in Gothenburg, and raised between three functional languages, Sa`id spoke mostly Arabic with his father, Finnish with his mother and grandparents, and Swedish in the interstitial plots of life. His grandfather is a classically trained musician, his father a Doctor of Environmental Economics; within the family as a whole, the mark of education, precision, and acuity pervades. Discipline, structure, character, achievement, Sa`id's family used this grid for generations, and his childhood, as I gather, was an endless pursuit for an actualization of it. As any child would, he looked primarily for his place by following the actions of his older brother, his parents, and in the guidance of his grandfather who he so dearly loved.

Before long, however, Sa`id and that grid met with some friction, one which still carries to this day. As it turns out, it's not in his nature to learn by guidance as much as by experience. And back then, climbing was not what it is today, especially in Sweden. There were no gyms, there were no guidebooks. And while the community of climbers in the Bohuslan may have had an ethic, if you asked Sa`id as a kid, he'd have told you that one-hundred percent, there were no rules.

You can imagine him, in his scrawny young savagery, a little Mogli, a man-cub filled to the brim with fire—puzzled by a grid that seemed to work for so many others, but not for him. He didn't fail at school, but this type of learning, the academic mind, was never his preferred function. Soon, Sa`id reacted to almost every structure and system placed around him.

When he finally got access to climbing, vis-à-vis a static sailing rope he'd bartered off a friend, a handful of old carabiners, the cheapest— which also happen to be the smallest—nuts he could penny-pinch, and a scruffy set of rock shoes, Sa`id was primed to explore all that was wild within him once again. He had already climbed every tree in the neighborhood, but they would not be enough. Even as a child, Sa`id understood that unto their own, rock and root each has a different soul, spaced apart by eons of time, elements, and earth systems. It was the ancient power which lies beneath rock, even then, that called to Sa`id, much in the way that Gnawa later would.

///

In December, the weather of Lebanon is swift, manic, and rumbles off the sea like a battle drum of long ago. Weather systems traveling unchecked through the Mediterranean—from deep water to snowy mountaintops—within the scope of a handful of kilometers, give birth to a spectacle of force unique in its own right. Storms around these parts are fantastic.

The human condition here is paralleled. Lebanon is magic and madness all at once, both the eye-of-the-storm and the sunset which shines behind it. Its people can be ravenous, and they can be angelic, they can inspire, and infuriate. The blades of grass are that thin, as we share the road with a half-million people heading south, toward Beirut on a bustling Friday just before Christmas. Sa`id, is no stranger to such a dynamic setting, in fact, his character is much the same. The glimpses you get of him fit each of the above human states. And make no mistake, whether you have known him for years, or just a few weeks, Sa`id's real character—deep to the Romani outer-shell—only ever occurs in glimpses. Today he's showing another shade.

Driving on the Autostrad along the coastline, we watch as lightning storms dance in Morse code behind sheets of rain, and across a purple horizon that seems to stretch out to Gibraltar. We'd been in discussion, again, about his past. Also, about spiritual climbing, as he might put it. For Sa`id, almost everything boils down to a kind of physics, a measurable and perceptible movement of forces. Life, all the glory of it, and all its energies are separated by mere single atoms at a time. Love energy, spirit energy, climbing energy. If it isn't raw, and you can't cut your teeth on it, Sa`id is probably not that attracted to it. What he craves, part of that shaman and hunter tuning, is the rugged cuts of life. He's far more into experiences that produce guttural sounds from people than those which produce language or long thought. That's what first took him into climbing, and it's also the core of his deepest identity, as a Gnawan.

"Since I was young, man, I just had this need for climbing, like I needed water! Music was like this too, but the way I had to practice it was all about structure. It was classical back then, it wasn't Gnawa, you know. I first learned music as a language of order and form. But not climbing. Climbing began because it was a way for me to act as raw as possible. Just like the sky here above us, man. I could explode when I moved, eh!"

A rain cell pitters just above us and the thousands of others on the slick freeway, forcing everyone to a pause just before last light.

"Nature I came to love later, but from the get-go, climbing was a way to erupt, not with anger, but with energy."

Like the electricity in our hair and across the hillside, as the rain pours down the slopes, I get it. He's reactive to the molecular level, not necessarily unstable, but full of energy.

Referring back to our chat the other day, Sa`id continues, "Yeah man, when I was on that beach with that girl, it all just hit me. What I get from climbing, and from music, what I find in Gnawa. This stuff is all about energy and healing, you know! Energy is important. People ask me sometimes if they know nothing about Gnawa, what's it like. Or, they'll ask about Sufi Islam, they'll ask why I'm a vegetarian even, who knows, they can ask anything. To me, it's all the same, deep down."

"How so?" I asked

"I think, people think I don't do this, or don't do that, you know—party, drugs, rage all night—because of a rule in church, or in a book. But, man, I love to rave, because I love what happens in a trance. The truth is, that I'm the guy shirtless and full of sweat on that club's dancefloor in Gothenburg, till the earliest hours of the morning, man, just raging! I can't help it! But the universe, for me, is big enough as is, mate. You don't need anything else in your system to access the heart of it, you know?"

There's a flash of lightning so big that it spotlights the entire 10 km bay of Jounieh, as he carries on.

"Choosing to follow a spiritual path is not about a book, man. And It's not about rules either, like on that beach. You and I, my friend, we exist in front of situations of total beauty, all the time, because of the outdoors. Out there you aren't accountable to anything your parents gave you. You aren't accountable to some big character, some fiction of a God either. He's not in somebody's book telling me not to do something, man! He's right here in this rain, with US buddy, alive NOW!"

As we settle to digest, the rain relents momentarily. Over the FM radio a man is praising, through bouts of song and verse, this great Allah we speak of, in exaltation. There's a mystic, slow hum of a Ney just behind him, barely adjusting its notes every few measures, and harmony, a haunting harmony that seems to echo from the very bowels of the canyons beside us.

Taken aback, Sa`id notes, "This guy is singing it, man."

"Sounds like something special," I add, acknowledging the weak spots in my Arabic.

"He's reading sections of the Quran, just here, and then he breaks into song," Sa`id says helpfully.

Intoxicatingly, vowels and notes are rolling off this guy's tongue and into the airwaves with immediate therapeutic impact.

Sa`id continues, "This guy is singing for someone he knows, man. This is not a song for the Gods of the written text alone. This is a song for a living God."

You have to agree with him. Listen enough to that voice on the radio and look around at this indigo horizon of storm and lightning, and it's clear pretty quickly that the God Sa`id finds in a trance, in the calcite squeeze of a tufa, and the respirations of cloud bands over cliffsides, is the same God holding these hydrogen bonds together on our windshield. The same one who not only gave a voice box to mankind but also gave the intellect and the knack to put other instruments behind it. One goddamn larynx, two-inches of anatomical meat and tissue, flickering out acoustics that are transmitted across the sky. All so that two vagrant fellas stuck in a storm, along with a half-a-million others, on a crowded road in an ancient land, can simply hear. The awareness of it all combined is a true delight.

"You know what I mean, man?" Sa`id says. "Life is the parade, eh! The real spectacle! And few of us ever really get it, man. There's just too much to measure!"

Whether he gets the whole picture or not, few, I believe, see it in the detail he does. Eventually overwhelmed by the beauty of the song, and aghast, Sa`id rolls his eyes in a shake of disbelief.

"It's madness, man. These humans, this road, this guy's voice, all of it! Madness!"

The plight of the shepherd is to care for the flock. The plight of the churchgoer, to stay within the fold; for there is indeed truth, and strength in numbers. But, the plight of the mystic, Sa`id's song, what I know about him from these little glimpses he flashes, his purpose, is to dwell in a beauty which has no rules nor regulations.

///

Gnawa, for most, is a practice of great mystery, both codified ritual and spontaneous spirit-craft. A musical tradition and a practice of faith, it is Islam, and it isn't. It is Fulani, Bambara, Sufi, Hausa, Berber, of the Mashreq, the Maghreb, and the Sub-Sahara, all at once. It is of the realm of the Djin, and spells, and sorcery, and healing, and yet it is completely human. Played for kings but founded by slaves, it embraces the Arab lineage, but only as much as it embraces Sidna Bilal's (Bilal Ibn Rabah) impact on it. Gnawa has symbols created by deeper symbols, and a subtext underwritten by a code of color, and energy, and spirit. In some ways, it chose Sa`id, more than he chose it.

At a concert, in a full house in Gothenburg, long ago, a man in traditional garb saw Sa`id standing out like a sore thumb. He walked right up to him, in the middle of a crowd, stuck his finger in Sa`id's chest, channeled all that is holy, and said one word. "GNAWA!"

"This guy just laid into me, man. Like in a movie, when a character finds out who they really are, it was a revelation, eh," Sa`id reflects, "He was like, sorry to bother you mate, but I've got news for you. You, are

Gnawa. I'm not asking, I'm telling. You've got it in you, my man, and it needs attention.

"That guy told me who I really was, in a word. That was the power of it. He explained to me why I am the way I am, why I need things the way I do, why I seek what I seek. It was wild. And you bet I paid heed. I dropped everything. For that summer, I studied Gnawa like I breathed in oxygen."

While Sa`id studied, he also understood that he could practice Gnawa his entire life and yet never fully control it. That is because its purpose is conduction, not manipulation. He knew it was never going to be something to master with his skills, but rather something to submit those skills to. Climbing, for Sa`id has been similar. It is not the skills he has that matter most to him, it's not what he can do with them, but what he can get access to, from them.

Sa`id has a deep need to connect to the parallel forces of life, one might say the spiritual forces—and that, above all, has directed his climbing. In fact, as much as he's sought to climb hard routes, he has been keener to use climbing as a means to travel to what he'd consider as powerful landscapes. In the growing list of over 45 countries he's visited, Sa`id has always looked for something more than just a tick-mark from a rockface. In fact, he has always wanted more than just the experience of the rock. The need to connect with the earth on an energetic level has always driven him more than the need to climb. You get the sense, with Sa`id, that he needs to vibrate down to the electron itself.

In his favorite places, where he keeps coming back, there is always the mark of the Indigenous wisdom—of ancient peoples. The haunts he has loved, traveled to, and climbed the most, all have a tangible sense of place—something unique, original, nonpareil.

///

Bear's Ears National Monument is such a place. Here, the night glows. The sky paints colors that make your microbiome move. For Sa`id, it's not only the petroglyph walls but this whole place which stands outside of time. That is because there are canyons here which will give no clue about a 21st century, or about a modern man. Rather, the clues here are about deep time and original man. For this, and the pure crunch of the desert on your teeth, Bear's Ears is his sanctuary.

Rolling out of the Creek Pasture campground, and on three days of consecutive climbing, Sa`id looks worse for the wear. That is, until I shuffle Mahmoud Giunea on the speakers to his total surprise. Grinding off the dirt track and onto the paved road, our tires spit up a cloud of desert sand, sending more of life's ancient molecules out over a traveler's highway. It's 8 a.m., early October, after a stellar sunrise, and it's about nine months on since our last rendezvous. Fall has just begun in the Southwest.

"Holy shit man!" as Sast-Demanio plays along, "Mahmoud is a legend, a real Maalem! Let me tell you about this style of Essaouira Gnawa and where it originates." Sparked by a handclap and a few measures of bass, Sa`id is fully riled awake. And, now engaged, within seconds he spits out a litany of factoids about ritual, about Gnawa, about the sacred Derdeba and the Lila. Once on, he can go for days.

As we pass the reservoir and the sun-blasted yellow cottonwoods, Sa`id belts out at the sky from his innards.

"Can't we just roam the desert with these tunes all day, until we start howling at the moon?" His Gnawan roots getting the better of him, he continues, "I'm serious man, climbing is definitely less powerful than these tunes are, and this place is, right now!"

With one hand out the window, he sharpens his gaze to the Western United States, to these Native lands, and shouts, "Rrrraaarrhhh!"

It's another single syllable moment. Layers of oil on a canvas bigger than any museum could house, all truncated into one, single sound.

Looking at Sa`id in the passenger seat, I see him for just a moment as the man he wants to be. Free. Sa`id loves climbing, but, his carefree has nothing to do with that right now. Here, now, staring out the window at the Bear's Ears (Bridger-Jack) skyline, lost in the dazzle of a million yellow leaves of old cottonwoods as we pass them by at 60mph, Sa`id is free precisely because his tuning is back in the keys of shaman and mystic.

In the last nine months, he's ticked a good measure of hard climbs and traveled far, although, most of it has been under the regimen of his career path. Driven more often than he'd like to admit to produce content, to stay relevant, and stay afloat in the landscape of professional climbers, Sa`id has climbed as much for financial security, as for pure expression. If you look closely, you can see that weighing on him. He never wanted to be the best climber, he just wanted to be able to keep doing it. And sometimes, that means climbing in ways that may not fulfill you most.

What I'm more curious about is how a place like this, a day like today, has a way of lifting all of that pressure straight off his shoulders. What exactly, is making him wear a shit-grin the size of the Sahara? Truth is there are thousands of five-star climbs just out the window, up to some of the hardest grades that humankind has achieved, and Sa`id is one of a select few on earth who could probably have a good rip at each and every one of them. Thousands of opportunities to make an ascent, to be recognized for an achievement, to push content to a sponsor, or just to impose his rabidity onto something, and yet, more than anyone present, Sa`id truly, suddenly, wants for nothing. World at his fingertips.

"This is the stuff, man! Just what I needed," he says.

Laughing back, I'm just glad to see him in the freeform I know him by. "Oh yeah?" I ask, "What exactly was it that you needed?"

"Ah man. This!" He claps his hands together to the beat. "There are 99 names for Allah you can invoke, eh. You know this already. In Gnawa when we clap, that's what we're calling out to." He claps his hands again, lip-smacking like he's savoring a dessert. "We've invoked it now, my man! And once the awareness is on, anything goes!"

We've invoked it—the magic force—because we've been busy clapping, and for the Gnawan, that's the action which brings two realities together. This is because written into the left hand of every human is the Arabic number 81. In the right hand, the number 18. Together they are the 99. Furthermore, in Gnawa, the left hand represents the akhira, the world beyond, and all that is of spirit. The right hand represents the world that is, the physical, the phenomenological. The clap marries them. The clap begins each song in Gnawa, because it is the clap which unites the two worlds together, and it's only in the two coming together that true healing and expression occurs.

"Yeah man," Sa`id continues, "Now that we've got Mahmoud playing, and we've got this spirit, and we're here in a land like this. Now we're talking, buddy!"

We sit in the car, windows down in an empty pullout beneath age-old canyon walls, and play that album entirely through, the better part of an hour. Afterward, when we do climb, Sa`id is on another plane entirely. The precision, acuity, and conviction you'd expect are all back with him. He moves like a magician, a charmer, like he's operating on that crack to gain access to another dimension. This is the climber he most wants to be.

Hours later, by firelight, we close the day with our own ritual. A purple moon has lifted from the horizon, mystic as it were, and cast long night-shadows across the desert floor. The earth glows in eggplant, a glitter of murex and bronze which tease one another across the landscape, as light does to dark.

Nightlight and campfire are all about impressions anyway, just the type of setting one needs to see the deeper sides of Sa`id's character.

Make no mistake they are there; they have been all day. But here, in shadow, these traits are no longer outshined by the animal instincts he presents with on the wall. Here, you see the inner Maalem; ancient, ceremonious, born for healing. Especially when he grabs that Guembri.

"You know what, man," Sa`id reflects while plucking a string. "There's something about this place, eh?"

"Something ancient," I offer.

"Hehehe." Sa`id snickers in the way only he can. "Ancient, and robust!"

He plays the opening bars for the tune, Marhaba, a staple of the Gnawan repertoire, as I find a means of percussion.

"You know what got me out of that funk, this morning?" he continues with the thumbsmack. "I was finally able to engage in this field of energy. It's everywhere. I had to remember that. That there's a lot more to climbing than just grabbing holds, right? There's something deeper. Something inside."

I can't help but agree as he continues. "That's the thing. To really get in, you've got to let go of the rational mind. All these thoughts, what am I going to do after this? What should I climb in Yosemite? What about my sponsors next year? What kind of man am I trying to be? Fuck, man. In the West, we embrace this thinking, eh. We are always there, in the mind, in science and detail, in thinking. But what does it serve us?"

Sa`id starts humming, then singing, gently, the first bars of Marhaba.

Marhaba, in Arabic, is a formal welcome, a greeting, and an invitation. It offers you to be in a place, fully, without tension. To be settled. To arrive in the now.

"The rational mind..." He trails off. "Here, in this Native Land, I don't need to think about any of that stuff. When I heard Maalem Guinea this morning, man, that was it. I arrived, finally. Aaaahhhh!"

Sa`id lifts off, immediately, into a jam. He praises the Berber, the Fulani, the Bambara, just as the song does, and fantastically wanders off into a free mind, a no-mind, jamming in Gnawa ritual for a good fifteen minutes for a single tune. In the deepest moments, it is damn right cosmic.

Gnawa is an exchange of call and response, and while I'm familiar which each tune, I'm not at a place where I can serve it justice. But, it doesn't matter. For each call Sa`id makes, the campfire itself chimes in. Where there would normally be long wailing echoes from the orchestra of krakebs; tonight, the cracking, splintering wood and the very sparks and bursts of the fire itself repeat after he does. Never mind the hyperbole, in some moments I swear that fire and Sa`id become one. Letting go as best I can, I also offer percussion and participate with him. Freely, as passengers to the night, we lose ourselves to time.

Eventually, as he closes the song and comes back to consciousness, Sa`id comments, "You know what it is, man? This desert is like my suit, eh. How do say this, you know, like the color in Gnawa, the Melk, the Saint?"

In Gnawan ritual, at a Lila, people only fall into trance and receive healing under certain musical and color-coded arrangements. Similar to an act of a play or a particular segment of a concerto. Each person has an energy that is healed by a specific type of musical mood, which is also associated with a particular Saint or spiritual liaison.

"Ah, your Suite!" I suddenly realize. "Like the equivalent of a classical music suite. It's your mood, yeah. Your theme. It fits your inner arrangement."

"Exactly!" he confirms. "That's it. A suite, not a suit."

"Just like in Gnawa, where we have a Melk, or the Mluk, the Spirits—equivalent to angels maybe. They are coordinated with a color and a Saint of Islam, and a smell of incense. Each person has his or her own spirit who enables them to fall into a deep trance. That's what this Native desert is for me, man. It's my Melk."

Sa`id heckles at the realization as he finishes, "Hehehe, for me, this is the place to be, man. I feel it. In my toes, in the sand itself. This is where I come for jedba."

The words of his inner Maalem. No mind, and free of the rational explanation, I see Sa`id, who he really is, in an impression by firelight. A side of him often overlooked by day. Just here, barefoot at a campfire, with a goatskin Guembri engraved in Tamasheq, I see his essence. The Maalem, the Gnawan, connected by the very keratin of his nail beds to the red warmth of desert sand, its crystals, its hematite, its tetrahedral complex of silicon, and oxygen. A soul as old as the earth we sleep upon.

///

Seven Hundred feet above the Yosemite Valley floor, Sa`id and I pause for a gear exchange after the Offwidth pitch of the Rostrum.

"Did you just lieback that entire crux?" I laugh at him.

"You got it, mate. I think, if you aren't placing gear on an off-width, if you are following, then you really don't have to be inside of it, eh." He jabs back with a smirk.

Happy to be out, happy for such immaculate weather, it is a California daydream come true. One of those salad days, completely in sync, light, and easier than it should be. Sa`id and I stare down at the Merced catching a ray of light—a champagne simmer between its banks—and both nod with appreciation.

"Quite the feel today, isn't it?" he comments with a raised eyebrow.

"Yeah, man. Must have been the ceremony last night," I chime back.

To the Southern Sierra Miwok Nation, it's a Chi-Tok-Non Kote-U-Pu. Last night, in particular, was quite special. Being the middle of November, the ceremony was designed to usher in the winter season, and, as these events have certain themes by design, the focus of last night, quite fittingly was transition.

Transition in season, in identity, in energy. A message that was not lost on Sa`id. He's been on that thread, the precipice of change, for two years now, maybe more. Since Castleton, surely, and probably before that. In every country and climbing destination he and I shared a rope, there's been an ongoing conversation. Whether to continue doing the next best thing, the next hardest route, or whether to live more on his own terms. Ultimately, as for any of us, that choice comes down to some measure of faith.

Will he be able to travel, not just climb—to feed off the waters of life in all the exotic places if he lets go of the sponsorships? Will a way be provided, or must he keep grinding? Can he abandon the ideals of one stage of life and step toward a new one? The permutations may be different, surely Sa`id walked into that ceremony with his own questions, but everybody, Native youth and elders alike, walked in with their own questions of life, too. And they are not so different from one another, after all. What is beautiful about Sa`id, is his quest. It is the fact that he seeks. That the first order of business upon my arrival to Ahwahne is this ceremony, is a joy. Most partners would get you right onto a wall, but Sa`id, gets you right into a ritual.

We'd been invited to the ceremony by Sa`id's friend, and local legend, Ron. The only requirements to enter: a sober mind and spirit. These rituals, just as for the Gnawa, just as for the Dineh, and for most ancient cultures, are sacred. Not to be clouded or convoluted by the fog of the psychoactive, the sedative, or the synthetic chemical influence.

Having confirmed our state of mind, Ron smiles at us, "We're happy to have you guys, as climbers, here, to see what this Valley houses in terms of the history of its people and the spiritual practices. I think in our generation we exalted the drug trip, which did a lot of damage to people, and a lot of us missed out on this part of it."

With the softness of a contented elder, Ron saids, "But we sure are glad you both made it, tonight. Come on in and join us!"

Walking into the log house, each person slowly circles the fire and pauses at the head of it. Per ritual, you take a handful of kindling and what smells like a mix of tobacco, dried sage and herbs, and spread them into the flame, unifying your energy with the fire. Contributing to the flame and connecting with it, this is a moment just between you and the forces that be; a moment to state your intention. The participants sit in a concentric, circular tapestry around the fire, with a clearing at the head and foot of the building. The ceremonies, which will carry on for hours, begin.

Sa`id looks as comfortable as can be, like he's been here before because, in essence, he has. This is not unlike the hallowed Lila. He's new to this expression of ritual, but he's quite familiar with the equation. There are themes, there is trance, there is music—ordered, sequenced, very specific layers of music designed to be played in a particular repetition. There is call and response. There is ritual with fire. There is healing.

The elder spreads his bushels of white sage across the pink flame. He looks out toward the crowd and takes a diaphragm-deep inhale, in a native tongue he says, "Experience. Experience the seasons change like the flame changes. Experience, The Way. Look into yourselves like you look into this flame. Like our ancestors have."

His chest rises. With all his authority, his eyes are surprisingly kind, as he spreads more tinder over the flames. The smell of burning sage and tobacco radiates while a communal prayer unfolds. A moment later, a fascinating chant begins from the choir, singing in a dizzying minor pentatonic slide across octaves, much like the Gnawa. The melody has a tribal repetition, is simple, harmonious, and is carried only by the rhythm of a single bass drum for backing. Like the Lila, I realize that each repetition has a purpose, each verse is a new layer, that each element of the gathering is structured for a specific communion. The chant carries on into eternity.

APERTURE ALIKE   155

A man in a trance circles the flame wearing a bear-skin cloak. He spasms in reflex arcs, abandoning motor control. Surrounded by a few elders to guide his trance safely, he channels the Bear-Spirit. At this stage, he's in deep. Is it a man we are watching? The Bear-Spirit come manifest? Or God Herself vibrating on stage? Perhaps all of the above. Not long after the Bear, other spirits visit by means of others falling into trance. Those who are raptured circle the fire in praise, and bridge the spirit world to our own, just as a Gnawan handclap.

It continues. Minutes, quarter-hours, hours. Time loses relevance. Trance, prayer, offering, and invocation simply sustain themselves. Sometimes the elders translate to the few among us in English, but for the most part the entire affair is rightly uninterrupted. There is no center stage, not even a high priest. This ritual is not for one to wield power, but for healing. Each portion of the ceremony is a complimentary design to the sequence which preceded it, and to that which shall follow. Only the true ideal, which is the people themselves making a divine connection, is served. Eventually, deep in the night, flames smolder to dust.

At the charity of Ron, the Miwok, the Ahwanechee, Sa`id and I walk out of that temple after hours of healing. We look up to an Ahwahne night-sky, cut clean by the blue and indigo trace of the milky way, that ageless glacier of the cosmos, as two children awakened for the very first time.

Looking out across the Valley, Sa`id pushes out a satisfied exhale. "No doubt, my friend. That was a hell of an event, eh. And the stars afterward, my God, are you kidding me?"

He grabs the set of stoppers of my rack, and lassoes them to his gear loops, pausing, "Plus, you had that sunrise this morning, huh? Tell me about that."

"Ah man, you can't imagine," I begin. "Something. Haha. We'll just call it 'something', woke me up just at the crack of first light today. I put on the shoes and started jogging East. Eventually, I stopped around the meadows, under the waterfall, and lost my shit at the setting."

"Yeah." Sa`id checks his knot, "What was that like, mate?"

"One hour of a quiet, perfect sunrise, man. Over sheets of thick fog, a full rainbow by the falls, and flocks of deer just checking it out with me."

"Hehehe," he encourages. "Buddy, that's the stuff we're after, eh! You keep channeling that and we might just have a shot at this after all."

This, that Sa`id is referencing, is the Alien Finish. It may only be 5.12 on a grade scale, but again, for someone like him, grades are more a suggestion of an experience than a standard of currency. The number doesn't matter as much as the context. You put Sa`id on a finish like the Alien, and he's not going to compare it to a romp up a cave in Kalymnos; he's thinking about the fact that it's legendary, the fact that it's onsight, the fact that his fingers are going in where Ron and Tony Yaniro's did. He's thinking about the focus to send but also the presence to pay it homage. That experience is something much different than just another 5.12 for him, and he wants every bit of it.

That has been one of the unique aspects of his climbing over the years. Sa`id doesn't just repeat routes, he courts them. He seeks out the classics, not just for the attention they merit, but for the history they provide. Watch him do it enough and you can see that even during an onsight, for Sa`id, routes aren't something to rush through. Neither is the process. He wants to have the best experience he can, the most informed, the most awakened because he's not just obsessive, he's reverent.

"I bet Ron would be happy to see us up here after a night like last night, too." He shares before take-off. "So let's do him proud, eh! I've got a feeling that I'm going to have to pull out everything I can and go completely a-muerte for this one."

Assured by the context alone, of where we are, I reply, "I'm sure you'll make it fine, brother. I'm positive. Just take some of that Bear Spirit from last night with you, man. You find that trance and it won't matter what the result is up there."

"We don't deal in results…" he sputters, quickly skipping moves into the roof, "we deal in the now, eh. Good reminder!"

Sa`id ventures out to the apex of the Alien roof, chest forward, the ease of a front-levered posture maintained by a single foot pushing plantar-flexed at extension. He makes one decisive reach and in a second, he has cut feet and rebounded his body position over the lip. A strong lock-off, one flex of total body tension, and like that he has sailed over the ledge and out of sight.

III

Kicking up dust on the campground trails of the Stawamus Chief, British Columbia, my partner, Nathalie, and I make out Sa'id's trusty tent. It's an army-green, one-man Hilleberg deep in the network of sites. Nestled among the ferns and the marigold mushrooms, there's a small gnome set up at the head of the tent. Its purpose is both welcoming the campground space and guarding the whole of Sa`id's material existence. All he needs in any country, for any project, is a revolving cycle of gear, a guembri, his clothes, and the laptop. We sit idly, for just a moment, until Sa`id comes running toward us from the deep cover of the forest, skipping and jolly as a Finnish folklore creature.

"Hey hey, my friends!" he hollers, "You guys found it!" He's all too excited, even by his standards.

While we've just arrived, he's been in the forest for almost two weeks already, and mostly in a solitary fashion—which is not the norm. Summers for Sa`id are typically social affairs. Trade shows in Germany, parties in France, music gigs from Gothenburg to Grenoble, the months tend to blur as the faces do. Compare that to the sudden quiet for weeks, of the old forest and a book at night by headlamp, and it's real downshift.

But this, the quiet, is exactly what he's chosen for himself at last.

Halfway through our hugs, I can't help but laugh at how rugged he's become. "You look like you've been held hostage somewhere, buddy."

Sa`id combs a lick of grease off his matted hair with his hand, and then stares at it. "Buddy, you have no idea what climbing alone in the forest will do to a man after more than a week! I've been completely stuck in my head."

He's taken on a project in the woods, which is atypical for him. On a short trip, he's normally the type to invest in a large volume of routes. But, as he's recently professed, he's trying to cultivate a more singular purpose. For how long, is anyone's guess. At the end of the day, there's no telling direction with a guy like Sa`id, but looking at him right now, helmet-hair and all, you get the sense he's willing to make peace with the notion of structure, if only a little.

That's probably a good thing, too. He's been scattered as long as I've known him, torn between trips to take, wooing women and chasing shadows. That freedom to roam, a life that's up and gone with the wind, is both where he lives best, but also where he wants the most. These days, you get the feeling he's looking for a new freedom. Right now, just for these three weeks, he is here in Canada for two reasons: to invest himself completely in one single route, for the pure redundancy of practice at something, and to create a deeper space for himself to silence the mind, and look into the next frontier.

"I can't tell you guys how good it is to see you both!" Sa`id shares, "But, before we get too deep into this catching up business, I've got an important question. Should I bring this beach towel or what?"

As you get to know the guy—the rope-stained hands, the dust plumes wafting from his pants, the expressions on his face, and the way he asks the question—it's hard not to love him. We could've gone to any shop in town to relax and be served a meal, but Sa`id wanted a beach. That's important for more reasons than I can explain.

Scurried into the car, in no time at all we're 10 clicks down the highway heading for the next bay.

Out on the beach, we are privy to an immaculate view of the Sḵwx̱wú7mesh Úxwumixw, the Squamish Nation. Half the Howe Sound glistens in a glacial, Prussian blue, the other in afternoon sunray. From our feet to the far side of the Sound there's a soft texture on the water, defined by depressions of light and dark, rippling from crest to trough on the turquoise surface. Symmetric beauty. With glaciers in the shaded distance as our audience and a lattice of lumber logs stacked on a sun-bleached shore, we recover the time lost between us.

"Look man," Sa`id reflects, "it doesn't matter how things go at this point, with this project, with the girl, with the sponsors, with all of it. I've just got to keep pursuing what I always have, you know, and that's to travel, to learn more. It's to put my energy, everywhere, cause it's what I do. I can't help it, man!"

Sa`id and I laugh at the revelation that his time in the woods has afforded him. The Great Concession, it seems, is to concede nothing. But it's true. Madness and Divinity have much in common, our bonds to the better of the two may exist on a scale finer than most can even magnify. To concede nothing and activate oneself fully in life. To attach nothing to the outcomes of what we produce. To have no other motivation for any activity which rests beyond the now, and how it relates to your fundamental ability to expand into this universe, is to live to a truth.

At the same time, living hard on self-will without the expansion will indeed drive a man off the edge. I've seen it. Grinding without concession, against a tide that one cannot with any force adjust, is madness just the same.

"You've been on both sides of the equation, haven't you?" I ask Sa`id.

"Ha ha, indeed mate. I have." He rips a piece of bread from our baguette and globs it with a broken chunk of cheese. "But! Then again, so have you, eh? You know all about it. You've tried the same thing man."

"Tried and failed like the rest." I respond, "But I'm grateful. It's what I needed to see what I see today."

Sa`id puts down the baguette and stares with adoration at the flushing tide, as it pools over the stones and his feet. Stepping in ankle-deep, he's got that same reverence he climbs with, and it looks like he's about to perform a Wudu before getting on his knees for evening prayer. He pauses, before the sacrament, and looks back, "Tell me what you've seen since then?"

"Since I came to," I reply, "I've seen my deepest elements, man. I've seen places like this. Beauty with no end. Constant revelation, constant flow. That's not how I see it all the time, but I know it's there. Incomprehensible, but inviting."

"Yes, man!" Sa`id exclaims.

"That being said," I continue, "someone once told me, that I can no more transmit something I haven't got than I can go back to someplace I haven't been. I gotta try my best, like you, to live all my passions all the time and let the results just handle themselves. But for me to do that, I've got to keep a structure, too. For me to embrace the ravenous I've also got to embrace the studious. Kind of like your Gnawa. The goal of the whole thing is to allow the neediest, the most wild and spiritual part of a person, to come out and make a connection. The point is to get the most fundamental, raw expression of a soul to manifest. And for that alone to happen, the whole thing is predicated on order, right?"

"Ah brother," Sa`id turns to me with his eyes alight, "Now we're talking about the good stuff, eh. The spiritual framework. The full expression coming from the full level of order. The whole package. You're right, too. Order is something I've resisted my entire life, but I long for it. In perfect sequences on the rock, in musical scales, all over. And yes, in Gnawa we hold order sacred. Every perfect expression is born from following some level of order. This is how we get there."

"Yeah man, all I can say is that since I turned to cultivating spiritual order, everything, all I ever really wanted out of life came, or came back, in spades."

"Mythic." Sa`id smiles at me.

He's now waist-deep in the water, hands gliding the surface. "Guys like us, man, what we long for is that order, because it yields the connection. That place where you can see there is no separation, in people, places, events, whatever. Where you can just see the energy of life, flowing, moving in everything."

"I'm just a student, man," I said. "The more I learn the less I seem to know. But yeah, there are moments where it all connects, and it doesn't even have to be in the mountains anymore. And that's the goal anyway, to not need to be on rock any more than one needs to be on a drug to find it. To simply be, in nature, or just people-watching in a market, on a highway in a car, it can happen anywhere. I'll be watching a leaf in the wind or a flicker of light and the shackles will just come off, man. "

"Yes, mate. This is the stuff of life." Sa`id affirms.

He dips his torso in the water, working out his own form of ablution, from arm to arm. At last, he commits entirely and is baptized, completely one with earth and water. Emerging anew, he looks toward the far shore and offers, "Mate, what you describe is what people testify to after a proper Lila. The way it comes upon you, the things that trigger your ability to see the truth. It's beautiful. You've got your own Suite, after all!"

As he comes to shore, he and I both notice a cove just up the beach and decide on a look. On our feet we continue our discussion, stepping across logs and skipping stones for simple delight until we come across a cottage-sized boulder. On instinct, we both scramble up the backside and spot a clean path for a rock jump from the top. Sa`id offers I take first go, which I do, from which he follows shortly after.

"How'd that feel for a first dip, buddy?" he asks immediately. Certain that he can tell by the whites of my eyes alone, I barely have to say a word.

"There's something so simple and healing about water, man," he says. "I can't describe it, but you got it right now, eh?"

"You're right, my friend, there is a healing. It allows you to see things. And I'll say this, man. Sometimes, when the shackles fall off and you get that sight, when you see the world as one continuous expression of the same energy, man, there is more of the infinite in just one of those moments than I'll ever have the receptors, or consciousness, to comprehend. Just like it is now. All I get are glimpses, man. But they're fucking precious. Little secrets. Little clues. What lies behind, beyond even this glimpse of a matrix, man, I can only dream."

A ray of light penetrates the saddle of the distant mountains and gleams onto a single pool of water just around the corner. On instinct, again, Sa`id rushes toward it. Excited steps take him over a series of boulders and driftwood, toward the cove just beyond the bend.

Just as he comes into the light, he looks back with brightened eyes and exclaims, "I know this feeling you describe under such a revelation. This overwhelming feeling. I've seen it everywhere I've gone, I've had it while breaking bread with others, when looking into the eyes of villagers, when quiet and all alone, too."

I can see him regurgitating millions of memories from his thousands of miles of travels. I can see his sense recall, the smell of Injera bread, the sight of Donso-hunters in trance, the clouds gathered over Mt. Fuji. The brilliant blue foam of crashing water against river banks in a valley outside of Ulaanbaatar, the ocean-colored eyes of indigenous peoples in foreign lands, the hallowed chants of Sámi orchestras. The crystalline shimmer of the Milky-Way from every place he's seen it. An entire flood of sense recall overloads him for just a moment, under that sunray, standing above the cove in the afternoon light; until he comes to, has a blink, and smiles back.

"And I have seen this matrix of which you speak, entirely. But right here and now, there is another one just beyond this cove, eh! So why don't we go see what that one is all about?"

All the talk aside, he's back to being just him, perfectly where he should be.

"I mean, come on, would you look at the lighting right now," he erupts.

As if on cue, "Rrrrrraaahhhhh!"

He jumps to the next boulder, and it's off and away. Sa`id the seeker, the one with the inner-Maalem, the dancer, the climber, the raver, the hunter, the shaman, the mystic; the molecular force who is always drawn by instinct to the next step, simply by natural attraction, floats off like a sandstone particle of dust between the rises of the Utah towers, bathed in light and blowing in the wind with a saffron glow. A god-damned revelation.

///

TALLY-HO

A tandem skydive is usually something of a carnival ride, at least that's what the boys at the landing zone tell me. As an industry cash-cow, it makes sense. Even in the seemingly thrill-crazed world of sky fliers, it stands to reason that the experience should be as exact and controlled a fear experience as one would have on a roller coaster at the local theme park. Even from 12,000 feet, with the earth sucking you homeward at a face-melting pace, the experience is by design, an avatar. As above, so below. A skydive is a cash-in on the fascination humans have with fear. It only flirts with the truth we innately seek from life. Most of what happens up there is premised on providing an experience without much of a craft. To ride the line and feel all the rush of being near death without ever truly navigating danger. Living to extremes, without getting any of the expansion. Now I'm not bold in any particular measure, but I do like the idea of expansion, and on a lark, it seemed, a good friend proposed we could have something of the sort.

As a qualified Skyman and instructor, Matt Blank's reputation walks well ahead of him in most situations. Considering I've known the bastard long before he first packed a chute, he seemed an appropriate guide if ever there was one. With a checkered past, we've had more than our share of ventures together, across many disciplines of the fringe sports. Over time, with enough hardships and the loss of a few friends, you could say that the deepest lessons we've each learned have come to each of us by our own means, as different routes to the same destination. Admittedly, I didn't see quite how this all connected when, fresh from a trip to South Africa, Matt strolled past the bay doors of the climbing gym, pointed his fingers at me like an Uncle Sam propaganda poster, and said with his standard grin, "Roman! I've got to have words with you, man."

Words? I knew well enough by that goddamn grin he wore that Matt had something up his sleeve. Chasing a speed record downhill on bikes and burning right through a series of red lights, rigging a maniacal rope-swing against the short-end of the safety margins, or bleeding mind-melting benders at the poker tables in Vegas while on a climbing mission; these were some of the suggestions one would expect from Matt when he needed to have words. Thankfully, most of Matt's propositions, lately, have had more to do with having a deeper life experience as opposed to just a renegade one.

"It's occurred to me, in the ten years we've been doing shit together, that you've never jumped out of a plane with me. And I think now would be an excellent time!"

No doubt, I had thought about flying the skies. But mostly due to not having the time or the money to afford another passion, I had always chalked up skydiving to something like the horizon: an experience faintly in my view but intangible all the same. On that day, however, sun bright and shining, I couldn't think of any reason not to. In fact, it sounded damn right appropriate. Not because I was going to jump out of a plane—Lord knows my fear instincts override the mainframe—but because it was a new experience to have with a good friend. That friend had spent more time, really living in gravity's clutches than most ever will. And because what happens when you're falling at terminal velocity—slave to one of the greatest forces in the universe—is a privilege. Because just as it is on the vertical fringe, in the sky there is also an entire human history, full of moments of deep awareness and realization. Because I wanted to share a page in Matt's great verse.

///

"I gotta say, I'm a little curious. Why now? " I asked Matt when he first proposed we skydive together.

Matt's eyes lit up, almost out of their place. He was uncharacteristically excited to talk about it, as if he'd been holding something in for days. And he had, at least for the long plane rides between Cape Town and Southern California. "Look man, I don't want to sound ridiculous or anything, but on this trip to South Africa, I realized that you and I are living in a very similar fashion." He paused looking for the right words, "You're all about the energy transfer." Holding his hands to his head, he searched himself again then said, "Well, that's what I call it."

"Energy transfer?" I questioned.

"Yeah man, like totally breaking down the bullshit in life and searching for the moments of vulnerability and clarity," he said.

In a matter of a half-hour, it all came clear. Through a series of questions about my own near-death experiences, and from having watched death in others, Matt showed me that the sum of our experience led us to a shared vantage point, a shared mission in life. We had, after all, both been through some incredibly barren low points in the last few years. Moments which made us both take a step back and reset our course. What that actually meant, for two guys who jump at nearly every opportunity to access the raw side of life, was whittling down all our outdoor activity and our relationships to a core. In the last few years, there had been just as many times where we did not jump, did not climb, or did not travel, as times where we had.

Somewhere, we had grown fonder of life itself than the legend of it. And while the output of total things done or achievements crowned may have slowed down, both of us would testify that our skills, experiences, and relationships had all sharpened. For Matt, the busier he got and more extreme his activities became, the less they delivered; in the end they neither hit the mark they aimed for nor could they be sustained. On a macro-view, Matt had said, losing his dearest friend and companion in the sport could have been reduced to simply living too large, to always doing the next thing, and not slowing down enough to ask why.

"Look, man," Matt carefully worded, "I've seen too many friends huck-off of exits and do bombastic shit 'cause of the legend that precedes them, or 'cause they feel like it's what the lifestyle of the sport requires. I've seen people run off for days on drugs hoping they pass enlightenment along the way. But you and I both know that what we've learned isn't something you find in your highs. Behind so much of our lifestyles, behind these sports which promote this idea of total freedom, are a bunch of characters trapped in fear. Less afraid of the sport as they are of their deepest needs, and of facing their insecurities. I've seen it and experienced it, and I know you have, too. That fear can drive people to dangerous places within the sport, and then next thing you know... it's like people do tons of extreme shit hoping it'll deliver a reward that only comes from participating in others. And when they lose sight of that, they can lose orbit altogether."

Compelled by his weavings, I listened further.

"And I feel like you understand that," he said, "because you went through the same thing in your own way. For years you kept doing it 'cause it was all you knew, and only in the near-death experience did you find it wasn't working, and that you had to start all over. You had to change everything because you were going to die if you didn't. What you found at the bottom was the experience you'd been looking for all along."

Matt paused momentarily, "It was always right there in front of us and we didn't know it."

"Damn right." I nodded.

"I mean what did you find in there, near death?" he asked, curiously.

"For me," I started, "Jeez, man. I guess I realized somewhere that it wasn't life that needed the modification, it was me. Life was absolutely perfect as is, the biggest, most vast explosion of energy and expression and beauty imaginable, but I just couldn't connect to it. What I was chasing after, the feeling I wanted, it wasn't a connection, it was an illusion. I was essentially trying by all the wrong measures to grab something I couldn't hold."

"Exactly!" Matt curled his hand in a fist.

Continuing, I shared, "For me, at the bottom and depraved, a few years down, there had to be a surrender. My turnaround required an admission that on my own will and by my own means, I am absolutely, inevitably, fucked to wrestle peace and satisfaction out of this life. But, at the exact moment I was ready and was able to let go of my trivial ways there was something far greater than I could imagine picking me up in the current. These days, if I'm fit enough for it, I see that current permeates everything around me, including you. I also know, these days, that it's not to be held as much as it is to be shared. That's what you mean by energy transfer isn't it?" I suddenly realized. "Giving it away."

"You got it." Matt smiled. "I just had this experience in South Africa with my partner where we put all our fear and insecurity in front of each other, and it was mind-blowing. For some reason, I thought you'd understand what I was talking about. Then I immediately thought about getting you in the sky!"

The fact is, after all we've been through, I know when Matt's tone is sincere, and I trust him to guide me into any mission. If he says there's something for me in the sky, I don't question his vision, I ask him what tools I need to access it.

///

The Sky-Shark is a mean-looking, retrofitted DHC-6 Twin Otter, short take-off and landing (STOL) utility aircraft, otherwise known as a bush-plane with a mean paint job. It seats about 19 people and sputters like a manky lawnmower cutting springtime air. Designed and first flown in 1965, it was originally meant for rescue and aid missions, but since being co-opted by nearly the entire skydiving community, the DHC-6 is as much a cultural symbol in a drop zone as a low-riding Chevy Impala is in East Los Angeles. Culturally speaking, when you are in one of these puppies, you are home. And that's what it feels like. Twenty of us packed to the gills, helmets and jumping suits on, the smell of jet-fuel over the tarmac; a quick gaze across the gallery, nothing but smiles.

In the cabin, it doesn't matter who you are in life down below. It doesn't matter what is or is not in your bank account, or whether you would or wouldn't normally mix in social settings. The only thing that matters is that you are doing something together. And so long as you are doing, you are thick as thieves.

Sitting inside that tubule, there's something to be said for communities where membership is as simple as participation. There's a new flier, named Jess, sitting next to Matt and me, and while she's obviously not in a comfort zone as the plane takes off, Sebastian, Trevor, and Matt—the motley and unkempt instruction staff—try to keep her smiling by telling jokes and keeping her in the fold. There's probably years-worth of collective free-fall time in this Sky-Shark at present, and Jess doesn't have a second of flying experience to her name. She literally cannot relate to the experience of everyone around her, but they can relate to her. She's the most important jumper, perhaps, because she's the newcomer, and the gang wants to show her that it doesn't matter so much what brought you here, at this point you just need to take action and you'll be flying. And once you're flying, you're in.

The Sky-Shark rises faster than your standard commercial aircraft, which means that in the cabin there's something like a full-tilt as we gain altitude. At this point, on a bench rather than buckled in an individual seat, I'm not totally hitched up to Matt via our tandem set-up just yet. And, as we climb and gravity begins pulling us toward the bottom of that bench, the sliding exit door is wide open, suctioning like a Hoover over old carpet. With a few thousand feet of gain, no parachute attached and no seatbelt, I'm suddenly feeling exposed, and based on physiologic instinct alone I am not in the least surprised to find a lump clotting in my throat. Regardless of my faith in Matt and the impending sequence we're looking for in the sky, for the first time of the day, quite palpably, my heart rate rises. Fear, the ageless friend of humanity, grabs holds of me, arm over the shoulder.

Now that our take-off has steadied and Matt has finished locking me into the tandem system, it's mostly an exciting wait-out, as I look at my wrist to make sure the altimeter is working. Sure enough, as bread and all things holy, it rises.

"Twelve and steady." Mark dispatches from the pilot's seat.

Just like so, and without a blowhorn or a trumpet sound, action begins. Quicker than a school of fish the crew whistle out of the gates. Fliers zap out of that cabin like it's a damned space portal and disappear instantly into the roar of the wind.

Immediately, time has ushered Matt and I directly off the bench and at the precipice of the wide-open, howling gates of life itself. Gravity awaits. 12,000 feet of it, compounded in force. That, and more free space than you've ever put yourself into in a singular moment, are just inches away. Were it a commercial flight, and were you fastened with a tray table and hot food in front of you, you might want to put a finger on the window and ponder something profound. You might find something like serenity, as you connect to the vastness of earth as it passes under you. But dammit, a first skydive is not like that, at all. It's more like you're naked and now is your time to look God in the face. For that reason, jumping willingly into that great vacuum suddenly sounds a bit more of a bold proposition than I expected. Wherever did we get this curious desire for everything at once? We long for rapture from our very bones and yet quiver from it all at the same time. There may well be an awakening, just one step away, but the threshold one must cross, from here to there, is a violent wall of sound and the rising ping of every preservation instinct.

///

One of the key features of Matt's tandem that separates it from the traditional model is that you, the newcomer, must lead the jump. When Matt and I sat there, for just that extra second, with the whole world beneath us, I couldn't just cross my arms in dreadful anticipation and make a shit-faced grimace with my eyes closed. Matt made it very clear from the get-go, this was our jump, sure, but it was my initiative which would get us from the cabin back to earth. Matt's tandem is not passive, and there is no abdication of rights or responsibility.

When explaining the gear set-up and canopy system to me before we had taken off, Matt said, "Look man, I'll go through every part of this journey with you. If you want to land safely, we'll land safely. If you can't make a part of this happen, I'll be here to help guide you. But, in this journey, you've got to make the choices. I trust you completely because I know your core code. Because of what we've been through, together. You respect life, so you'll choose life. When it comes time to pull that chute, you'll choose to live. But just know that our friendship is deep enough, that if you decide not to pull that cord, I am willing to take that journey with you also."

He wasn't fucking around. And this was no consumer-brand jump.

This was all the friendship experience I had bargained for, and then some.

"I want you to know that none of this is safe in as much as climbing isn't safe. But, as you know, it's not dangerous either, if done correctly. There is a real aspect of risk with each skydive, and you need to know that going in. I'll show you all the parts of the pack, the harness, and the chute so that when you are up there you are making informed decisions about our lives and doing so on an informed timeline."

So, step one was simply to look that unknown force in the face and make a conscious decision to go. In these moments, it is important to me to recognize that while I do, in fact, have plenty of fear, I can also take action despite it. I know that if executed correctly, it is a reasonable, perhaps even enjoyable activity. I also know death is not the beast I once feared, but rather, a new transition of energy, possibly even awareness, in a universe bursting with both. I cannot imagine what the experience will be like just outside that door, but, at the same time, I cannot imagine not doing it. I know I must. Matt, understanding the sacred nature of the position, has left it all to me. He would not rob me of that precipice, of that position, nor the power within it. Rather, he's most satisfied riding shotgun, joining in as first-witness to real-life experience. Strapped to my back, Matt is fully prepared and awaiting my countdown, allowing me the chance to fly with eyes wide open.

One deep, steadying breath. There is peace in every moment, I mantra from within.

One more to recognize my excitement. Let us enjoy this, I remind myself. For life is a joy.

Action.

My brain fires a charge.

Action is ultimate, action is now.

The Sky-Shark flies through the California sky but we no longer fly with it.

///

If you asked Matt, he'd tell you we exited just fine, no errors whatsoever. But, for me, who was expecting something like a slow-motion, frame-by-frame equivalent of a perfect cast on a fly-rod, it was a hot mess. Brutal, in-fact. Wind seemed to flood in from all directions, with decibels from hell, and my entire body felt rudderless to navigate a course. A sudden loss of agency, gravity seemed to swirl in from all sides, seemingly pressing me upwards, downwards, even sideways with equal force. It was not serenity and it damn well was not as advertised. Not in my mind. Like a ship on full keel, center-point and ballast lost. My levels of input and response to the situation were unreliable, at best.

Forty-five seconds happens fast in sky time. Really fast. I was aware of it, maybe even too much, as I tried to find the stillness of the moment and handle the supreme speed of it all at once. Thoughts and biofeedback spun faster than a slot-machine through my mind, and I was only seeing them in passing as freefall and terminal velocity set in. No chance to grab it, gone before you even fully see it.

But, considering the speed of it all, the view was still exceptional. Between the wind-folds on my shitty goggles and the warp of the horizon with the altitude, I was lost, visually, in a fish-eye lens. Earth itself bending like a spoon in the matrix within my field of view. For just a moment, it was glorious.

Forty-five seconds though, pass in light speed, certainly faster than time does. Truly a sensational platform for a human being. I mean, how many new sensations can your five senses take in all at once? The mind can't catch up to the experience fast enough to even project a framework upon it. Phenomena pass without register.

For a moment, I am a child. Born without a clue, enamored by energy from all directions. Perceiving but perception-less.

Into the freefall, I was just trying to check some basic boxes to enjoy it as it happens. I was having trouble breathing, not due-to panic or hyperventilation, but I just couldn't seem to regulate what went in and what went out. I pondered if the remaining 35 seconds is enough time to hold my breath and pull the ripcord. Might be, I thought, but what if I pass out trying? Matt might pull the chute, sure, but the whole point of this is to have an experience and not to hit overload.

Just, fucking breathe, I reminded myself.

But breathing wasn't the only offset; my alignment was still questionable. With the collagen and skin on my face blasting in waves and ripples to the backside of my ears, I realized I was in proper position—arms out, chest forward, head to the horizon—but I still felt zero control up there. Like a wind-spinner flurried in all directions. I was desperate, coveting for just one single moment of steady. The entire flight has been a betrayal to the one aim I had; to move with confidence through positions of danger, to navigate with grace, to dance. But this, this was not the fucking dance.

Matt grabbed my hands from behind me, just for a moment, only long enough for me to realize they were not fully open. Immediately, my fingers expanded, and my wrists relaxed. Just. Like. So.

Finally, it came as desired. The mechanics of my position steadied with a modicum of balance. That current I spoke of earlier, which picked me up in a position of surrender, now lifted my wings. Without struggle, I could feel the totality of gravity from a singular plane. Pure, distilled, energy. Incredible amounts of awareness and stillness, at the same time, occurred somewhere between ten-and-seven thousand feet. I worried not for perfecting the flight, not for execution, not even for realization; not for my ability to take it all in, as if it was anything I could ever grab in the first place. Falling at 120 miles per hour, I understood that my time up there was perfectly what it was, passing. Where I looked or fixed my gaze was simply where it went until I fixed it elsewhere. I carried no concern, nor questioned the merits of what I was doing while in flight.

I was, for a moment, able to simply accept the beauty that which I could not catch.

///

"Why do you exist?" Matt had asked me as we drove toward Perris earlier that morning. He was already prepping me for the moment of truth. His tone was gentle, it wasn't intended to threaten the ego or to debate something without value.

"Think about it, why do you exist?" he repeated, even softer. "No pressure, but I'm curious to see how you respond. I've gotten a lot of different answers from different people."

Even if it wasn't threatening, coming straight out of the blue it was a big ask. Because of that, I balked, just for a second, then took my best shot. "I don't think you want a response that addresses the other parts, the purpose-driven stuff. I mean, I can tell you what I exist for, where I find the greatest value in existence. But, we've already covered these things. I think what you are asking is as simple as this. I exist, because I choose to exist."

Matt nodded slowly, his whole face, five o'clock shadow, and the cheeks behind it rising with cheer.

"Yes!" his eyebrows lifted, "Exactly."

"When we are up there today, falling out of the sky, remember that! It sounds simple, ridiculous even, but it's just as profound as anything. We exist because we choose to. It might sound basic, but that is exactly the same choice you and I had in the face of death."

"And that's what we'll be facing anyway," I suggested.

"Absolutely," Matt responded. "This skydive is a perfect situation for guys like us. And that's what I want you to appreciate up there. It's not just a thrill-ride, it's a choice to live." He continued, "I've known you for over a decade, man, and I know It's not the adrenalin you're after, but the awareness. I don't think you want the most sensational skydiving experience; you want the most powerful one."

"And for you, that all begins and ends with identifying the choice to live?" I asked.

"Yes, because in this equation, up there, you are forced to make a choice. Time necessitates it. And when you make that choice the first thing you need to ask yourself, is whether you are choosing to live, because of something like love; or if you are choosing to not die out of something like fear? And they are different responses. It's the same outcome on paper but there's a different formula. One to be aware of, for sure. Fear can drive us to live, but on the long timeline, we've got to know what we're living for. When we do, I believe we find greater satisfaction in the choice."

Matt kept on. "You already know that real death is not just physical. You already know death in its worst form is disconnection to the source. Because you've already died, a lot. You felt it. You know death is more of a direction than an event, and that direction is steered by choices."

"So, what I'm encouraging you to do with this today, is to let it serve as a reminder to always act from love, and not from fear," he said.

///

At 6 ,00 feet I reached for the golf ball, the grab-device which sits about hip-level on the pack and unleashes the parachute, but found only air. Instincts got the better of the moment and immediately, I panicked. Every follicle from my little toenail to the back of my neck rose like a scorpion's tail, and I had ball of sick the size of my fist stuck in my throat. Fuck.

Steady, I thought. Time is on your side.

I whipped my hand back and tried it again with no luck. Afraid to move even an eyeball, for fear of throwing us into a tailspin, I gingerly turned my left wrist into my field of view to check the altimeter.

Five thousand feet. I watched as that needle dropped into the red zone, then I tried again. Still empty-handed.

"Don't turn your head and body back looking for it." Matt had told me at ground-level during our training lecture. "Keep your form, stay balanced, and trust it will be there. You will find it, because you will have to."

Alright, I thought, I've got to do this. If I don't find it this time there may not be another chance at it.

Feeling less than an inch away from a full meltdown, every god-damned instinct within me wanted to kick and scream in a panic—a familiar sentiment codified from a life long-lived in struggle. I could feel the fear creeping in, the nauseating invasion of desperation, breathing right up against the rise of those frozen follicles.

But just then, I took one small, fraction of moment, and paused the frames in the slideshow. In a Deja-vu, I remembered. Right there, even on the way to dying, pending an action having or having not taken place, everything was truly okay. The entire scene. The instincts which were screaming for attention, the brown earth rising from below, everything in sight and everything inside of me, was all good to the most basic level. That I need not be overwhelmed by fear. That death may just be another mirror of life. Because how you go into it, and your experience of it, will be an extension of how you've lived in the first place. Life, and birth, are such an obvious transfer of energy and awareness, why wouldn't it be the same on the other side of the coin? The logic may only make sense to those who have experienced death in others, or who have been quite near it themselves, but it is a logic all the same. It is less dogma, than experience. It cannot be articulated as much as it can be felt, which presents no problems to a flier. Because up in the sky, truth is a language of the heart.

There is, after all, only one constant as I know this universe, and that is revelation. So, calm yourself, steady your hand, and be at ease in a world that was never anything but beautiful.

I traced my right hand back to my hip, as slowly as I could. I found Matt's hip behind mine. I traced further up until I found the pack. I took a deep breath, I envisioned my fingers themselves had eyeballs and I found that motherfucker of a rip-cord at last. With a steady hand and the world before my eyes, I paused for just that last moment, enjoying the journey of 8,000 feet and 45 seconds I'd just taken. Then, as confident as when I jumped out in the first place, I pulled the chute.

///

"I'm going to the top and taking everyone with me." Matt always used to shout.

It's a quote from his grandfather. Matt would say it at the forefront of every dangerous situation, like a cartoon hero, with a hand outstretched for glory, just before action. It was his rally call. In fact, it still is. But there's been a huge shift in the way he operates with it. In the past, the practical outcome of this quote looked a lot like Matt was flying hard-and-fast through life, and hoping to pull along a few others in his airstream; whereas today, it's obvious that taking others with him is the priority, and that getting underneath others and holding them up to a new level is the focus. And the summit, the "top", isn't a fixed place you aim for, it's where you end up as a result of doing shit for others.

I'm not sure if Matt's tandem set up is something every new skydiver should have, or if it's a commercially viable model, but I am sure that it is good. It balances the weight of the thrill with the responsibility of managing the experience; no less focused on the extreme, but more so on the expansion. After all, for Matt, this whole falling out of the sky business is just a parable anyways, perhaps an avatar; a simple event used to illustrate a moral, or even spiritual lesson, a version of a deeper reality.

Back on earth, and after one of the more memorable hugs on our track record, we propped up for a photo in the Sky-Shark. "Dude, this is so righteous. I can't wait to show this photo to our kids fifty years from now!" Matt joyfully shared.

For a guy who used to say he'd be amazed if he made it past the age of thirty, it's a striking commentary. What's most profound about Matt, is that for all he's done in life—and he has done volumes—he is still entirely full of new beginnings. By the time you read this, without a doubt, he will have transferred into many newer and deeper spheres, just as he did after losing those closest to him in the skies. His model is less about growth, in the linear sense, as it is about expansion.

For me, in equal measure as a friend, he's a legend. Sharing the sky with Matt was tantamount to blowing brass onstage with Fela Kuti, holding a beat with Tony Allen, a rope with Robbins, or a wave with Aikau. On the drive home, rather than reveling in the experience we'd just had, we focused on what we were doing. On speaking honestly with one another. The gratitude wasn't about having just done a skydive, it was about being in a conversation, in a car. After all, the same stuff was happening between us, it was just the circumstance which had changed. There was no need to hang a laurel on that skydive any more than there was to take another one, because the friendship was the reward more than the freefall. And that's right by my code. Falling through the skies or catching waves in two-foot surf, it's all the same for us, because at the end of the day, it's about who we're with and where we go together. Having been through all the space between heaven and earth we call ourselves the fortunate, for we know them as one in the same.

///

ONNA BUGEISHA

In a lot of ways, Faith Dickey is beyond metaphor. An original. Though that might not be the first impression you're likely to receive looking at her. The kind, seafoam eyes, her sun-bleached hair that shoots from brown to dirty blonde in straw bundles, and those country freckles, give off all the ease of the California surfer girl, and at the same time, all the grounding of a rural countrywoman. That is, until she speaks. Behind her sincere, articulate charisma, lies her childhood; Texan roots, immutably expressed in her soft country drawl. Under that genuine charm, pleasant as it may be, lies a unique character. Craftsman, artist, survivor, the layers run deep and often bleed. A woman, why not start there? Not by my or your definition, but by hers. A woman, and a hustler. Raised by a single mother since she was three years old, among many lessons, she learned young not to wait for life but to pursue it. And she did. Between 2009—2014, Faith consistently held and set new female and human world records in her preferred sport of highlining. Walking across gargantuan spans far above the ground on a 1-inch sewn webbing, in outdoor environments equally compelling on virtue of their severity as their beauty, was her passion, and unsurprisingly, her métier. And in that pursuit, she was without equal for a very distinguished amount of time.

At the height of her powers, she was globetrotting, gunning between festivals and setting world records. She established new, artistically envisioned highlines all across North America, the European Alps, and the sandstone towers of the Czech Republic. She gave Ted Talks, started women's highline festivals, and carried sponsorships which she networked into a complete professional package. The first woman to do that, also. She was featured in print, online, and in film, all over, including and famously, on a harrowing stunt project for a Volvo commercial advertisement in Sweden, where she walked a highline, about 50 feet long, strung between the tops of two 18-wheeler semi-trucks going 40 miles per hour, barreling straight for a tunnel that was cut clean by a center divider. While every single step in this triumphant arc was met by her exceptional level of focus—consider the attention needed to cross the gap between those trucks—a lot of it, admittedly was never even a goal. As much as it could have, that entire sequence in life kind of just happened. It was not planned.

Today, here and now, at the peak of summer in the year 2020, what you need to know is that she is that exact same person, even better in many ways. The fact that you'll now find her, at least 4-5 days a week, putting in 10-hour shifts and running up a fluid volume deficit by means of slinging food tickets in the grease pit of the Kill Bill yellow-painted, Quesadilla Mobilla food truck, in Moab, is almost inconsequential. Except that it is an exact demonstration of her endless pursuit of growth. Who and where Faith Dickey is today is less the kind of thing which begs explanation as it is that which begs further decoding. She is one hundred percent, showing up for life in ways most of us lack the courage or the modeling to. And—if we're keeping the Tarantino imagery going, she is still a female hero, a warrior of the feminine order, ala Tomoe Gozen. That she hides in plain daylight is even better.

Most days, Faith comes home from work in a half-dried soak of sweat and walks up the four steps of her porch into her humble, tiny-house style studio. She'll give a kiss to her partner Michael, and then head straight for either the garden or any of the other hobbies she keeps. Among them, refashioning, retooling, and restoring anything she can get her hands on, from scrap metal which she'll turn into new fencing for the chicken coop, to gutting an entire vintage Airstream camper for God only knows what future glory. She's always in motion; behind every humble aspect, she's honing a craft.

That's exactly as it was when I pulled up to her house, fresh from the 12-hour drive, famished and bordering on delirium. On the twilight of a balmy, 90-degree evening, we sat on the porch for a round while dinner finished in the oven. Shortly after, with food at the ready, we moved to the quarter acre of open space that is her front yard, and sat at the quaint dinner table while, just above our shoulders, a roughly 100-ft, sunbaked-beige slackline fluttered in the evening breeze. Like a picture frame strung on a wall in a hallway you pass every day, it stayed in the periphery, for the course of our entire three-hour dinner.

On the table, with a fantastic array of her garden's harvest spread before us, Faith welcomed me to break bread with her. Under the fold of two large cottonwood trees, and with the gentle silhouettes of red sandstone towers framing the background, we dug in. With an exceptional offering of mixed chards, greens, kale, cherry and heirloom tomatoes, beets, potatoes, summer squash, and roasted peppers divided between a farmhouse salad and a rustic take on a ratatouille, conversation came easy. In minutes, we were straight into the business end of both her and Michael's backgrounds.

Faith and I had been in correspondence for some time and had always gone deep on the details of our emotional and lifestyle landscapes, but we hadn't ever buckled down and talked history. Knowing only a little about the life she had fashioned, before her current era, I was interested—to put it mildly—in the details of her traverse. In short order she has gone from rural Texan, to international record-setter, to an Alice Waters inspired, farm to table homebody taking on earthworms and mycorrhizae.

///

Of the innumerable details of one's childhood that forge our persona, perhaps it is impossible to really know exactly what, or who, or how the events of our youth shaped both our better assets and our inevitable liabilities. While she may not remember it precisely, Faith will tell you that from the moment her struggling, abusive, alcoholic father left, and in the events following his absence, she came to learn most of what she knows in life by force of rude awakenings. At three-years-old, Faith and her older sister, Christina, along with her mother, Linda, packed it in, becoming a traveling survival band.

Life, at the early stages was characterized by high tension, insecurity, and fear. In the span of a few years, Faith recollects, they moved an estimated 12 times. Never in one place, and unable to foster a home base for more than a few months at a time, life was a roulette.

"Gosh," she said at the dinner table, "I remember we'd go anywhere for support. Shelters, care organizations, I definitely remember standing in front of church congregations with my mom, asking for help. It was wild. We could barely pay bills, and often when we left to a new place, it was 'cause we hadn't."

Whether by eviction or by the rising cost of rent, Faith and the family never had a fair footing. During those days Faith's mom also worked to her limits, taking every odd job available, which resulted in a familiar, parental absentee equation. The family ran the wheel of poverty, as one would suspect, where ends and means simply don't match, and the collateral damage of each penetrated deep in the nooks of Faith's mental framework. Too add, her mom, Linda, developed a very real hoarding habit. It was a manifestation of her clinical diagnoses, anxiety disorder, and O.C.D., which were ultimately expressions of a deeper mental health landscape. The exacerbations of their financial struggles did them no favors, and in this regard, life, for Faith and her family, was a bitch. Unforgiving, relentless, impossible.

But there was a buffer. "I was fortunate to attend a unique elementary school in Austin, on my mother's insistence," she shared. "The coolest part was the duration of it. It was a very small class of students and we were all aware from the beginning that we were all going to be together, like a team, for years to come. It was also special because in that model the focus is on the entire child, and on educating by means of teaching the students to look within themselves for answers and authority."

For Faith, school forged an ability to focus on the long play of relationships, and to look for team-oriented individuals; a growth model that still serves her to this day. She is very conscientious about who she surrounds herself with. Still, school aside, childhood was rough, and those insufficiencies at home eventually trickled over.

In an early memory from her youth, she recalls, that a friend came over after school one day so they could study together. Before they could find a place to sit, it was clear to her friend and Faith alike, that the hoarding dysfunction of Faith's mom had advanced to a fire hazard level, with piles of material stacked floor to ceiling. It was an embarrassment. And not by spite, but more from shock, Faith's friend couldn't help but share the news with her classmates. From that day forward, Faith had to do a lot of soul searching, to cope with her new stigma as the girl with the really odd family. It was an unfair ask for such an early age. Certainly, there are worse childhood's out there, Faith knows. But growing up in all the wrong ways, and all too soon, is no small crime to the great human capacity for wondrous imagination.

By the time she was eighteen, Faith understood that her only chance to define the course of her life was to get out of mom's orbit, and out of Austin. That's not to suggest she wanted nothing to do with her. Faith still has a relationship with her mother to this day, and looks forward to caring for her as she ages. She'll tell you she learned an indescribable amount of wisdom, and ethic, from her mother's modeling. How to really work hard, how to be an independent woman; a damsel without the distress, a princess with no need for a prince. She taught her to stand up, have self-respect, and to march through the trials of life even when you want to crawl.

"There was an unquestionable amount of values I learned from my childhood," she concluded, under the dim glow of her strung patio lights. "I learned about resilience, about the ethics of work and standing behind your word, and about how to love. But I still had to leave."

"Because you needed to establish your own pursuits, I imagine?" I asked.

"Yup," she laughed, "Mom would have found every reason to keep me from doing the things I wanted. Not because she didn't love me, but because she couldn't help but worry. It was just a part of her illness."

"So, what came next?" I asked.

"Well, Lucas," she started with a smirk, "In a very short time I decided I needed to study fashion and move to New York. There was a prestigious school I had my eye on, and I even got accepted. But it was wildly expensive!"

"And?" I asked.

"And I made a resolution. At one point, and mind you this is at 18-years-old, I had five jobs and was working an average of 80 hours a week. This continued for about a year until I burned out completely. I mean, I was trying to save enough for two years of room, board, and academic costs, but I was way out of balance. It's something of a recurring theme in my life."

The way she talks about it, you get the hunch she could've done anything. Design and art held her attention, and she did love the idea of it. You could see why. The notion that it was a craft to hone, something for her to quietly chisel. The notion that you could reframe concepts of who wears what, of self-expression, of beauty even; that's all right in her wheelhouse. While she might have been the next Nour Hage, you also get the feeling that Faith just needed something to aim for. Whatever the target, the rubber met the road on Faith's ambition and industriousness shortly thereafter.

"So, having exhausted myself to the edge," she continued, "I drove home one night after working too many hours and burned it all to the ground. Not intentionally, of course. I was so tired I passed out on the road and flipped my car completely, just totaled. I was fine, somehow, but the ambulance and police came and next thing I knew I had taken all the money I'd worked my ass off for, for school and rent, and I'd dumped into a pile of bills. I was gutted."

Not one to wallow, she found a new beginning. In her spare moments, while working those couple of years, she had seen a group of people slacklining in a park and had even tried it a few times. At that point, she could walk a basic line, and it dawned on her that she had a contact in Europe who was doing the same. With what little money she had left, Faith booked a ticket, one way. On a lark, it was off to London to meet a guy she'd been hopelessly romantic about, forging a half-laid plan to look for direction while walking her little slacklines.

"That all sounded really good," she laughed, "Until, wouldn't you have guessed it, things didn't work out at all with the guy, and the well ran dry. The pound was exchanging at a 1:2 ratio back then, so just landing in Great Britain took half my savings. I found a humble flat to rent, got a job at a local pub and worked my ass off, grinding the hamster wheel all over again, drinking beers and getting nowhere."

Back to square one, on her own, Faith put in the equal measure of trust to the higher forces as she did to her footwork on the slackline. She had no idea where her life was going, only that when she was on the slackline, it didn't matter. Within a few months, and with a little bit of grace, she made one single contact—an American Expat, living in Berlin, who pointed her to the Czech Republic. Acting on her namesake, Faith booked a ticket, looking for something like a community, guided only by her inner sense of direction.

///

Next day, just after lunch, we drove out of the swelter-lands of Moab and up the La Sal Loop Road, about twenty clicks into the high country. With Michael and Faith in the front seats, I took in the views above Mill Creek Canyon panning all the way out to Canyonlands National Park.

"I'll tell you, Lucas," Faith turned from the passenger seat, "things have changed a lot since those days. The sport is entirely different."

When Faith arrived in the Czech Republic, slacklining was still a young sport. Established in the heart of Yosemite Valley from as early as the 1960s, and mostly in the 1980s, by the intrepid wall climbers during their rest days, slacklining was developed simply to improve balance for aid climbing, and had nearly no rules and even fewer standards. The idea that it would evolve into its own discipline with a variety of records, ethics, and aesthetics would've blown the old-timers away. If anything was certain when Faith came around, circa 2009, it was that slacklines were rigged a certain way, with a certain tension—not so taught as a tight rope but not too loose either, right in the middle.

"That all changed about five to six years ago." Faith said. "Lines got progressively looser, and records fell all over the place. But more than that, the sport changed in how people saw slacklining. People started taking more to performance than they had in previous generations. While that was empowering for a lot of people, and it probably attracted way more of them into the sport, it was a departure."

"Sounds a lot like an old surfing transition period." I offered.

"Right." Faith agreed, speaking from her handful of years in Central Californian surfing. "It's a lot like that, people got really into doing tricks and creating feats, and the way they actually rigged the lines was a reflection of that. The looser lines made it easier to do that stuff, not that any of it is easy. But once the sport moved in that direction, the old high-tension system was suddenly seen as this archaic style, almost useless."

"It sounds like the sport settled pretty quickly on the progressive side," I said. "And that happened in surf culture, too. Although, personal style in surfing is pretty en vogue right now. There's definitely been a movement back to free surfing and cultivating a variety of equipment, surf-style, and wave styles, too. People see both the waves and their ability to express themselves on them as a fluid system. But in my experience surfers tend to have some parts of style ingrained, whether that be a top to bottom approach or just committing to staying in trim."

"I'm falling into the latter category on that analogy," Faith declared. "I think you're right, and perhaps slackliners and high-liners could use more of that perspective. It's lovely to think that everyone can express their art out there on the line in whatever way they see fit. But like you said, the trend, these days is definitely on the performance, and doing that requires rigging a loose line. For me, though, you sacrifice some of the aesthetic beauty when you rig loose."

"How so?" I naively asked.

"Well, it's just a function of the system you use," she started. "Loose lines still require back-up lines, you know."

A back-up is a secondary line. In the older style, it was rigged at similar tension and was almost invisibly placed under the primary line. Every 8 feet or so, it would be taped to the mainline, which gave the effect of reinforcing the primary, and visually, aesthetically speaking, the entire system looked like one seamless, taught slice of webbing cutting clean across the sky.

"Today's lines are so loose, they don't lay in space the same, and the back-ups underneath them are even looser. People still tape the back-up to the primary, but there are these large curling loops of slack created under each section. Performance-wise, what that gets you is a looser, lighter line."

"And how does that enable the performance?" I had to ask.

"Well," she began, "Think of it this way. If you were to take an old, tight set up, say a 200-foot line, and you were to flick it with your foot, you'd create a relatively strong wave of energy. Immediately, that wave would travel down the entire 200-foot line, rebound off the anchor and then come rushing back to you with even greater force. If you were standing on that line, you'd have to receive that force. You'd have to balance it. That balancing requires really good technique on the part of the highliner."

"And that's not the case with a loose line." I realized.

"Yup. The loose line will distribute that force. This means, in theory, you can make more mistakes, you can have a technique that is not as developed and get away with it. That was hard for me to accept because what other people saw as performance enabling, for a long time I saw as technically weaker. On top of that, the lines themselves just didn't look as presentable, and for me, slacklining was always about that clean element of it more than trick-lining. My focus was always on an inner sense of harmony, and on walking as beautifully as possible across a striking backdrop of nature, on a line that looked beautifully constructed."

Arriving at the pullout for a local crag, we unloaded our climbing packs and began our hike under a glorious patch of aspens, as Faith concluded. "You know, I think that was a tough period for me to accept because there was so much change happening in the sport, and within me. But, I do believe that the beauty of highlining, like surfing, is that it is an individual expression. It's not up to anyone to tell you how to walk a line, and there is no right or wrong slackline, unless it's not rigged safe, I suppose. Other than that, the whole sport should just be about expression, about defining your own freedom. However you practice it, at some point it's going to require a level of craft. And I guess my hope for kids these days is that they embrace a wide variety, some might say even the old variety of highlining, just the same way surfers do nowadays."

"Well," I said, "They call it soul surfing for a reason. I can see how that idea translates up on the line. A well-tensioned high-line just looks and surfs like something straight out of Makaha in the sixties. It's classic."

With that said, we finished our descent through a dizzying maze of aspens, flickering like champagne bubbles in the wind, and made way to the cliff. Faith and Michael gave me the honor of having the first leads for each climb of the day, another gracious extension of their hospitality, as we sampled the vertical terrain. Climbing with the two of them was an effortless joy, a perfect way to gel together on a warm summer afternoon. Easy climbing, with the occasional steep thrill, tempered by a long dive into Faith's early travelling days. It was, after all, a golden age that Faith unwittingly walked into the day she left the U.K. for that slackline festival in the Czech Republic.

///

Looking back, it feels a lot like destiny of some kind. Faith, the meager city girl, had nearly no relationship to nature in her youth, nor had she traveled. She'd never felt the rush and wanderlust of the road, nor the dizzying freedom of having home be wherever you choose to lay your head. She was just an honest, hard-working young woman, looking for something to connect with.

At the festival, Faith met two critical figures, an American Expat named Jordan, and a Polish stud named Yannick. While Faith had gotten way past the white-belt levels on slacklines at ground level, she found highlining, for the very first time, was light-years out of her league. Or so it felt. Faith failed utterly, but it gave her a drive for improvement, giving those difficulties no chance against her stubborn grit. She also clicked, lock in key, with the boys, and in no time a team was formed. The three of them became an outfit, joined at the hip on a single mission, to learn and grow together. That began with traveling to the alps, a first time and life-changing experience where Faith, with all the wrong equipment for their amateur climbing ambitions, found out what it means to be a human among giants. A lesson in exposure that would soon pay dividends.

Within months of that highline festival, Faith had graduated to her own beginnings of mastery, to the point where she was suddenly walking high-lines that only a lunar cycle sooner she would've pawned off as impossible. One day at a time, stubbornly, quietly; wax on, wax off. The beginnings of her now famous, impeccable technical skill were fashioned in those anonymous lines. That's where lightning first struck. In the fall of 2009, an opportunity arose, from Grolsch Beer of all institutions, for Yannick and two friends of his to have an all-expenses-paid, sponsored trip to the U.S.. They'd planned to revisit the classic American high-lines of lore, and, if all went well, to establish new lines of their own. Without any level of sponsorship, Faith and Jordan decided to join, paying their own share out of pocket. This trip, on the order of just a few months after Faith had first walked a high-line, and less than a year on from moving to Europe, was her coming of age.

"I honestly didn't even consider myself good, and I definitely wasn't setting out to break any records," she said as we revisited memory lane.

But history tells it otherwise. When Faith arrived back in the States, reaching for the last of the dimes in her pocket, she flew into Texas first, to pick up her beater Honda Civic which she had purchased after the bad car accident. Barely making it out to Ahwahne (Yosemite), she reconnected with the team and within no time at all, she found herself above one of the highest waterfalls in the world, Yosemite Falls. Three thousand feet off the deck, with one single foot standing out on the line that connected her to the top of the Lost Arrow Spire, some 55-feet away.

The Lost Arrow Highline was a coveted feat, described as a Holy Grail and other spiritual epitome by the originators many years back. First crossed in 1985, by a fella named Scott Balcom, it had at that point only seen two female crossings, first and notably by Faith's idol, Libby Sauter, in 2007. Fresh out of the beater Honda Civic, with lactic acid burning in her legs from the monstrous hike and rigging job, Faith stepped out on that line and was immediately blown back by a howl of wind rising from the abyss beneath her. But she maintained. Steadied, by the invisible sorcerer's wand in her hands, she gently floated the whole of her life's balance with subtle, graceful curls of her wrists, as if a conductor on stage. Men, generally speaking, wrestle up there, they fight force with force. But not Faith, you will not see her flagging her limbs out far off the line. She fights force, not with strength, but with a soft, feminine response. Without fail, completely competent where she had been a beginner just a few months earlier, the sum of those quiet, anonymous sessions paid return. Faith became the first woman to walk the Lost Arrow Highline, first try, a unique feat in all the world.

Later that same trip, after having walked all the classic Yosemite Valley highlines, the team went to Moab, and Joshua Tree to spin history further. In Moab, perhaps to nobody's surprise aside from Faith's, she established a new distance record, for females. Held by her hero, Libby, until then, this was female world record number one. Not only was history being set above ground, but underneath, in the moments between, Faith was falling in love. Sure, she and Yannick had grown into a deeper partnership, but even that couldn't match the love she discovered in connecting to the outdoor lifestyle. Empowered in such radical fashion, suddenly so apt, so able to engage with the wild spaces in life, Faith found something like purpose for possibly the first time. She was hooked, rose-colored, drunk goggles and all.

In Joshua Tree, a month later, circa December 2009, Faith and the boys set up a striking line across two of the more attractive formations in the park. When they rigged the back-up behind it, taping it to the mainline every handful of feet, they took their first measurements and found to their surprise, they'd just rigged a potential world record proposition.

"Never in my life," Faith described as we sat for dinner back in the front yard, "had I thought I would do something another human hadn't done. No way. That just wasn't in me or my life plan. I've always had a psychological make-up counter to that. And I'll tell you, it was truly humbling."

First point of fact, she means it. For all the swelling of persona that might come with being the best at something in this life, with being an actual standout among almost 8-billion, Faith is sincere. She takes nothing for granted, largely due to where she has come from. Second point of fact, she is an original. And she proved it again when, on that evening in the magical twilight tones of Joshua Tree, she stood up past her teammates Jordan and Yannick, and walked the full 67 meters (~220 ft), without fail, right into the record books. Faith completed the full, men's and women's, human world-record distance on a high-line. Records she would hold, redefine, and refashion—all things she's best at—for another six years.

Perhaps better than the record itself, according to Faith, was having the chance to meet her idol, Libby. While that highline was still up, a few days later, Faith met Libby who was on a climbing trip in the park, and invited her over to the line. It was a connection she'd been aching to foster. A woman to woman, positive role model on the front edges of the sport. A dream.

"Well, that sounds incredible," I said, "The idea that you got to achieve all of that, see all those places for the first time on that trip, and meet Libby. They say you shouldn't meet your idols because they'll let you down, but it sounds like it was quite the opposite."

"Oh my god," Faith exclaimed, "It couldn't have gone better. But I'll tell you, I learned something from Libby, too. In a way, she kind of did let me down, but only because she didn't fit the expectations I had placed on her to be just as manic about highlining as I was. I was just so wrapped up in it, it was all I could see. But Libby wasn't, and she was already engaging in all this other stuff in life."

"While you were entering the peak of your expression, it was probably hard to see that someone who'd had a world record, and been so established in a sport, could just as easily turn in other directions away from it," I said.

"For sure," Faith agreed. "When Libby struggled on the highline we set up, it blew me away. It wasn't because I had become 'better' than someone I looked up to, it was because she didn't seem to care that much about not being able to do it. She was so free of it. I couldn't understand it. It took me years."

"Until you had to find something deeper, or at least something else to strive for," I suggested.

"Absolutely. Looking back, I was just in love with the first thing that came my way, I mean, highlining is amazing, but it's not everything, and Libby was already on another plane. She's a cardiac nurse and a badass who does her job incredibly well. She's always pushing herself, she travels to give aid to people, she's an activist, and, she still manages to crush. Libby's still my idol in life, for sure."

The dichotomy presented to Faith on that world record line, in Joshua Tree, would take her years to walk. Frankly put, Libby had a wider, deeper purpose that Faith was still looking for. And no length, no span, no record distance walked on a line could separate Faith from the need of that wider purpose. But all things in time. Faith was raging in life, and when you are flying with the unstoppable feedback loops of acceleration underneath you, you look only to set further goals. You do not ask yourself of their value.

Faith was at an all-time high, the tip of the spear. The Best. Period. Not best woman, the best. How could she not run with that momentum? With so many moments in life, in her childhood, defined by struggle, by inglorious and insecure epochs without the means or the ends, where she'd never seen a woman come from the shadows, into a boys club, and redefine the terms of engagement, how could she not consider that as purpose? In many ways, it was.

Faith was driven by a few core components. The beauty of being one with nature and exercising a craft, out there, up high, for sure. The ability to be a role model for other women, absolutely. And the gift of being a functioning part of something bigger than herself, of being a part of a team. If you ask her, that was the most distinguished element about her rise. That it was not alone.

Yannick and Jordan went with her everywhere. With the new sponsorship she'd acquired when they returned to Europe in 2010, now as a team holding records, Faith jumped in capabilities. Trips were sponsored, expenses covered, media outlets were drooling for content, festival and event organizers were calling her for contracts; the list went on. From 2010—2014, in successive cycles it was Europe, Czech, the Alps, the U.S., Moab, Joshua Tree, Yosemite, Cuba, Germany; board the flight, open the book, smile at the customs kiosk, passport stamped, check. Faith went everywhere. But always, with the team. "We were as fundamental to one another's success as a good diet. We did everything together, and that was the fount of our energy. It was a group thing, collective energy more than it was any one person's." She shared fondly. "I think that's the best part of coming from the schooling system I was raised with, because more than anything, what it gave me was this desire for community. To do things with people, not in competition against them."

There are a lot of friendships of convenience out there, especially among the dirtbagging type. But what Faith attributes as the key to those four years of running-and-gunning is the real thing. Partnerships, on the long play, was the mission for her and the team, from day one. That single, organic thread, perhaps, is what separated their outfit from the others, and what pushed all of them together, further, higher, and longer than any one of them could've gone alone.

"There was no peak too high, or gap too long for us to set our sights on. We rigged and walked everything. I kept setting and resetting records, too. But not because I wanted it as much as it was just a consequence of the three of us pushing each other further. It really was an incredible time," she shared. "Those were special years under what felt like a completely unstoppable force. We just got after it in ways neither one of us could've imagined."

Those, indeed, were the salad days.

///

Unloading from the cars, the following day, Faith, and her friends Chelsea and Nicole grabbed the daypacks and cinched the laces on their trail shoes. Guided by the team trail-dog, Finn, we set out for a hike at the trailhead of Warner Lake. Once again in the high plains of the La Sal's, outside of Moab, we sought good company and better shade from the toxic pulse of midday's sun.

As we started hiking, for what we were told would be a short jaunt out to a nestled alpine lake, Faith and I continued in discussion, rewinding the tapes to get a feel for the slow, steady unraveling of those golden days we'd spent the previous day highlighting.

"What can I say," Faith began, "It was working really, really well, until it wasn't."

"Ha ha," I laughed with familiarity, "I know exactly what you mean."

"Yeah. Well, I guess it was a three-pronged series of events. First, there was the team element. Yannick and I had split up, and even though we were all friends, life started taking all of us to different places. Second, there were the injuries. They crept in, and I lived in a lot of denial for as long as I could, but the truth was, I was working myself down. And third, the sport was changing, a lot. That might be a two-parter unto itself. But the end result of it all burned me out and left me juggling a divided life I wasn't sure about. I was part-time in California, and occasionally part-time with trips back to Europe. Never really happy with either."

First, the team. As she mentioned, the romantic venture between her and Yannick fanned out, as happens, somewhere in the fog of all the busyness. With Faith taking jobs all over, in some semblance of celebrity, and with Yannick having his own needs in life, equilibrium wasn't easy. Jordan, their good friend and the original link between the two of them, also had his own opportunities. After all, while they had been a sponsored team for a handful of years, they were barely getting enough to keep the party going. The option to freewheel at a net-zero on the balance sheet might sound like paradise to most dirtbaggers. But do it for long enough, with a little seasoning of age, and it won't matter who you are, you'll start asking some questions of direction. It just happens that way. The team was still something like a family, probably the closest one Faith had, but they couldn't keep up what they'd started. Life was moving on. It always does.

"I'll tell you, it got lonely out there," she shared. "It was an odd realization, that I had friends all over the world, in every place I went. But there were a good couple of years there where I just kept finding myself alone at the end of a day highlining, or after some party, and feeling like there was nobody out there but me."

"I'm no stranger to that," I replied, "I can't tell you how many nights

I sat up in my tent alone out in some distant place on a climbing trip, baffled how in the span of a few years, and all in the same tent, I'd gone from king of my own world to a prisoner of it."

Next, injuries. As Faith put it, she trampled and abused her knees for far too long, and without any recovery. Five years, maybe more, lugging heavy packs up alpine ridges, to the tops of distant cliff bands, way the hell out there. Always wanting to earn her keep on the team, and to prove herself as capable as the boys, Faith often packed on 2/3rds of her body weight whenever she went up to rig a line. That behavior, and the endless sequence of standing up on those lines, bit back at her. In highlining, you skootch your bum out on the line, just past the cliffside, and from a seated position, almost in a lotus pose, you squat press yourself in a quick but very intense pulse until you're up to your own two feet. Do that 50—100 times a day, five days a week, for five years without any major yoga regimen, active injury prevention, or strength training, and you're simply going to flame out. Faith hadn't felt good on her knees since she was still paying off the car accident bills.

And lastly, the two-parter, the sport, and profession itself. While she was mostly injured, walking half-mast, at best, for those last couple of years, circa 2015—2017, the sport had changed around her entirely. As mentioned previously, highlining and slacklining both moved toward tricks, flips, bouncing charades, and other tomfoolery. New techniques which, while eye-catching and by no means for the beginner, were not something Faith felt drawn to compared to the soulful standards she'd began with. On the one hand, she had to concede, it was a progression, and it brought people in. Yet she knew, still knows, the new standards of rigging made foundations and good technique easier to bypass. People who lacked the technical prowess on a standard landline at ground level were making remarkable gains, to the point where the records she'd worked ages for quickly became irrelevant. Faith almost did, too.

That was the second part of the crisis. Her place within it all. Just as quickly as she'd taken the helm, the sport was leaving her behind. Conversations to acknowledge the variety of styles up on the line were not taking place, which meant that no matter your craft, if you weren't rigging and sending lines with all the razzle-dazzle of the new wave, your practice, no matter how disciplined, was not validated. As a female, she'd already spent years fighting for just that, some validation. It wasn't easy to find, not in a male-dominated outdoor sports industry where her femininity was only as good as the clickbait it produced.

Faith hit a crossroads. She spent months on trips, alone and without her team, asking those larger questions of herself. Longing for connection but lost in a new wave of highlining norms, while walking on broken tissues and wasted cartilage, she suffered. She was getting lapped by people younger than her and struggling to even stay relevant. Often, she would spend an afternoon on a line just for the sake of a good photo she could send to a sponsor, then end up beating herself up about it at night. She just couldn't find the soul anymore.

"Must have been pretty hard," I said, "I mean, not only were you injured, chronically, but you were basically expected to perform at this new level, without having had the time to practice it. That's an unfair pressure, just to stay relevant in something you weren't even sure you were enjoying anymore."

"Definitely," Faith agreed. "There was a real long period there where I wanted to give it up completely. I mean, for something like two years I just wasn't able to have anything close to a good experience with it. Whether by the constant, debilitating pain or by the mental tension because my motivations were all over the place, there was just nothing about it that was enjoyable. And if I'm honest, my ego was busted up about it, too."

Faith shared that while she was never in competition with anyone, truly, there was a good few years where other women weren't even coming close to what she was doing—she unwittingly got comfortable with the status. It's an insidious thing having a reputation walk in front of you. Getting that ego smashed put her defenses up, both to critique in the sport, and to allowing others get close to her.

"At the end of it," she concluded, "in that last year or two, I was living kind of off-the-grid in San Luis Obispo. I was trying to move on, but still taking any highlining jobs that would come my way because I couldn't let go of it. I was so torn up with pressure and expectation, and I'll tell you, right then, I thought back about Libby, often. I began to understand why it was important to have other things of value in life, other ways to push yourself. That's what really put me on a new track, the realization that I had, in a lot of ways, gotten everything I could've from highlining. I didn't have to give it up, but if I wanted growth in life and new happiness, I realized it was going to have to come from a different path."

An hour and a half, and nearly 2,000 feet of gain later, Faith and I stopped at a turn in the switchbacks, looking to Chelsea for some direction. Turns out, there'd been some confusion on the objective. Chelsea thought we were just on an aimless hike, while Faith thought Chelsea was leading us to a lake. Nicole and I were just along for the ride, so we didn't have a clue. But now that it had been both a decent time and distance. and since we were outfitted with no more than a daypack and some small rations of water, we found it was worth asking what on earth we were actually doing up there. As it turned out, Burro Pass, a nice respite between Mann's Peak and Mt. Tomasaki was just a short skip above, at which we decided we'd call a highpoint.

Up at the pass, Faith and the girls made a special note to mark the occasion, setting a timer on Faith's phone to snap a photo of the four us. When the clicker counted down to zero, Faith and the ladies, connected by some unspoken and unified exuberance, all jumped as high as they could, while my sorry ass was left on the dirt. It was fascinating, not because I looked the fool, but because without saying a word to another about it, all three of the women just understood on a gut level that it was a moment for celebration. It was some kind of magical feminine telepathy straight out of the hive mind, and it blew me away. It's notable because from that point forward, for the entire trek back, those three women hiked in ways I can only imagine women do. The feminine expression out there simply is different. Every bit of their conversations had only to do with steps they were taking in new directions, about self-improvements, goal setting, and figuring out ways they could keep one another accountable to pursue those improvements. Something genuine, egoless, and only about connection.

It's a theme for Faith, and something she intentionally put into practice more than eight years ago. Always aware of the barriers to entry for women in life and sport, Faith used her platform to build something at a time where infrastructure was lacking. Of all the aesthetically superb and beautiful lines that Faith has ever rigged and walked, many, she confessed, were in the enchanted woodlands and mystic sandstone towers of the Czech Republic. It's where she had both fallen in love with and spent so much of her time highlining. Outside the town of Ostrov, Czech Republic, Faith started the women's-only highlining festival. Running strong since 2012, her festival has changed the lives of countless women from all corners of the globe. When considering the best things she's ever done—in a sport where she'd held and set, then reset, world and female records—she'll tell you, It's all there in Ostrov.

"Without a doubt, Lucas, the most fulfilling and beautiful thing I've done in the sport is that festival. It means the world to me. To be bonding with, and building up, other women, is a dream. We don't care what your ability level is. We don't care who you know. We just want to connect and make you better to face the world you're in. Whether that's on a line or applied somewhere else in your life. Hopefully both."

The exceptional pride, the kind that cannot be taken from somebody by material circumstance or even by injury, is the pride that glows off Faith's face when she talks about that Women's festival. And rightly so. It is a bright spot of her life. As we hiked out of the aspens and made way back to the cars, you could see that same glow on her, having spent hours around a few good friends and fellow women, circling simple themes and working out ways to edify one another.

An exemplary, refreshing take.

///

Back to Moab after our hike, and back to Faith's journey to find a new path. When Faith moved to Moab, about three years back, it was less to rage in the endless delight of the desert—a reason many take to these canyons—as it was to slow life down to the essentials. A task that proved difficult. While she had just started dating her partner, Michael, which was a joy, other aspects of life were piling up. Faith faced an eerie repeat sequence to her early days, when, in a period of 12 months, they moved between five separate apartments, trailers, even resorted to renting parking spots for a place to sleep. The toughest reality, for the both of them—as Michael had also carried sponsorships in his past— was the financial shortfall that came as a result of transitioning away from the profession.

Still, even with the manic transitions around her, Faith turned inward, journaling, and reading anything she could get her hands on. Nature, fiction, Taoist and Buddhist works, even the dreaded self-help aisle, everything was game, as it should be for a curious, hungry mind. What she found with the help of those tools, and her part-time therapist, was centered on her co-dependent streaks through life, and her proclivity to run headfirst into it. She realized she had always operated full on passion, but perhaps without the balance.

"It's odd that I've made a living slacklining for so long," she laughed in irony, "I've always been able to tell when I was in or out of balance on a slackline or a highline. But there's been little of it outside of a 1-inch webbing in my day to day. I've proven it a tall order to live moderately."

"Another place we can agree," I sympathized.

"And perhaps that's what I wanted the most, that's what drove me in all those quiet hours, long before the big trips and sponsorships."

"Well, exactly. That's why it's sincere when you say you weren't trying to break or set records, at least not at first. It sounds like you were pulled into it because it represented something deeper you were lacking," I suggested.

"It's true," Faith confessed with a smile, her soft country drawl giving admission, "And for a time, it worked, like we said. For a time that was what it gave me. But it wasn't sustainable, because however deep on all the other levels of performance and focus, it was still topical to my inner needs. Highlining was never going to address those things; although it could give me a lot of other awareness, and craft, even a spiritual practice. But to get what I needed I had to work directly at it, and that stuff had to happen off the line."

It's true. The amount of complex, high-performing, and exceptional frameworks she learned to operate with while up on those lines, is beyond measure. But as she noted, for balance in life itself, to get away from co-dependencies and learn how to live with moderate, assured wisdom, the metaphor failed. Nothing she could do on a highline could give her that. That work required something longer than any highline, record-setting, or not. It required time. Not only time, but also faith, because on that line you do not have the foresight of the finishing point. You simply do not know where, or if the work even ends.

In Moab, Faith finally settled in for the long play. She and Michael cultivated something intimate, special, and most importantly, honest. In their partnership, they forged an assurance and a simple commitment to work deeply on the darkened spaces, together. How they foster that, the particular tools and habits they operate with, are theirs alone. In Moab, Faith also moved slowly into what are now established directions. She simplified, and she did the inner work. She dealt with those long-standing injuries and the psychological motifs. She came face to face with all that self-limiting talk. She was, and still is, selective about who she lets into her life, and she has taken the steps to build her body back up. She has found, to her joy, a great learning, more in the practice of climbing rocks than in the practice of walking on a line between them. And, perhaps most importantly, she traded a lot of time and tools of the highlining life, for a simple, dirty, unapologetic one with her fingers in the earth, gardening.

///

A few hours later, near sundown in Moab, Faith invited me one more time to share dinner at her place for an evening as warm as the company within it. I arrived up the now-familiar steps to her studio and greeted Michael who was helping in the culinary preparations. From the distance of a football pitch, Faith hollered out from her happy place.

"Lucas, come check out the growth on these tomato stocks," she yelled.

Cast by the fading crepuscular rays of twilight behind her, the purple tone and almond shape of the sun closing over the cliffs, Faith was simply the happiest I had seen her. Completely alight, sunhat, shears, and woven basket for the harvest.

"You still haven't seen my garden," she smiled with invitation. I skipped in her direction, past the chicken coop that she had reassembled out of spare metal, to the perimeter of her most personal project.

Faith's garden, like her, is an unsuspected bounty of life. Held together by reclaimed wood, fencing grates, even abandoned sets of snow skis, she has mosaiced the fragments available—much as she has in life—

to construct a place where growth can happen. It is lush, fully bloomed, interconnected, and well designed, a deluge of many-colored splendor. Upon entry, a cornucopia of tomatoes—heirloom, cherries, grapes, and tomatillos—share eco-balance with squash varietals, cabbages, root vegetables and leafy greens. All of them, in balance. Faith, as any farmer will tell you, knows that it all begins with the soil. Tending to the subterranean, unseen elements of a garden is the most important action. Even when bare, before a new crop rises and you could swear it's all just a pile of dirt, an empty garden with healthy soil is all stuff of life; it is the landscape of promise.

Faith's garden is a beautiful, inner cultivation. A physical demonstration of where she really is in life, today. Beautiful enough, that as we harvested dinner for the evening, a fallow doe gracefully hopped a neighboring fence and snuck under a tree, just beside us, to see for herself what all the magic was about.

Finally, in the dark of night with those warm, strung patio lights aglow, and joined by Faith's neighbors, and Nicole, we sat and shared dinner. The one-hundred-foot, sunbaked beige slackline flickering in the evening breeze, was still just a fond part of the periphery. Right there, at the splendid table and surrounded by the small group of her inner circle, Faith was truly at home, a long way from those childhood roots in Austin. We broke bread, played musical instruments, and laughed about the many small fortunes in life, wanting for nothing.

After a long conversation, near midnight, Faith noted the hour and began winding down our time together. She had to work in the morning, as another round of the sweat-fest in the food truck beckoned. It may not be setting records, but it is a place where she can apply practice. She has come to embrace it, even. Spending all day dealing with tourists, who pawn her off as some nameless clerk behind a convenient fast-food order, both moves and excites her. Because it is not forever, and because it keeps her humble, and hungry to move forward.

Faith Dickey has embraced the entire journey, and she is aware of the full circle of orbit it has taken. There is no question, as a life stage, that she is right back at the park, quietly building the foundations of her craft, traversing into a new mastery. The difference, this time, is the awareness, the choice of it. With all the focus and creative energy inside of her, Faith is bound to excel at anything she commits to. That much is obvious. All she needs is to refine that sense of purpose. Without that, without purpose, she cannot get into those extra gears.

Slacklining and highlining were never her plans. Where it took her, how her life magically upended and became an international, world-record-setting odyssey that it was, she'll never regret. But she knows today that she has extracted the full measure blood from that stone. She knows what the pinnacle of success looks like, feels like, is like. She knows that ultimate success is not measured by financial bounty or some far-reaching prestige. She knows that those metrics do not fulfill, and because of that, they are no longer her targets. She's not interested in playing the finite board.

"Slacklining may have nothing left to give me," she shared, contented. "In the sense that it can no longer give me the purpose I'm looking for. But no question, it has given so much to me." Faith looked lovingly over to Michael and concluded, "And for that, I'm truly grateful."

With just the three of us left on the front yard, the neighbors having gone off to bed, Faith awakened in an epiphany, and shared, "Damn, Lucas, it's been three days and you still haven't actually seen me touch a slackline."

Convinced I'd already seen all sides of her, I deferred, "No need, Faith. It's late, you aren't warmed up, and it's dark. I'd feel terrible if you hurt yourself or something."

My concerns, to no surprise, had zero effect to keep Faith in her chair.

She may not walk a line to answer life's larger questions these days, and the profession may have nothing left to give her on the inside, but these facts do not betray the exquisite pleasure, the love, she maintains for the practice. Body, in motion. Faith strapped on a headlamp, pushed into a muscle-up, and then straddled the slackline. Skootching, then pausing in the lotus for just a moment, she transitioned onto a single base leg, and Chongo-started up to her feet.

Quiet but for the sound of some West African blues gently playing on the speaker behind us, and the fluttering waves of crickets in song, Faith took on a new dimension entirely. I'd seen photos of her on a line, most of which captured a specific strength of focus, a slight tension even. But in motion, just there, her movement was a thing of revelation. With remarkable, intoxicating fluidity, Faith space-walked across the line, lit up only by a silhouette which grew smaller and more distant as she drew closer to the old cottonwood some 100-feet away. Poised in frame, just like so, she moved so gracefully you'd sooner call it the dance of another species than anything human. Turning, about-face, at the far end of the line she stepped into a deeper flow state, something of an extravagant, oceanic ballet—hands filled with a holy spirit, with some force which only the waving sea anemones may fully understand, she synchronized all parts of her body into a lucid orb of movement, her wrists and fingers especially, weaving, storytelling, interacting with the force of life in soft curls and pronating bends—the whole of it, beautiful.

They say, the greatest act a samurai can fashion with their own sword is to put it back into its sheath. To arrive at a place where the entire craft of it can be expressed without once putting hand to hilt, is the mark of the true warrior. Watching Faith gently step off that line, and transmute back into human flesh, back in disguise, I understood. She is completely, still there. The records, the fantastic, the sensational, all of it abides just under her fingertips. She is one hundred percent, still a female hero, a warrior, a total samurai of the feminine order, Onna Bugeisha status.

And she's hiding in plain sight.

As she came off the line, I had to go into just one more train of thought with her.

"You know," I said. "In my own efforts at life, in the closest thing I've had to a flow-state or a purified practice, I've had what some might call an experience of no-mind. But it begins and ends, just there, in the mind. For me, it's a welcome departure from our Western ways, which are usually dominated by rational thinking. When it clicks, it seems to drop the critical self away completely, leaving an abyss which I hope will be filled by some supreme flood of emotion, some joy, or deep abundance. Often, when I'm there, the awareness of it comes too soon, and the bubble bursts. But still, I hold out. I practice."

"That's sounds right," she said with encouragement. "So, what's the question?"

"Well," I began. "I'm just curious if you've ever had something like that on the line. I wonder if you have found that those experiences, the ones rich with pure emotion, do indeed abound? And if so, are they available to all of us?".

"They certainly are there," she began, "And they are available. They take a lot of practice, but I promise you they are out there. I'll say this, too. While there are floods and emotions you can't imagine, there's even more."

"There's what?" I stammered, dumbfounded. "How so?"

"What I can tell you, from my experience, is that you can get to a place beyond even the swell of pure emotion. You can go further than the mind, further than the emotion, into a place that is completely devoid of a narrative. In that place, I'm there only as much as there are antennae, as much as there is sense perception; to hear sounds, to feel wind, to note the rise of the hairs on my neck and my arms. But the senses don't serve me, they serve to acknowledge a present beauty and fullness. That's it. It's not me having an experience. It's not a divide between myself and my environment. It's nothing that can even be narrated over, there is no *me* to even swell with emotion. Just a radically pure, awareness. That's out there for you, and everybody, too. I know it."

Lights out, dinner served, completely astounded. Her pièce de résistance, is that she knows all about that transcendental space. That she's been there. She's found the place where words, like narration itself, serve no purpose. She's accessed the quiet chamber and stayed there long enough to see her nature.

I looked over to Faith and realized exactly why she is an original, and, why she is beyond metaphor. And that is because she's been to, and come back from, the exact place which is also.

///

CREDENCE

In life, so little can be assured to us, that we learn not to wait upon our wishes. Visions are for the romantics, and dreams, are just that— unfounded. Best intentions, best plans, and roads well paved, often take their own turns. End results, we learn, are the object of fools. Process is what we get more than achievements. But every now and then, in some act of the cosmos, the hands of the almighty reach down and do for us what we could not do for ourselves, in a script beyond our machinations. Somewhere in the mired fabric of every single day, in the lowlands, the doldrums of every one of our individual lives, there is that clever, invisible hand, leading you and me both to that next moment of revelation. It is almost always unseen, but be assured, it is always there. Rapture, in this life, is designed for you, too.

This is a tale of such an intervention. A message from the netherworld, that place we've all been and that place we're all going. A little suckle of nectar coating a single day in the lives of two partners and waxing it eternally in a golden chrysalis, far above the mark and the reach of time. Suspended, into something deeper, longer, rounder than a single day. This is a collection of life moments, bookended by the incidents of time on a single climb in a single place. Time, that enemy of mankind, it turns out, is the very hand of God. It spins for us, not against.

///

At 4 a.m., the High Sierra RV and Mobile Campground outside Bass Lake was pitch black. The stars that spun overhead just three hours ago, at the close of the firelight, had curled clockwise in slow-motion, like the hour hand itself. By the crown of Cassiopeia, they bent in unison, to our North. Freeze frame. Before anything else, before the headlamp flickered on or the coffee water boiled, I took the deepest breath I could. Because just that moment alone, that pitch black, quiet, and starry moment, I had learned in the last few years, was something of dreams.

That breath was cold through the teeth and clear as could be. It passed right though the ethmoid, and populated a million molecules of nitric oxide onto every fiber and branch of my brain stem.

It was needed. Because the mind rambles without direction, without guidance. That pause alone, that moment to pay attention and decide to draw the first breath with something of intention, was something I had only really recently learned—Somewhere between late-night study benders and predawn wake up calls. It's a part of the process of living with skill, on the lowlands just as much as upon high, which I wouldn't have accounted for back when all this was just about showing up and climbing rocks.

Butane alight; the hollow sound of the JetBoil cut through the quiet of night. Dave, longtime partner-in-crime and overworked third-year orthopedic resident at the local level-one trauma center, rose awake in a mixture of his regular predawn grimace and his boyish glee. With less hair and more wrinkles than he had at the same time two years ago, he and I both wore the seasoning life had given us. Being short on sleep might have hurt, but time was on our side—though we weren't sure if the weather was. Not minding a forecast of rain, we were Ahwahne-

(Yosemite)-bound because this was going to be our only window of opportunity to get to the Valley together until sometime in the next year. It is the first weekend of October.

"How's a bit of Yirgacheffe sound, Dave?"

With a slight kick to his tent and shake of the poles, I nudged him to slide out of his sleeping bag.

"You and your Ethiopian vices," he laughed back. "I'd be happy for some."

///

By 5:30 we were just above the Tunnel View. From the comfort of the car we sat and watched the sunrise over the Rostrum pullout in all its California splendor. The morning light show, the rosy golds and that tint of lilac in the sky and on the east faces—that was the stuff we'd been missing the most. And considering our windows to the outside life were short and long between, we'd realized that it wasn't the Tunnel View or the rocks that were fleeting, it was the colors that amplified them that were. Like your life, daybreak and its unfolding will never be repeated.

"Sure is a hell of a place to have a coffee and catch a sunrise," Dave laughed over a small patch of Irish Mist on the windshield.

"Yeah, I'd do it again. Drive up here just for this," I said, with a sunray straight in my eye.

"You think there's more rain coming from those guys over on the north rim?" Dave pointed out the foggy side of the dashboard above his thermos, at a gloomy band of clouds.

"It doesn't look good, man. We might get hosed on this one. But we'll make the best of it either way."

It had dumped heavily during the hour drive in from Bass Lake; pellets and all. Especially where we'd parked. With mixed clouds, noticeable humidity, and soaking wet topsoil, you'd have to muster a particular optimism to put climbing in the forecast. But one thing Dave and I had both seen is that it isn't so much the—ism which determines outcomes, as the mark of time and the willingness to keep the space.

"Let's give it an hour or two and see where it stands. It's a hell of a morning from where I'm sitting, and it's only gonna' get better," Dave suggested.

Contented, we sat and ran the highlight reel, spinning tapes across the sky, pondering the time since we'd first been on the Rostrum back in 2016. Climbing or not, it was all the morning we could ask for. So good, in fact, that we hadn't noticed the makings of that chrysalis spinning at our feet.

///

The highlight reel wasn't just the winning moments. Life is as much defined by what doesn't seem to go your way as it is defined by that which does. Sometimes, I'll grant you, those frames are filled by the Beauty Revelation, out there in nature. Other times, often, they are moments far darker. But it has been our experience that these, too, are highlights just the same.

Since I met Dave, in 2015, he's always been on other commitments beyond just climbing, most notably medical school and residency. For a guy who's a rather quick study on cracks and how his fingers fit among them, who's got an engineer's mind and capacity to tinker well with gear, whose workload capacity is in the highest percentiles—in another life I always figured he could've been your next trad-climbing hero. But Dave learned long before I did that his greatest commitments weren't going to be while tied to a rope or wearing rock shoes.

Much of his process, in climbing, has been riding that line. It has been adventuring, not with caution, but with responsibility. He's always answered to something deeper when making his decisions up there, and he's a prime example that it's only a conquest of the useless if you decide it is. There is, in fact, a lot that's up for grabs in the vertical world, and Dave is a case study on the notion that when it all comes clean, it boils down to life skills up there.

Since Dave's first go at the Rostrum he's endured endless workloads in residency, years of a long-distance relationship, countless cases of life and death, and all the other threadbare moments that come with a life in medicine. In that same time period, I've juggled capacities of my own, gone back to school for a nursing profession while working multiple jobs, lost some family members to age and lifestyle complications, and then nearly lost my life partner and her family in a Godforsaken car wreck down the road outside the Valley. She and I grabbed each other by the holy between us and worked our asses off to restore a life that's integrated and involved. Our plates were full, no doubt, but no more so than most others out there. Life, we learned, will mold you from all sides, and it will do so as it pleases. Climbing can't help but take a peripheral place on the greater stage.

With an Amharic soundtrack and a thermos, we sat in that car, pierced by light-beams, and ran our tapes like a goddamn Folger's ad.

///

Two hours later, with clouds still looming, it looked as good as it was going to, so we decided to rack up. While closing the trunk and shouldering our packs, a scruffy college kid in black jeans peered out of the only other car at the pullout, a banged-up old hatchback, with some curiosity.

"You guys going for it?" he questioned.

"Yeah man, figured we'd at least give it a look from the top of the third pitch ledge. What about you?"

"Ah no, we're not here to climb it. My buddies are setting up the

APERTURE ALIKE

highline. We got rained on pretty good last night, but you guys should go for it!"

We zipped past him with wet boots and a chunk of idealism, down the familiar path which is just a couple of football pitches in length, past the clusters of trees in the snaking single-track, until the rocks overwhelm the soil and it cliffs out. Further down, in the steepest bits in the gulley, we laughed about the second time we'd been on the route, when we'd managed to get all the way down to the rappels before we realized we'd forgotten our harnesses. That folly only bested when, after hiking back to the cars and back down to the rappels again, we realized we'd forgotten our rope, too. This time, at least, we'd checked all the boxes.

At the ledge below pitch four, we got our first look at the face—that lovely orange and copper neckline—and were surprised to find it only a little wet in just a few sparse patches. We'd found some luck, after all. In no time we'd rappelled clean to the Valley floor, pulled the ropes, and set up for the opening pitch. First, lead on my side of the line.

With a kiss to the stone, my two hands pressed to the face of the rock, and a quiet moment for my own internal ritual, I made my intentions known.

///

Pitch one is nostalgic. A faded snapshot of you and an old lover. It takes you back, every time, to who you were and the way the world looked in a different set of eyes, once upon a time.

It took me ages to lead that first pitch, especially the small chimney up top. I was as new to the wide stuff as Dave was to medical school, and when he noticed I'd slowed pace considerably, he asked with some concern, "How's it going up there, buddy?"

With my helmet over-cammed in a flare, tight enough that I could feel my spit rebound back at me when I spoke, I answered, "Apart from being whole body stuck in this squeeze right now, I'm not too bad. It just kind of feels like I'm the actual chest tube that's pushing a thoracotomy."

Slapping about, cluelessly, up there, there was a certain comfort in knowing that Dave understood. Not just the reference to the procedure, but the newness of it. He was just wrapping-up his first stint in the E.R. At year one, of five, he was even less experienced at medicine than we were on Yosemite grade fours. Getting his first taste of emergent cases, from CPR compressions in the E.R.—sometimes on patients who didn't make it back to this side of the brink—to his first practice performing amputations, it all took from him. In particular, the week before our first go on the Rostrum, it was the thoracotomy he performed that really stuck with him. Like many firsts, as you push about with a chest tube between the intercostals of some other persons' body, where you have no real idea what it's supposed to feel like—you don't forget it.

There's another strong memory with that first go. Pitch one also always reminds us of Jesse. On that first round, back in 2016, while Dave was leading the second pitch, another party started up beneath us. And on the front of that pursuit, wrapped up in delight, was Jesse. Shirtless, carefree, Pacific-Island tan with a samurai build and a handful of anime tattoos, Jesse went hand-over-hand on the opening boulder problem like a bird dancing on water. This guy could climb Valley 5.12 in his sleep. It was impressive, but the beautiful thing was how he climbed the easiest stuff.

Right in the middle of the first pitch, there's that patch of enormous ease, five-point basic, by Yosemite standards. Jugs, rails, cracks, and chicken-heads the size of dinner plates for feet. It's a geologic wonder zone, all thirty feet of it, and Jesse was well aware. He slowed to a glacial scale and walked vertical on that flake like an old man in a garden; fascinated, curious, and mindful, pausing to muse the diorite knobs as a poet muses a flower. In complete comfort, he'd feel, trace, and comb sections of the face between his slow moves. Relaxed, balanced, a water lily on a windless pond.

When Jesse looked up to anchor and spotted me gazing at him from above, he just smiled, and shared a sagely laugh.

"Yo, man, are you serious right now? I mean, come on, how cool is this rock, right here?"

His focus was beautiful, his flow, untouchable. Pros don't even pull it off that good. A free, harmonious human expression, untamed and alight, Jesse was transcendent at that moment, whether he knew it or not. Didn't matter what other high-mark of art or what other high-mark of tragedy was going on with the seven billion, right there and then, on pitch one of the Rostrum on a warm August morning in Yosemite Valley, humanity had no fuller expression. No shit.

Jesse was a reminder, still is, to walk that garden. That's climbing at a rare level.

///

Traversing down, delicately, across the water shoots and to his left, Dave shuffled across the sopping dyke as a man walks a plank and arrived at the crux of pitch two. The sun was just coming onto the face down there, illuminating the slick patches, as he placed his lower foot on a smear and then high-stepped the other foot to a small rail for the mantle. That's when he made his wrong move.

Under pressure, Dave botched the sequence from the rail, leaving him out of balance to place the crux piece, which was just as off-center as he was. All things off-kilter, he hastened toward letdown, and nearly set off for the crux moves before he'd had a chance to collect himself. It suddenly looked a lot like a déjà-vu, because he'd been here before, exactly.

I'd seen him, just like so, hanging by a thread and out of his wits on this exact pitch in this exact light. Back then, he rushed it, got too anxious. He wanted the chance, at the least, to fail falling. And he did. Dave ran headfirst into that crux going the wrong direction, and a moment later, he cast off like Peter Pan, flying through the sky in a race with his own shadow, the two of them destined for one another and a slab of rock fifteen feet below. The fact that I didn't have to question if Dave had learned the pause of life, in the space between those two leads, made the moment all more satisfying.

The consummate part of his lead on that pitch, two years prior, was his commitment. But there's more to a life well led than simple abandon and commitment, however rare and valued they may be. Two years removed, neither Dave nor I were in a place to be relying on strength alone to squeeze us out of pickles. Back then, though, watching him go all-in on that lead and stand up to his full measure, was a revelation. It was a pure focus, singularity, attendance to this exact moment. That part of it, that was righteous, exact, like the first cut a chef makes at the prep station, like the long carve on the shoulder of a wave the surfrider makes to reestablish momentum and trim. But this time around, more than commitment, it was the presence of mind to hold action, to not go at life with valor alone, but instead, to pause when agitated, and reestablish center; that's what shone.

Moments like that, life lived on that plane, always work in our favor. Just as it did for Dave. Instead of going full bore, Dave reversed a move, took a deep breath, and reset that crux piece. He then set himself assuredly, under that seam, took hold of the moment once more and led right on through—he and his shadow both, a déjà-vu no longer.

///

In its regular form of ascent, pitch three is the longest journey you take up there. Fifty meters, or maybe it just feels that way. The point is, it carries, uniquely. Like a run without a distance to meet or a time to be achieved. On that pitch, you can get steady, go long-form, reach into something deeper than a rock face, and think in the larger pieces. You've got the space and the time to do it.

Two years had passed since I'd last had that lead, and in that time, life had taken from the both of us. Just three weeks prior we'd been up in the high country, Tuolumne, together, for one of our regular sub-24-hour weekend escapes.   Having only shared a rope four times, in the whole year, we jostled up Fairview Dome's Regular Route in a half an afternoon and felt proud to still be able to travel fast and free up a big chunk of rock, even if it was only 5.9. Life had us pinned, fully overworked. But even then, a day like that, running train and doing it not for its difficulty, but for its luxury—you don't forget that kind of freedom. Especially when it's elusive. The entire reason that days up on the line, for us, are as Cadillac as they come, is because more than our time on a wall, our entire friendship has had that mark—give yourself entirely to a cause beyond your own, go at it completely; but insist, always, on living all your ambitions. And live them, to the lees.

Multiple days a week, Dave would get twenty-four-hour shifts in the hospital, while I had stacked blocks at the restaurant, a second job, and then school. How that became the norm, I wasn't sure, but I do know that the last couple of years had a succinct busyness that I'd honestly never grasped. I'd always been halfway capable of mustering up a grand effort for something in a single moment. But doing good work, honest living, and sustaining it? That was the stuff of legend for a guy like me. What I'd learned, from Dave's exemplar in his rotations, was that you could, absolutely, get to a place in life that is both full of commitment and yet full of enjoyment. The memories I have of that fucker, on numerous occasions, passed out in the driver seat of his car in front of my apartment—too exhausted to even turn the engine off once he got into park—are among the high points of our friendship. Not because they were the brightest moments, but precisely because they weren't. In one way or another, that's what our friendship and our partnership on the line has always been about. Either affirming the other to go further, deeper, and longer with each dive, or being present enough for each other to insist on a surface breach when the air got too thin and the pressure too heavy. Looking up at Dave leading pitch three and knowing all he'd been through in the past few years, it was impossible not to root for him.

Nearly at the top of the pitch, coming to surface after that long corner, Dave looked suddenly absent, overwhelmed. His shoulders buckled and so did his knees, as if someone had just added a pair of anvils to the gear loops on his rig. Then a foot slipped. With only his left hand and his left foot in the corner, he started a barn-door skid off the wall. Yelling both in surprise and abandon, he cried out, and somehow—fuck if I know—checked the slide. Something, it seemed, was working in our favor.

///

Near midday, the sun and clouds began to mix, as lovers do, over the Ahwahne (Yosemite) Valley. With a storm clearing and with the greater forces on display, perspective was inevitable. Up on that ledge and footed at the robust tree trunk of life, Dave and I sat still.

There is a memory I've got, first time up, when Dave and I sat in the same posture, with the same anchor pieces, the same awe and the same wonder. Waxing it up, just like so, the two of us asking, looking, thinking out loud.

"You know, I sometimes wonder, what if?" Dave had said.

"What if?" I exaggerated his inflection, as a follow-up.

"What if I just stayed right here, this stage in life. It wouldn't be that bad, right? Or what if I went back even? Lifeguarding, like before. There's nothing wrong with that, right? There's a nobility in it. It's honest work."

Dave sunk with the weight of that first year of residency. Nervous to embark on his next pitch, the next five-year process, without the chance to even pause and take time for himself. He was wondering if he could rationalize, or even hope to find peace or a sense of purpose, in a life that shortchanged his ultimate potential for something just a little more forgiving.

All of us, men and women alike, doubt our course. And never so much as when crossing a new threshold. That's just human instinct.

"I mean look at this, Jesus! It's incredible." He rambled with his inner poet awake.

"Look at it, man."

"No doubt, Dave. The temptress is at hand for you today." I laughed off the drag of a cigarette.

"I know," Dave sobered. "But really, look at us, man. What a place to be."

The doctor was fixed on the notion. Place. This place, of all of them, on this ledge. Exactly. At this stage in life, on this precipice of the next one, at this time even, in human history.

When Dave referenced our position, he wasn't at that moment just appealing to our kick-back at lunch hour on the Rostrum. It was the exact place in life that he and I were both in. It was the financial insecurity, the long-distance relationship, and those goddam hours that don't end. It was me and Nathalie coming out of the jaws of life from under that semi-truck, with her family. It was working two jobs and keeping your head down in the process. It was this exact place in human history where we have the means and the tools to explore our limits on the vertical. It was the relationship to nature that Dave and I were both trying to keep each time we ventured outside and up beyond. It was the relationship we had as two guys, budding a partnership, tied together by gumption for life and 9.6 millimeters of rope, taking a shared journey sixty meters at a time. Hell of a place to be, exactly.

When Dave stood tall, hands wide to the sky, and affirmed the whole world before his eyes on that ledge, that day, he and I both knew it would be a Herculean undertaking to marry the richness of the outside revelation, with the commitments of a medical practice. But, two years on, all our affirmations still stood. Yes, to this place. Yes, to the privilege of being that underlies any human experience. Yes, to the winning lottery ticket that birthed us at this moment in humanity. Yes, to partnership. Yes, to life plugged-in, not dropped out. From the speckle of granite that was digging into my toe to the wisp of cloud that was zooming across Tenaya in the distance. Yes. Yes, to that ledge, to that view, and yes, to the crucibles we carried.

"I'll say this, man. For all that society, my parents and my teachers put in on my behalf over the years. For all the structures that ever supported me; for all they put in, for everything it's taken to get right here. It would be downright criminal for me not to finish this process."

Dave knew better than to follow his feelings. He understood something in the value of commitment, and over the years I took his experiences under direct study. If pitch four, as a crux pitch, would indicate anything for me this day, it would reflect to what degree I'd internalized those truths.

That lead, especially when busied by life apart from the walls, had always been at the peak of my prowess. As such, executing its crux sequence had always been more contingent on a steady mental faculty more than it had been about anything physical. It was less about what I did, or did not do with my digits, as it was about where I was internally, and what I was willing to experience. Tap into that, as Jesse did, and you have something deeper than performance alone.

After skirting the line between free-climbing and free-falling by measure of a few nano-forces of smear and smudge, on the initial seam; I found the reservoir I needed and stayed in that deeper space. A surprise, at least, to me.

Surely, it was not mastery on display up there, but it was an affirmation. To my surprise, there was no fall, no take, and most deeply, no conflict.

With the two years away from the wall and all the lessons it brought, with the pains of life, came the tools. A man can appeal to hyperbole, and if you ask me it's only proper form to speak to the grandeur of our imaginations, but I'll say this sincerely: one-hundred percent, no bullshit, every successful moment we had that day came as a result of the life that Dave and I both had been living off the wall. Of that I was and still am convinced. Absolute.

///

Two pitches and a couple of hours later, the team-free was still on, but only just. We'd both been inches from the slide, beginning with my effort on the fifth.

I've always had that lead, and while I've never fallen on it, I've never led it without thinking that I wasn't about to. For me, it's always been one of the most sustained workloads of the route, and there's just one spot, just under that final little block, where I can shake out and find a modicum of repair. This time, though, it wasn't coming. I writhed in there for a good two minutes, noodling, panting; losing. The only thing I got from it was as much pump in my working hand as relief in the free one. A zero-sum prospect, at best. I wasn't recovering, I was burning out.

Just as I decided I'd get on with it, my feet slipped, completely blind, karate swept right under me; and just like Dave's moment at the cornice of pitch 3, I honestly can't say what force kept me on that wall. Just barely, by the fold of the last papillary ridge, I stayed. By all accounts, I should've been ten feet lower with a kilonewton of tension on the line. The fact that I wasn't suddenly struck me, and with that awareness I plunged deep into some unknown well, and twisted each ankle and hand jam with more purpose than I knew I had, gunning it for the anchors.

Dave had another moment of truth all his own, too, on pitch six. The off-width. Each of us had only successfully led that bastard once, and considering I'd strung the last two pitches on my yarn, we agreed it was best led on his end. But as he got started, things got tight. Coming off a clean follow up pitch five, something which he had only done once before, Dave was now climbing well above his expectations. But he was also nearing empty. When he onboarded the big cams and that harness sunk to his knees, his hope turned.

"Ah, buddy. This feels like a bit much, suddenly," he stammered.

I gave him an affirmation, as best I could, "I know you're good for it, Dave. I'm right here, with you."

Truth is, right then and there it hit me, I had wanted this for him a lot more than I realized. Surely more than my own success. It would be a heartbreaker if he fell.

Crossing that plank in the opening traverse, he was at last on the edge. He moved for the first time like a man who had something to lose. Like he really wanted it. Which was beautiful. Dave fought for it, at that traverse and for the rest of that pitch, nearly falling but somehow surviving—precisely because he had something to lose. We may not have expected such a performance, but it was obvious to both of us at that point, that for each moment of grace that got us that far, we had an obligation to marshal our best efforts. Anything less would belie the grace itself.

///

One of the brighter slides on our reel was in the Spring of 2018. Three days, a couple of work shifts and five final exams away from the end of the semester, Dave and I sat for lunch. Frayed at the midpoint of my wick, which I'd burned for sixteen weeks at both ends, and nervous as all hell about the outcome, I sought his counsel.

"I can't tell you how impressed I am about what you've done, Dave."

"What do you mean, man?" he shrugged.

"I just mean, getting into medical school, or nursing school, it's pretty fucking competitive out there. Not only that but what you've committed to since getting your B.S. in molecular cell biology: the four years of Med School, the five year residency, the research year outside of that, and all the fucking time you've had to dedicate to your learning as a result. The fact that you have a life that's so well composed outside of it all. It's unbelievable."

"Well, I can say that like you, I just took it one task at a time, for starters," he said encouragingly.

To finish my point, I continued, "Look, maybe this is just because I'm at the beginning of all this, and at such an older age to be a student, but I'm amazed that you had the discipline for something even deeper, the maturity for it, at a much younger age. I would've never been ready for this stuff in my youth. And, I'm pretty nervous that if I fuck up on these last exams, I might miss that 4.0 that you need to get into these programs."

Dave paused, as he often does, and smiled. Probably because he delights in process and he could see that I had unwittingly faceplanted right into one.

"Man, that's funny," he began. "You've got some mountains to climb, even now, between this lunch and the end of your exams this week, for sure. But, I'm telling you, man, it's been my experience that you'll be just fine."

"You're telling me you never got anything less than an A?" I asked.

"Buddy." He continued, "I did not get the best grades out there. In fact, I barely even got into medical school. What I can tell you is that as I look back, I can see that there was always the hand of something else to help get us to where we are going. Make of it what you will."

"And what then, do you make of it?" I asked.

"We can't just endlessly worry ourselves about all this stuff, dude. It's a shit ton of work, for sure. But you've also gotta' trust that you're doing all this for a reason. It's a purpose we're plugging into at the end of the day, and in my experience, life or whatever you want to call it, accommodates."

"So, you've been right here, too, then?" I questioned.

"Absolutely. I mean, you're probably working more than I did outside of school. But yeah. You already know it, man. The best part of a deep process is that it's where the magic happens. So, I'm just saying, whatever grades you get, you already know you're giving it your best shot, and you already know there's going to be a way provided. It's how it all works. In the meantime, we do our best to live our lives completely and not just shut ourselves indoors for four months at a time."

Dave nailed it.

The thing is, we've probably had that conversation a half dozen times in our partnership, on a rock face or in life at large, and we've each been on both sides of it. Life is not static. Knowing a truth, experiencing it even, one day, does not exempt you from needing to experience it over again. The beautiful thing about partnerships, we've learned, is that when tethered to our common good and the affirmation of the other, there is a succinct joy in the freedom to swing between each side of the fulcrum.

///

There may be no better representation, in climbing, of the commitment to a process, than the action of offwidth. By nature, it is both hard work and good work. Elbow-deep Calvinism. Dave endured that process, as he's endured many before him, and I was fortunate to follow in the same fashion. Now, near mid-afternoon, we stood just two short pitches, maybe 150 feet from the summit block and a rare collective success.

The first time we were up there it was another story entirely. I'd been handled, completely smote by that offwidth to the point of seeing stars. With black and blue cigarette burns over the technicolor slides, I retched at the anchor till my face found color again. When Dave proposed my lead on pitch seven, the final 5.11, I sunk into my harness until my rib cage pushed my shoulders into my ears. It took me fifteen minutes just get the gear on my loops and the chalk on my hands.

But this time, things were different. We hadn't planned for any of this, especially not the last two pitches and who would be charged with each lead. Like prizefighters, both of us might have been out on our own feet already. But, before Dave could make a stand and do something characteristically noble, from the moment I backed-up the clove hitch on the anchor, I knew I was going to take that next lead.

"I'm pretty amazed, man. Check out this view," Dave started. "You know, this anchor is always special for me, 'cause you can see to the tip of El Cap, and if you go left you can finally see the 'Separate Reality' roof."

After a moment of scanning, he chimed in again, "Remember that time we drove in at twilight and climbed that thing (A Separate Reality) in the dark?"

"Absolutely, my friend."

"That's right, you were sick that night, too, weren't you?" Dave remembered.

"Sure was, man. Still don't regret it, though. Two years and we haven't been back on it since. These things are hard to line up."

"Yeah," he laughed, "I'll tell you what man, I'll never forget belaying you above the crack and seeing your headlamp peering up through the overhang. There were these cars hundreds of feet below you, driving along the Merced, and then your headlamp, alone, lasering up the crack out of the pitch-black abyss like a marquee spotlight. So good, man."

"Well, my friend." I started while putting order to my rack, "I know how much you love that spot on this pitch, right before the end, and I'm going to enjoy watching you take it all in, Especially today."

Dave looked suddenly surprised, as he came to, and realized I had every intention on the lead.

"You sure you want this one?" he asked in concern.

With absolutely no ego, he offered to take it, just as I've come to expect. Because he gets partnership. "If you aren't feeling it, man, you don't have to step into this one, at all."

If I was a betting man, I'd say each of us only stood a 25 % chance to lead that pitch free of falling, at that point. Even for the follower, odds couldn't have been better than a coin toss. It seemed only fair, after all the work that fucker had put into life as whole, that he had the best shot.

Checking my chest pocket to make sure I had a cigarette at the ready for the final alcove, I smiled back to him, "I'm truly happy to, Dave. I'll see you up there."

That moment might be the highlight of the day. Maybe. Because right then and there, I think it's fair to say I had something of a pure heart. At the least, a better heart. And beyond all the sunsets and summits out there, that's probably what I've always wanted the most from the great wide spaces. A better version of me and the capacity to care for someone else's success more than my own.

///

At the very top of the seventh pitch, just where the best exposure and the best climbing clump into a final ravine, in that corner, I reached my limit.

It all came down, as it always does, to the last gasp. My mitts were greasing, my knees and ankles buckling, too. With a final lurch, the last possible pulse before doom, I slapped at the sloping ledge and kept it in hand. Crawling over the top without a trace of grace, I hugged my entire surface area on that stone like a human-sized plunger and used all the primordial muscle memory in my mitochondria to ooze and squirm my way to the anchor. Done.

Extending the anchor position a moment later, for a better view of

Dave's climb, I glanced out to the summit ridge and came to a surprising sight. The gang of highliners who had camped out the night before, were finally op on their lines. My view from the alcove, sitting some 75 feet below their webs, but hundreds of feet above the Valley floor, was a luxury I suspect I'll never earn. Rays of light shot into the base of the Valley, and earth itself awoke for the occasion. Everything was aligned. Goddamn it, Dave had to send!

He set off easily enough through first half of it and in no time climbed out from under the headstone to the midpoint of the pitch. But quickly, it got heavy. The next 15 feet of his follow, for me, just turned to a series of snapshots. Still frames. A shutter clicked, and he was up another ten feet, grimaced. There was a wide hand-jam that looked like it was not connected. It clicked again, he was still on but he was trying harder than I'd hoped. When I came to, Dave had just released a grunt so guttural that it echoed from his biliary tract. He made one more move, aghast, and nearly buckled-off when reaching his foot out to the stem.

It's not a good rest, not when tired, but it was something. It's the steepest 20 feet of the climb, at almost the highest position. Six and a half pitches, at least, whirls under your wide-open stance just right there. With each leg reaching about 45 degrees, stemmed out on each wall at your side, you look down at the triangle between your personal parts and you see the entire route, plumb. It bisects both your nostrils it's that true. And that, even while gassed out of his mind, is one of Dave's favorite places to be on this blue marble. That's the sweet spot. Full realization, full presence.

While Dave had been at his limit, Alonzo, the fellow on the line who'd walked himself about halfway across the 400-footer, had also been watching.

"Guys! Holy shit," he had shouted while Dave was in a grunt. "The view right now is out of this world."

It caught my attention, so with one eye still on Dave, I looked up just in time to see Alonzo out there in orbit. Just as I looked over he did a one leg, reverse-squat; after which he sat, balanced on the line, and reached a free hand into his pant pocket for his damn cell phone. A work of pure fiction.

"I gotta get a shot of this, guys. You'll love it! I don't know if anyone ever gets to shoot this wall from this spot. You gotta see it."

Sure enough, he took a slew of them; consummate photos that he later sent to Dave and I, which were just as immaculate as he promised. And that—with Dave looking down his favorite view and Alonzo out there shooting it—was the moment it all clicked. That's when I knew Dave had it. That's when I knew we had it. The world, and Yosemite Valley was a Fall-colored snow globe pierced by rays of light, resin sapping every round of the sky, every contour of the retina, every membrane of every cell and every ounce of the heart. With fifteen feet to go, Dave was not fresh, but he was also not capable of letting go. Not anymore.

He didn't.

///

Together again for the final belay exchange, we took our time. Could've been thirty minutes, maybe more. At that point it came down to saturation. We had been off this wall for years, away from her, busied. Finally, on a day we both realized we'd never quite live again, on a hands-down classic, without a single other person or party on the wall, we had no other place to be. Up high, in an alcove filled with bird shit, one pitch from the pinnacle of a two-year journey, we sat with a view of the world that only time can give.

"Remember that trip to Mammoth, in July?" I asked.

"Oh boy," Dave mused, "I think I slept more in those two days than I did anything else."

"Yeah man, you'd just been nailed by a 100-hour work week. And neither of us had climbed since April." I reminded him.

"Do you remember that shitty, 30-foot, 5.10a we you got on?" I continued.

"God," he laughed out loud, "at that crag-let? That wall that was too short to even be called a crag. Yeah, I remember. I got completely shut down on that thing, right? And, just two weeks after that you took that nasty knee injury, didn't you? That was a terrible set-back."

"That's right, man. I got pretty beat up by life this summer. But so did you. Do you remember what you said right in the middle of that climb, though?"

"Not really."

"Dude, you were in the middle of one of your dozen takes on that thing, fifteen feet up with a pump from hell, and you just sunk at one point, and said, 'I gotta' be honest, the Rostrum feels pretty far away right now.'"

"Oh Jesus, that's right," he exclaimed.

"Yeah. Look man, just a few months ago I could hardly walk, and you could barely stay awake to drive yourself home from a work shift. You slept for eighteen hours at a time if life gave you the window, and, you were convinced you couldn't climb 10a. But here's what I know, man. You and I both kept this place in mind, we always left space for it. For this."

Dave's trademark joy, the kind that you see from a child rather than a medical professional who deals in trauma rotations, erupted.

///

The first time we were up there, Dave took me by surprise when he offered that I lead the final pitch. He was a hell of a lot fresher, but he also understood something. Clued into the special moment of solace the lead climber meets upon summiting, Dave wanted me to have that lead

CREDENCE

because he knew I needed the appointment in life more than he did.

"It's your first time on this thing," he had said, "You should be the one to top us out."

I took that lead begrudgingly, but at the top I quickly understood the gift of it. Now, on our last bidding, I was happy to keep that reservation for him. This, the final lead, was designed for him.

As I shoveled him off and checked our belay systems for the last time, I reminded him, "Climb well, focus, and enjoy, my friend."

That last pitch can get you in a hurry if things aren't right, and we both knew it. With that in mind, Dave tempered the excitement for his final push, understanding that he best not count his chickens yet. But, just then, Dave also caught a surprising updraft that neither of us were ready for.

"Dude, I think I tore my pants right down the middle, somewhere in those last couple of pitches. Maybe in the offwidth," he jutted out. "And the situation is getting interesting, quickly."

A moment later, he added, "This might get full exposure for you, man. Fuck. I'm sorry."

Sure enough, the bastard had ripped his climbing pants clean at the underscore. Now, as awkwardly as you can imagine, he was shuffling across the deck and under the massive overhanging roof, in full-squat, like some bashful child off the schoolyard—each move tearing the seams just a little more.

The moment he traversed past the roof and made the push move out of the overhang, that fucker's man-parts went freestyle like a goddamn kite in the wind. From the belay, as half his body was now trying to do a muscle-up into the crack, all I could see were his legs, the gear on his harness, and his wide-open manscape, savagely swinging a thousand feet above Yosemite Valley.

You could not script it.

///

Two-and-a-half years, thousands of hours in the barrel at the hospital, and one pair of torn jeans after his first attempt, Dave completed his free ascent of the Rostrum. For me, the honor was just being a part of it. The guy with whom I'd learned about partnership, had achieved something I knew he'd been dreaming of. That alone, without the manic beauty, without the sheets of light unfolding around us, without the whole thing being framed by a Yosemite Valley which is so damn rich, not just in its history but in our history, would've been just fine by us. Could've called it right then and there. But the team-free wasn't done, yet.

I followed, gently. Made that last traverse under the monstrous overhang, chose my momentum with caution when popping up for the mantle, and paused as much as I could for every breath I needed. And it's a good thing I did. Because just then, right at the lip, and for the rest of the pitch, I got a set of cramps in my forearms so bad I damn near had to climb the thing with my elbows. Like an old clunker with no grease in the gaskets, I sputtered down to the last mile. Fifteen feet, 10 feet, the last curve, the final pull. I looked up, and anchored to the tree, extended off to the side with a long shadow cast against the orange glow of the stone, was Dave. Shit-eating grin for days. Eyes alight with the heavens. All time.

We'd successfully freed the Rostrum, a Valley tradition, together.

///

To suggest, even for a moment, that it got better than that, might be overkill. I know.

But it did.

After an emphatic hug, Dave and I sat under that tree for ten minutes, buzzing to the last electron above a strewn pile of rope and rock gear.

When the light rounded behind us, we stood up and caught our first view of the highlining gang, a whole host of them, bouncing like shooting stars in a flickering light show staged from the West. They had the entire network of lines up. The 400-footer, the 200-footer, and the 75-footer.

At the far reaches of the 400-foot line, a fella named James was up to his feet, and we watched as he tracked a single beam of sunlight between two long clouds, at exact pace as it sunk into the lower of them. From the east end to under our very noses, James dazzled, taking in more photons than a goddamn astronaut on a spacewalk. An incandescent spectacle of human potential and natural force.

Unwound by it all, Dave and I both reached into our pockets at the same time and dialed up our beloved. You just had to. The utter, boundless energy that shot through those series of moments at the summit, had to be shared. It was ravaging, it was underserved, it was overwhelming, overflowing, it was opulent. Light like you've never seen. Cavernous depths of shadow, and grandeur, and contrast, and light. Christ himself could not have come into this world with any greater glory.

We put Nathalie, and Kate, live on the screens and scanned for them the entirety of the horizon as we fumbled for words, tripping over our own tongues, lost in the inexplicable joy of such a champagne moment of life. We needed to acknowledge their presence, with us, because we knew it had also been a journey with them. The last two years of each of our lives were undoubtedly connected, by an innumerable collection of choices and events, by a string of life spun by the friendships we'd preserved in order to forge for one another, a life of substance. Dave and I could not help ourselves, because there is perhaps no greater human instinct than to want to collectively share that simplest, most unsuspecting human experience. Joy. They needed the reminder, just as much as we did, that all the glory and the invitation to it, was the true work of reality.

Breaking the moment, one of the highliners, a warm and curly-haired fella', shouted to us from the promontory with an offer.

"Hey, you guys just free the Rostrum?"

"Somehow, we did," Dave said.

"Ah, dudes, that's awesome. How you guys planning on gettin' back across the notch?" he asked.

"Probably just rappel into the ditch and climb up the ramp, as usual," Dave answered.

"Well, yeah, you could. But you know what'll really cap it off for ya?" he grinned.

Dave and I looked up at each other with disbelief, as that gentleman continued. "See that 75-foot line right there? There's no one on it. I know you got all the gear with you, so probably can't walk it, but it would make for a righteous Tyrolean."

Evening light and a stranger's invitation will make a man do a lot of things, and even though Dave had never done a Tyrolean, he wasn't about to miss his chance. There's a type of happiness that comes from a deep process, and then there's the type that just comes with a surprise. Simple delight. Right then and there Dave had both, and so did I. Seeing it radiate off his face, bronzed by the twilight, as he set up for the Tyrolean, was a reflection both of his deepest self and his innermost child. Foolish of me, perhaps, to separate them in the first place.

I set off before he did, as a demo, and was out on the land side of the rig when Dave jumped off from the spire. And, in a moment, all glory, became all too human. Dave darted off the point like he was expecting to ride a zipline, but sunk to zero speed, immediately. You just knew the poor guy had some other vision in mind. But here he was, now sunken with a leash—his daisy chain—overextended, reaching up for the tether, floundering out at sea.

Dave found his way back on the line but was struck down after just a few feet of sliding across it. A set of leg and arm cramps he couldn't contend with got the better of him. One lurch at a time, Dave wormed his way across that Tyrolean for the better part of the sundown. Exhausted and alight, with balls flappin' out of his britches for a handful of unfortunate strangers to see, Dave made it across. This was life completely unscripted.

Truly, one for the ages.

///

Men and women alike, we don't get that many of those days out there. Nobody does, not like that. At the car, we tuned out of a plan completely, stuck in a corporate spell of thanksgiving, fully undone. No idea what to do next.

I thought back to the first time we'd climbed it. I was reminded of the drive home and how the sunset that day was so golden I couldn't imagine a truer color. How we passed a stretch of land after Fresno that was full of cornfields, stretching east for what seemed like ages, past the Sierra's themselves and all the way to Nebraska, and how those sunbeams cut right through each one of them with detail and a sequence that looked a lot like intention. I was reminded of that same stretch of land, covered in rainbow and twilight, when Nathalie, her family, and I, all drove home from the week-long hospital stay after that car wreck. I remembered the purpose in that sky and the promise of it. And, I remembered all the long hours and uplifting phone calls Dave and I had shared in the past two years. The low spots.

Dave and I swung between bouts of breathlessness and laughter. In haste, we unfurled our packs and followed a violet sky that pointed in only one direction. Just a minute later, at the bottom of the Tunnel View, we'd driven ourselves right into the apex of an alpenglow which was radiating on another spectrum entirely. Some shades, some arrangements, are expressions of things deeper than nature. For the light and color alone, right then and there, surely there will never be enough cones and rods in the human reception.

We watched, muted, on another planet entirely.

On instinct and at dark, after the headlamps glimmering on the high flanks of El Cap had closed, we drove up the 120, across the Tioga Pass and down the Sherwin Plateau, eventually camping at the foot of Mount Tom, in Payahuunadü.

Waking the next day, still aglow, we walked with embers in our feet, capable only to partake in the simplest of pleasures— watching daybreak over Mount Humphrey's, passing soil through our fingertips, boulder scrambling in the Buttermilk country, and getting lost in the smell of a gluten rise, fresh off a pinch of bread from the Great Basin Bakery, when pressing it to our noses.

That partnership can be more than what happens on a rope. That keeping the space for something is, unto itself, an act of faith. That time, the old devil, works for us, with us. That revelation, that rapture even, in this life, in this time, is designed for you, too. That two lucky bastards could've walked right into that ball of wax, that golden chrysalis, by just showing up for life a day at a time. That life accommodates. That somewhere in the mired fabric of every single day, in the lowlands, the doldrums of every one of our individual lives, there is that clever, invisible hand.

Make of it what you will.

///

NIHALGAI

In *Dine Bikeyah*, the ancient land of the Dine (Navajo) people, all is sacred. This life, this world, all of it, was born of previous worlds and unfathomable histories. For the Dine, the telling of those histories is just as sacred as the stories themselves. Who you share them with, how you share them, when you share them, all of it. That next breath pushing out the brim of your chest cavity, sacred. The eyes which squint as you read, sacred. The matter you see around you, the space it occupies, the materials which make up the chair you sit on, the sound you are hearing right now, the last thing you touched. All of it. Sacred. According to the Dine, the life you see in front of you, from wherever you may sit, is no doubt as complex, as revolutionary, and as full of lore as it is full of atomic particles. There is equal life, equal story in each particle under your nose as there is a unit of mass, or force, or energy to measure. There is an entire world which glitters for us all. Whether you see it is another story.

Shaun Martin spins a fast turn into the parking lot and settles his mud-covered Jeep right in front of me. Forty degrees out at 7 a.m. here in Chinle, Arizona, with the sun just rising from the east. I open the door to see his warm face and straight black hair, regal as a mare, shining at me with a welcoming smile. Dine, I think to myself. Beautiful.

Jumping into the backseat with my partner, we join Shaun's lifelong friend and running mate, Harold Bennally. Spinning out of the lot, we head east toward the Great Spirits, as dawn cracks the first sight of sun over the wet Canyon De Chelly. It's been raining for nearly a week straight, which is perfect because when Shaun talks about the Ultramarathon he's created and how he wants it to serve as a means for outsiders to get to know this place, this is exactly what he has in mind. Thirty-five miles of it, in a historic, verdant maze of undulations. The Canyon De Chelly is to the Dine, the cradle of creation; it houses a grand litany of their most precious tales, as well as some of their most tragic. In each of its dendritic offshoots, there are highlights of mankind's best, and worst.

This time tomorrow there will be 150 runners covering every inch of it. The intrepid rises, the near-purple varnish of the Wingate stone, the colossal greens and yellows of the Cottonwood, the Berbere-hue of heaven's soil, all of it. There will be glory, there will be inspiration, there will be suffering, and after this week's rain, there will be plenty of mud and water. There will be great plains to traverse for the 150 lucky runners who've come from as far away as Perth, Western Australia.

The Dine are familiar with traversing great plains. Since time commenced, theirs was a wandering path. Not only have they traveled far in this world, but in others which have preceded it. They've communed with the Great Spirits beyond time in previous worlds, and they've moved between worlds. Theirs is the plight of a mystic people.

We've gone about three miles into the Canyon, each turn a little better, each mile a little deeper, each bit just that touch the grander. The walls, their color, the trees, and their shapes; the further in we are going, the more we are getting. A labyrinth.

"Look at this, Harold," Shaun exclaims, "these are good spirits with us today."

Shaun kills the gas as abruptly as he had been pushing it and enters a prayer.

There is a layer of pearly-grey clouds breathing across the rim of clay rock. It takes dawn light on its upper sheet and reflects into one of the corners of still-wet rock.

"Amazing," I suggest, "these clouds are a dream."

"Yeah, what you are seeing are cloud people. When they gather like this near the walls, and after a storm, they are sending us blessings," Shaun explains. Shaun romps back over patches of broken double-tracks at full speed as soon as his prayer is finished. We're ripping down the Canyon at a suspension-busting pace, as if he's driven, and ran the damn thing a thousand times.

To be ready to commence the weekend's events there are a hundred things to do between now, and the runners' orientation meeting at 4 p.m. this afternoon; tagging all seventeen miles of this Canyon with bright-orange trail markers, every 100 yards apart, being one of them. Time is certainly not on our side, hence the eco-tour gone wild. But, whenever what we see what Western society calls an animal; whenever a squirrel, or a horse, or even an ant-hill comes in view, Shaun always stops.

"These are insect people, my friend," Shaun notes a small colony near a robust cottonwood. "I'll tell you what man, that tree has seen it all." He's got a trademark oaky-ness in his voice, that of an elder in the making. "Yeah, so, with the insect people, it's important for us to pay homage to them also. In fact, in our narrative, they were there at the First World, before we had bodies, and First Man and First Woman were only known as Spirit People. At the beginning of creation were the insect people, and we Dine, we recognize their value as fundamental beings. They are sacred to us."

Shaun looks torn for a moment, but quickly settles with a conclusion. "You know, it's almost funny to us, to see how scientists have only in the

APERTURE ALIKE

last few decades come up with terms like 'indicator species', and how people are now paying attention to the bees." He breaks into a warm smile. "Because you can just see a Dine elder shaking a stick going like, 'I told you so!'" He aggressively waves his hand , imitating his grandfather. Shaun's laugh trickles into oblivion as we burst over another mud-crossing from the snaking wash. He does well to manage the conversation and its content amid a skull-rattling safari. "But," Shaun adds, "what we have in our culture and how we see the world is not in conflict with what the scientists see, [the car thumps against its wheel-wells] maybe we just use different tools to measure the same stuff."

That's a key point.

"Wow, Harold look at the crop on this field." Shaun admires a small plantation at a tiny offshoot, just beside a traditional Hogan.

"That energy from the soil people is good this year," Harold speaks with a smile, "I'm glad to see the rains came when they did. It's very good for these people."

"For the people living in the Canyon?" I ask naively.

"For them too." Harold patiently smirks. "They aren't the only 'people' living in the Canyon, you know."

But the Canyon is unique in its status. It is one of the only living National Monuments in the country, and there are about 40 families who still call it home. They plant their food, they live off the grid or have gone solar, they maintain traditions, and that is a damn special thing. They continue to do something completely their own and they do it in a privilege unique to them. Their Hogans (the traditional home and ceremony setting) their histories, their traditions. A white man, a Westerner, or any other non-native cannot just walk into this Canyon, nor even dream of calling it home. Tours along the Canyon are only by reservation, must be guided with a native, and must be either in a vehicle or on horseback. One does not just go walking along this canyon looking for enlightenment, not unless your history is its history. And to me at least, that is a damn special form of respect.

It's not that the Dine culture isn't welcoming or hospitable, it's just that there is so little of it left. It must be preserved. The culture of the Dine is as much in the people as it is in the land itself. Each one of them; the beautiful, the hard knocked, the black-haired, the under-dogged, and under-represented, is a reflection of an ancient tribe in a modern world. They, the people, are the artifact as much as the Anasazi petroglyphs. The depth of that reality cannot be overstated.

We trek past the famous White House, a perfect remnant of Puebloan history, and watch as a band of horses feed just near the small creek crossing below it. Stillness.

"The morning rises on the four-legged people," Harold observes with glee.

"Ah!!! Yes, my man, I'm beginning to see things more as you describe them. What a treat, indeed." I reach out and affirm to him with my hand on his shoulder.

Further down, just after ruffling the feathers of a gang of beautiful wild turkeys, by scaring them off the trail, Shawn lightly proclaims.

"Man, there's just so much life in this place, you could see why our ancestors came in times of famine, in long winters, or when they were fleeing colonial control. This place is so rich, so fertile, it defines us."

The mood is only broken when, through a thick brush, a couplet of bush-coyotes run south across the double-track path. Well, I see coyotes. What Harold and Shawn see is The Great Coyote Who Was Formed In Water, and First Angry. The guys look at each other, then back at the scene with reverence. My naivety about the bush-coyotes does little to affect its importance on them. Shaun walks ahead, out of the Jeep, and spends a minute beside the coyote tracks in what looks to be a prayer, before he eventually spreads soil over the tracks to cover them up. This happens time and time again. They interact with nature; they do not just observe it. There is a humility in their tradition, and it is obvious in the presence of other creatures, or as they know better, in the presence of other "people".

By the time we make it fifteen miles deep into that Canyon we've traversed the plains of all beings, we've told histories of creation, we've talked of birth and seasons of life. We've covered everything a moment could allow. For almost every occasion, what the West would call an object, passively, or what the West may call as living, by definition of a genus or species, such as a tree or a piece of rock—has an entirely additional name and story. For these guys, life is so much more. They see two worlds where most only see one. And all of it is sparked or transitioned by the landscape and the people, two-legged and four-legged, within it.

"Sure is a magical place, Shaun," I say to him.

"Ah, just look at it, man," he replies.

Here is the first awakening. Here in the Canyon, in Dine Bikeyah altogether, behind the poverty-stricken veil, a worldview for the ages still smolders.

As we pass the mighty Spider Rock, home to the benevolent Spider Woman—she who gave the gift of weaving to the Dine people—we step out of the car and tag the path leading up toward Bat Canyon before turning back to retrace the previous fifteen miles. Coming from someone who spends quality time on the vertical plane, Spider Rock is immaculate. Just, immaculate. It is pristine in sculpt, uniformity, location, and surrounding. Having said that, looking at it in context to the people who hold to its legend, it's clearly more than a peak, it's a sanctuary. It makes perfect sense that it should not be a measure of man but a reflection of something more divine. That's why they don't climb it. Some summits shouldn't be clouded by sport or achievement. Looking over at Shaun, I see a parallel. He's competitive, and he's gifted, but a lot of what he does isn't on the level of sport as much as it is in the realm of spirit.

As we note the weather, a perfect forty-seven degrees, he shares stories about Spider Woman, Spider Rock, and the histories of its neighbor, Face Rock.

"I bet you can run on a perfect plane of meditation in this canyon, with these stories lighting your path as you go?" I remarked.

"You got it. Absolutely. Often I'll start at our home in Chinle and run straight up Monument Canyon up to the rim and end up at our family's traditional Hogan."

"I'd imagine the Hogan is a place for meditation and reverence during a run like that, right?"

"Completely," he replies.

"And, I bet that detour up Monument Canyon adds a few more miles as well?"

"Oh yea, it's about another ten in total, but you know how it is. On the good days when you're clicking that's exactly the kind of addition you want. By the time I get back into Chinle, with a stop at the Hogan in the middle, I'm restored."

"I don't care what you're ailing from in life," he begins with an inflated hyperbole, "you take a run like that and you're getting medicine."

Shaun pauses and looks back at Spider Rock. "On a day like today though, just-after-a-storm-blue (there's a word for that, too) oh man, you'd go forever."

Just talking about it, and the thought of a journey like that in conditions like these has made both our skin crawl. The trained athlete is tuned to recognize the right conditions for revelation as much as the right conditions for physical capability. That's what just tickled both our arms. Some might call it a rush of sympathetic innervation to the arrector pili, but for Shaun, there's a spiritual being who fired the synapse behind each rising follicle.

We jump back in the Jeep and make haste. However, today is not for us, it's for preparation. There are still 150 runners from the world over, and today our job is to ensure they see as much as possible in this Canyon, tomorrow. And that goes way beyond the glitter of orange trail-markers flying in the wind.

///

Back at Shaun's house in the afternoon, we empty his storage garage for event set-up materials. There are two Super Duty trucks and a mobile trailer which need complete packing; and, within an hour the small group of us manage. Despite all the attention Shaun has drawn in, it is amazing to see just how small this enterprise really is. Shaun has been filmed before, and this weekend's IMAX team is no exception to his recent attention. He's been featured in newspapers, magazines, online and in print, and his event is the envy of most in the Ultra community. But when you look at all that fanfare and the thousands of people who registered for it, it is mind-blowing to see that the entire event boils down to a handful of people doing everything at home, by hand. From the "Start/Finish" sign to the blue-corn mush and fry-bread at 5 a.m. All of it.

Shaun is only the tip of the spear, so it's a pleasure to meet his wife, Melissa, his two children, Maverick and Isabell, and his parents, Lisa and Allen Martin. Shaun's father is a legend, a medicine man, a maverick in his own right, and a giant in both spirit and physical regard. With that in mind, when you put him next to the ten year-old Maverick, his grandson, it's pretty hard to discern who's got the younger heart or the greater capacity for mischief.

Shaun's mother, Lisa, of German heritage, was described to me by a few sisters of the support crew as, "more Dine than most Dine." The heart of a saint, who came to these lands a long time ago to understand more than to be understood. Her level of genuine character is impossible to miss. And, Melissa, of the Yazzie clan, is an obvious anchor and provider to Shaun. Their energies highlight one another, and the marks they've made both shine on the sunspots of their kids' faces, in equal measure.

As sunset turns twilight, we light a fire beside the stage of the main amphitheater at the Cottonwood Campground. The 150 runners and their significant others, the film crew, everybody, is excitedly hanging onto the moment with anticipation as Shaun takes the stage.

"Ya'at'eeh." Shaun begins.

He goes into a minute-long introduction, completely in Dine, to commence the weekend and the ceremonies; only translating the message back to English secondarily. It is exactly what the people want, as well. The smiles on each of their faces are a testament. They are here for the privilege to run a Canyon which is normally off-limits, sure, but beyond that, they are here to have an experience which begins in the heart. Dine speak this language.

"Tomorrow, in that Canyon, what you'll experience is sacred for us. The walls will sing if you listen, the sky and the earth will guide you, the Spirit People will hear your chants and see your effort, and they will commune with you."

It's an honorary commencement. Shaun continues for half an hour, sharing his history, the race history, and Dine history. He makes it clear that more than a race, the Canyon De Chelly Ultra is a cultural and spiritual experience. It always has been, fundamentally.

"Suffice to say, things were not going well for me that year, in 2012, and in a trance on this run through the Canyon I asked the Spirits for guidance. I asked for direction." Shaun painted from the stage.

"In the midst of this weather, the time of day, everything ruby and orange, and this female rain in the sky, I ran into a band of horses." The tears begin to reflect the spotlights in his eyes as he opens up to the crowd of strangers. "And, in an occasion of pure blessing, that band of horses let me into the center of their fold, right alongside their young colt; which is impossible. Seriously. It does not happen unless by divine action. And we ran, together, under that sky for miles. I cried like a kid the whole time. It was so beautiful. And, that's when I understood that my purpose was to share with others what is sacred, just as the horses had shared with me. I knew that for more people to understand who we are and what we experience as Dine people, people had to come here. They had to see it. They had to fall in love with it. And so, here you all are."

Among many heartfelt sentiments that Shaun shares throughout the night, this draws the greatest response from the crowd. He goes on for another hour, between segments of testimony and ritual provided by his father Allen and Melissa's father, William, who sings over a Dine drum. All are inspired.

In the dark of night, after the ceremony finishes and the runners trot back to their hotel rooms, Shaun and Melissa, along with the family, pack up the amphitheater and head home for a family meal. As is common practice in the Martin home, along with that meal, they'll all sit and recover the days' events together; each of them sharing their favorite part of it as a means to center their gratitude.

Chinle at dark is a band of souls looking for light in the wilderness. In the canyon you can dream big and touch the Holy People, in Chinle you touch the Hwéeldi. It comes in different shapes than it did in Bosque Redondo, but it is visible. The town, as a statement of infrastructure, does not always shine. And the pathways one sees at night are not just street alleyways, but of greater directions; footprints of those still on a Long Walk. One hundred and fifty years ago, the Dine nearly vanished; forced to exodus in an ethnic cleansing prescribed by the American Government; a journey which covered nearly 400 miles of suffering and loss. Through blistering summers and desolate winters, plagued by disease and erased from human consciousness, they walked. Today, that path is still plagued.

There is a deep, palpable force in the Navajo Nation, that of insidious vice and systematic depression. There is a unique poverty here, one which is not just material in nature. These are spiritual places, and the poverty is much the same.

At 10 p.m. on a Friday night, there are only so many places to go. At the local Denny's a rush of High School students flock the gates for a post-football game hangout. Sitting at the bar, with a view through the expo window of the kitchen, you see everything. Line cooks dropping tongs in a meth-driven neural misfire, a shift manager working triage as the wait staff goes under the weeds. A server, in a body suffering from years of poor health choices, literally out of breath from walking the floor with a water pitcher for refills; a busboy dropping cups off the dry-rack and picking them right back up from the floor without a rinse. The ship gets carried to abandon without the rudder.

From the management to the kitchen staff, to the wait-staff, there's not a single ounce of pride in the work in front of them. Mistakes happen quicker than they can be corrected, hot plates fly around the expo window, people laugh, others shout. It's a perfect, hot, mess. The realization suddenly strikes, that this is more of an outlier than the norm.

As Shaun had mentioned earlier, "Nearly everyone here [in Chinle] has been unemployed, is unemployed, or knows someone unemployed primarily because they don't have an education or any means to get to work. And, the reason, chiefly, why they don't have that education is tied to substance abuse or an inborn level of poverty in the family that has affected them personally, or that they are busy managing in someone at home."

This, at Denny's on a Friday night, is the current working class. These guys are the ones trying. Completely in the cycle, they grind the hamster wheel, slowly, burning molecules of hope like adenosine triphosphate in a spiritual equivalent to cellular respiration; the byproducts being helplessness and isolation. Under the Bikeyah sky, isolation from the great elements was never the intended state. While reality here is polar, one must not forget what the Canyon just down the road teaches—that this a land of revelation.

This is a hard reminder to keep on a Friday night. The lack of infrastructure, the health problems from the obese, the diabetic, the drug addicted and the alcoholic, show on even the youngest faces of a packed restaurant. There is a sense of imprisonment worn on the shoulders of kids barely past puberty. The Dine look as shadows at times.

"You can't get much around here in the way of healthy choices or alternatives to the norm. The depression flows through everything, even our food. Nothing comes to the Rez that isn't prepacked, genetically modified, hydrogenated, or just full of chemically processed junk. Melissa and I will drive all the way to Flagstaff every other week just to get stuff we can feel good about eating. These kids today, have it all against them." Shaun had said.

All against them. The Hogan where they'd get a real education has been replaced with the butt-end of an American public school system; the endemic varieties of corn which sustained their people for thousands of years has been replaced with the cheapest thing on the supply chain; the world of giants and mythology, which bred a proud people and an even richer heritage, has been ground to something worse than any socio-economic metric could measure.

In an earlier insight, Shaun had also shared, "It's pretty obvious when you pass through Dine country, man. You saw all the muddy, abandoned cars and buildings in each town on your way in. It goes on like that for hundreds of miles, you know? And there's no large chunk of land devoted to agriculture in that space either. You can get the same level of depression from a large-scale look at land-use as you can by picking up trash left in the alleyways. Bottles, needles, all of it. It's all an expression of the same pain. Just look at it."

This is the second revelation. This is Navajo Nation. Poverty is a

Navajo trait that is a function of a Western construct. Richness is a Dine substrate that lives, but only just.

One only hopes that the lucky 150 of tomorrow's race can see both the sublime and the subtext in this place.

///

Morning. Five a.m. and the fire sparks under an indigo sky. The Milky Way, or the Great Bag of Stars thrown by the Mischievous Coyote, glitters over a vast Dine horizon.

"We've got our own legends up there, you know. For us they are the So-Dine e', or Star People," Shaun says while pointing upward. "I think almost every indigenous culture tells stories from the stars. And in ours, like others, that guy some people call Orion, who we call A]tse a]ts'oosi, or the slender one, is still a hunter, and he's still got a bow. I think there's a lesson on how to be a hunter or warrior in the skies for all peoples."

When he says hunter or warrior, I take it that he means it as Don Juan would've said it to Castaneda. Not that every culture was bound to promote warriors and wars specifically; but that each culture will foster warriors and hunters because each society values those who will go to the depths of any and all experiences. There is more to being a warrior than taking life.

"I'm transposing the world as I've seen it in other cultures on top of the map you've laid out up there, and I'm just full of wonder," I replied.

"Yeah man, we just see the things this way because it's the worldview we were given by those who brought us into this place. We follow what we've been taught, like keeping the path to the fire open to the east."

The cardinal directions have a sacred positioning in Dine culture, and in this morning's fire, a clear path must be maintained directly from the fire pit to the east, where the Holy People reside and arise with the new day. What you may see as sunrise is in-fact an explosion of holy energy, each morning, longing to reach out to you and your life. Even when, as the ceremonies begin, the runners and families all gather around the fire, the path to the east is cleared all the way to the horizon. This flame, is sacred; as are the prayers that shall spring from it. This flame will burn for each runner and will only be extinguished when all that is meant to happen out there in the Canyon, happens. When this flame ends, the run and everything holy about it also ends with it.

"My father is going to bless the ceremonies for us all now," Shaun says to the gathering crowd. Dine culture honors all people, and all genders. In fact, those of non-binary expression have a special place in their creation histories and their culture. This is apparent when Shaun's father takes the head of the ceremony, humbly, and says. "We'd like to pray for all people today. We'd like to bless all the runners, all women, all men, and all other expressions among us. In our culture all are equal and we ask for blessing and vision to come to all who run today."

Allen was famed for his running long before Shaun was. During a period in America where segregation was preferred but integration was the stated aim, Dine children were forcibly removed from their homes and put into State Schools, designed to Westernize their sensibilities and provide a 'proper education'. Allen, along with many other students, famously ran off from Leupp, at the western end of traditional Dine boundaries, and trekked back home on multiple occasions per year. The estimated distance, about 100 miles each time. Not bad for a kid yet to finish puberty.

"They were telling me lies and calling it education," he reflects, "they said things like my forefathers built this country, and my forefathers made these laws. Well, I was old enough to know that wasn't true at all. My fathers didn't build this country, even though they helped save it in the Great War. And here I was being fed by lies. Here I was, punished and told my own language was forbidden."

Back then the parlance was, kill the Indian, save the Man. Allen successfully ran off from school on several occasions, but others his age weren't so fortunate in their pursuits. Death from the elements, and starvation, was a real outcome for his fellow classmates.

For the Dine, time may not be a linear path as it is for those in the West. However it moves or however we move within it, it is clear that great distances have been traversed since Allen's time as a child and the world as he finds it today. Today, he is elevated. Today, he is blessed. Today, people travel the world over just to hear the expressions of him which are uniquely Dine, and not Western. Today all that would have once been squashed from him is precisely what people long to learn. They want him for his mysticism, for his shamanic nature, for his elderly wisdom as a Dine and not a western man.

"We want you all to know, that we are truly a loving people," he begins. "But some things for us are very sacred. Too sacred to be shared by today's devices. We believe that these moments, right now, are sacred and so are the people who are present to share them. Because of this, we ask that when we pray and sing and bless these runners in the next ten minutes, you all put away any phones or cameras. These songs, these prayers, are sacred and should remain with all who are here."

The entire crowd silence themselves and their ambitions to record the experience out of respect for Allen and the life he and his people have endured.

What commences is sacred. It is beautiful. It is a gift to observe. In the space in which the blessings occur the fire cracks and the sky moves from indigo to violet. The Holy People hear the prayers and rise to meet the blessed who run this day.

"In one-minute, this thing is going off and I encourage everyone here to scream and shout and call out to the East with everything they've got!" Shaun yells just a moment after the blessing ceremony.

Runners slurp up a last cup of blue-corn mush, chug the bottom of an electrolyte solution, bend deep into the hamstrings, and pack into droves at the start line. Headlamps get turned off and packed away as dawn shows more orange than violet.

"Remember. Running is a means to celebrate. Running is prayer. Running is a teacher and running is a healer." These are the four tenants of Shaun's paradigm in the active life. "So take this with you, on the count of ten…nine…eight…three…two…one…Ya'at'eeh Abini!!!"

Horns and shouts erupt, runners' feet pulse off the muddy floor, heartrates rise, and the Holy People to the east look upon the Canyon de Chelly with pride.

Action.

Immediately Shaun, along with last year's event leader, Greg, past finisher and photographer Todd, and I, pack into the Jeep and fly up the Canyon via the rim road. Shaun has it planned to be at each aid station to greet the runners and encourage them. Fifteen minutes in, he gets a text from Harold—who is running the course entirely in moccasins as a tribute to the Dine before him—that there is even more water in the Canyon than yesterday when we'd tagged it.

"There's going to be a lot of teaching today!" Shaun laughs back to us while standing on his third tenant.

We stop at the Tsegi overlook three miles in, to see Dustin Martin, also of Dine descent, easily ahead of the pack on a wicked pace. He's covered roughly three miles of muddy flats in eighteen minutes and will soon be at the first corral, the White House aid station, which is at mile 5.5 by Shaun's estimate. Wanting to arrive ahead of Dustin gives us about fifteen minutes, based on his current pace, so we pack in and make haste.

At the White House overlook, Shaun rifles out of the Jeep, and Greg and I follow. We've got a one-mile descent down ragged switch-backs and a 700-foot elevation drop, followed by a half-mile of undulated

Canyon-flat to cover in under ten minutes. Within seconds we're at a blistering pace, surfing the Canyon at ankle-snapping speed, as much with momentum as with footwork. Shaun's skill in navigating this terrain is evident as he remains perfectly in balance and sways with each cut of a switchback. Greg, to his credit, follows with a casual generalship on the stone as well.

At the base of the descent there's a small tunnel which hides all daylight, and against the odds of all foot misplacements the two of them charge through it at pace, without even a second thought.

Fuck it, I think, marshaling the whole of my Dine scrambling skills, which I've emulated from Shaun in the previous one-mile of our running together. One must be swift in direction, firm in decision, but light upon the earth all in the same stroke. I burst into the void of the tunnel without compromising my pace purely on measure of faith to the Holy People and come to find I am rebirthed without harm.

On the flats, the revelation continues as Shaun truly bursts into form. It may not be at great distance today, but it is an honor to share a stride with him. His form is like one of the Canyon's sacred four-legged people. It is his terroir.

Shaun prays when he runs. His feet move, not as runner's feet but as pilgrim's. It is not Western prayer, this is Dine. It is communion with the holy from a place of humility. Take one step with all your being. Holy dance. Breathe out your spirit and be settled. Holy prayer. Wind prayer, and breath prayer, and ball-of-foot and body prayer. His feet carry with beautiful pace, he strides long in full awareness. Creek pass prayer. Sand prayer. Earth prayer. Behold, the way this world now shines to the pilgrim who passes through it. He is connected.

We'd made it just in time to see Dustin fly by in first position and to take photos of the first 100 runners in the Canyon. Already, shouts of joy were echoing across the membranes of the Canyon walls in an inspired ostinato. This just 5 miles in. Stuffing our backpacks full of the runners' cold weather clothes—which they'd now abandoned in the light of day—we ran with purpose back to the Canyon rim.

At the top, Shaun paused, before loading the backpacks into the hatch, and pulled out a heavenly band of red-tailed hawk feathers. He crossed to the Cardinal directions, to the four sacred peaks of the Dine Bikeyah, and bowed in prayer and thanksgiving. Pointing the feathers in each of our direction, to bless us, he spoke again to the holy people.

Opening a larger box, Shaun revealed an equally holy, single eagle feather, nearly twice the size of the hawk's. Like an amulet, he again pointed it in the direction of each of us, against the tide of the howling desert wind, and blessed our paths with native incantation.

Breaking the silence of the sacred moment, Shaun spoke. "You guys are a part of something special right now, and I do this to give thanks to the Holy People for the event today, but also to give thanks for you guys and to give you blessings."

Sensing my impending question about the Spirit People, the hawk and eagle people, Shaun added, "Of course, for us, these instruments connect us to the sky people. And, these instruments, they are alive, you know. When we experience a beautiful moment or a beautiful day, we do not just leave them in these boxes. They've got to breathe, they've got to come out, they've got to take in the life on earth. They need air just like we do. So, we take them to these special places and we maintain balance."

That fucker's Beauty Way is brimming over the cup with which he holds it. The source, no doubt, runneth.

///

At the top of Bat Canyon—the 1,200-foot climb which marks the midway point of the run—we gather with our binoculars at the ready and peer down the Canyon's walls. With a free moment at hand, Shaun points out the various offshoots of the Canyon De Chelly and the Canyon Del Muerto further to the North, giving clues to the artifacts in each offshoot, and the histories—both personal and of legend—which they house. With Shaun's guidance, a simple look across the landscape yields something of magic. With time less linear, history lives before your eyes, when multiple images are then transposed onto the same landscape, that of time in its fluid state, one sees beyond just colors and the three dimensions.

Breaking this guidance and epiphany, the group of Dine volunteers who make up the midpoint aid station shout in unison, "Shaun, here comes Dustin!"

Dustin, who has held the fastest stride since the Ya'at'eeh at the starting gate, is of a special composition. He's originally from the Gallup area and has been a creative force and voice of the Dine for years. He earned a degree at N.Y.U. and returned from the Big City to work as program director of Wings of America—a grassroots organization promoting native youth development by running. He's a fully committed activist, passionate runner, and wild soul. In this last year, he's run at a great distance to remember the Long Walk, and to pray for native lands with the Bear's Ear's Prayer Run Alliance. He is a soul alight.

This becomes evident when he pauses at the very peak of the climb, overlooking the Canyon, and enters formal prayer. If he cared about this event as a competition, he'd be 300 yards down the switchbacks in a matter of seconds, gaining a larger lead on the hungry pack who chase him. But, Dustin, is here to fulfill the spiritual experience within the run. He pauses at the very precipice of Bat Canyon, overlooking the northern horizons of Dine Bikeyah, and pulls out a small vile of corn pollen from his pocket. Deep in prayer, he quiets himself for a full minute or more, exercising his Beauty Way, before crushing the pollen between his native hands and inviting it to catch flight in the Holy Wind. Now this, before us, is less a race leader as a true leader. This is a hero the Dine youth so deeply need.

He is not the only one. Among the many runners are other Dine, Hopi, Apache, Osage, and Cherokee. They too have come to demonstrate and to practice a cultural expression as much as a physical one. As the runners' pass, Shaun points out a former student of his, who makes it to the peak of the climb with a smile as broad as the Dine sky, and comments.

"You see her, she's done it all. We won tons of competitions when she was on the team. But more importantly, she spent her entire time in High School running track, working a job, taking care of her sick father, and raising her younger siblings. She lives an hour from Chinle and would wake up every day at 5 a.m., prepare things for her family, get on the bus, finish homework, do school, run after school, work, take the night bus back home, and do homework under flashlights when the generator ran dry. She probably ran on five hours of sleep for four years straight."

Shaun paused a moment to allow me to absorb it, then finished. "So, yeah man. I couldn't be prouder of her. Where she's at today, being the first to get a degree, but still keeping her Dine traditions, she's doing it. She's done it! She's changing the cycle. And, when her younger siblings see it, they know she did it, and they know it can be done. It's so important. Nothing she'll encounter ahead of her will be as difficult as what she's done. Hell, man, this race today, for someone like her, this is just a nice day out. It's barely even training, physically or mentally. Just look at her man; total pride and freedom."

The pure, endemic pride that Shaun exudes when sharing these types of stories—of which he has many—is the stuff of great humanity. This is the third revelation, that cycles are less broken as they are absorbed. In patterns of human life and suffering, there is something of a law of mass and energy conservation also, such that any depth of depravity can

Lucas Roman

be catalyzed into its equal level of restoration. Nothing is eliminated as much as it is refashioned. The fundamental elements of the greatest joys in life come from substrates of the greatest pains. When a turnaround occurs in these lands, when a cycle is shifted, it shines to the depths of human capacity.

III

In the Third World, where First Woman and First Man came into their current physical form, there was much magic. Great forces of attraction produced even greater sequences, as it was an age of birth and becoming. In the Third World, much was revealed. The great Spider-Woman—who today is seen as a benevolent overseer to the human people—was herself in a quest of self-discovery. The complexities of her eight-legged form, no doubt, contained a magical function, but what that exactly was, remained unknown.

The Holy People advised Spider-Woman, telling her that within her was the entirety of the universe, that she in fact, could weave a map of it—that she could connect all within it by way of a geometric narrative, by way of a multi-dimensional, interconnected pattern. Having never seen such a map, nor experienced this within herself, she knew not what the Holy People had shone her.

Shaun himself, during his only major period of injury, questioned his direction. For months, he wondered, deeply, in doubt about his purpose. His primary tool, his way to celebrate, to pray, to be taught by the Holy Ones, had been removed. All his life, from the very blossoming of his youth, he ran. He ran to emulate his own father's strength and perseverance, and he ran well. Better than most. It was clear that Shaun had a gift, but with this career-ending injury, as it seemed, what was he to do? Who would he become?

Like Spider-Woman staring at her own eight-legs in total mystery,

Shaun asked the higher order, "What, is my purpose? What of all this talent? What of this universe inside?"

In Dine Bikeyah, running is essential. This is because at the core, it is a spiritual practice, and they are a spiritual people. It is how they come to communion with the divine, how they worship, how they achieve balance; it is how they receive revelation. These are a people who learn, truly, by their feet. Like other indigenous societies, they have always used it to connect to the higher order.

Back at the finish line, I break bread with an elder and close friend of the Martin family, John Curley. Well into his fifties, John exudes a peaceful wisdom from every cracked pore of his native skin. He shares tales of running as it relates to some of the Dine legends, and how it relates to his own history. In every major turning point, it seems, he's found the equations of life most satisfied by running. It still carries on today.

"Yeah, I ran this event a few years ago and it was a great experience." He's looking at the horizon where the first runners should be arriving shortly. "It really helped me get some vision and training for my other runs lately also. I got back in touch with the long distances from this run, and now, I'm running my age in miles each year during my birthday."

"Holy shit, John. That's incredible."

"Thank you." John humbly looks down at the floor and sweeps a brush of sand with his feet. With his boots made of aged leather, his hands in the pockets of his rugged blue denim, and the sacred turquoise neckpiece resting on his easy shoulders; when you stand and have chat with this guy, you know without a doubt that he's a legend. Not because he is famed, but precisely because he isn't.

"The way I see it, it's my spiritual practice, you know. It's how I learn things these days. I need that long-distance, that open space. It helped me when my father passed, it helped me when I was looking for direction. It was my teacher. And you know what?" he shifts his gaze over to Shaun, "It's just the same for that guy. It's been a big teacher for him, too. He'll tell you, everything he ever got when he needed direction, he got in the running."

"That's totally true." Shaun followed up when I asked him.

"It's been fundamental, man. Like I told you, from the injury to the recovery, from the first Ultra to the press articles, from starting this race to becoming a parent, to getting my position at the school...I ran in every situation. And those runs, specific to each big shift in life, were always the deepest experiences."

When Spider-Woman, it is said, was out during a beautiful day among the Holy People, she noticed a small young tree. The mark of this shrub, even amongst the greater Cottonwoods, moved her. She wrapped her hand and fingers around it, longing to know its beauty further, to engage with every bend and branch of it. When she released the connection she had made, to her surprise, she had spun the beginnings of a web from it. Immediately she reached out to other branches nearby and began to make greater connections. As she moved from one beautiful brush to the next, she knew, suddenly, that she could forge great patterns and ageless shapes; she realized the gift which the Holy People had given her—that the universe was within her and that she could map it. That she could connect all beings.

It seems too convenient for the narrative, but this is exactly true of Shaun. You could hardly deny the coincidence. What Shaun found when he was broken, was the spark he needed. It was the injury that led him to move to Chinle with his wife and pursue teaching. That was the first branch, a beautiful, small sprout among the great causes he'd imagined he might champion. As an educator, aside from coaching, he's earned great accolades and changed countless lives. And as an educator his fire pushed him to seek not one, but two post-graduate degrees. From this position, Shaun re-entered running. When his brother suggested he run his first "Ultra", just for fun, Shaun didn't have to try too hard to win it in record time. This event led to his first press coverage, which led to greater attention to his people and his cause. From there, the growth was exponential: news, media, short films, features in full-length films, the connections, and the web expanded brilliantly. The core of the web had been spun and what followed in each layer of the tapestry radiated from this center. At each new expansion, however, the same questions had to be asked of himself, by himself. The Beauty Way is deeply personal in this regard. Are his motivations pure, is he ready, and can he maintain the balance of the Beauty Way when taking the next step? These answers, for Shaun, are found by running, by praying.

The afternoon haze paints long strokes of light over the sky, which will soon be aglow. John and I continue a discussion along with Shaun's father, Allen, about Shaun's development in those critical years while small bands of runners emerge from the Canyon. As each runner passes the finish, Shaun gives each one of them, individually, a warm hug, and takes a moment to give a congratulation to each. He then ornaments each runner with a turquoise necklace which he and Melissa have made themselves, as a symbol of the Canyon run and the spiritual experience it provided. Many of the runners cry at the emotion of the day. All of them gently bow in gratitude as he places it over their necks, thanking Shaun for the privilege; and some of course, simply rejoice and celebrate while interlocked with him. Shaun does this, adds this personal touch to the experience, to all 150 runners. From Dustin, at just over hour four, to the last finisher somewhere near hour ten. He's weaving again.

At the finish line, at last, you can most truly see the work Shaun is doing. It is in the experience he's provided the runners. It doesn't even matter what brought each of these participants here, because each is finishing with a unique experience. An experience that is deeper and richer than anything they could have foreseen. They've been moved, shifted, like Dine cycle of poverty, to another plane. They've learned from the feet upward.

Just after the award ceremony my partner and I drive back up to the Tsegi overlook to catch the peak of sunset over the Canyon. The sky is legendary, mythic; and that's no hyperbole. Purple people, blue people, sky people, long-band cloud people, gold people, hawk people, Holy People. It is unfathomable. As we park the car and step-out we notice one of the men's top-ten finishers, Yatika, who is representing the Osage and Cherokee tribes from Oklahoma, in a bit of a trance. He's painting, frantically, beautifully, on a large sheet of canvas. It is a stunning representation of the overlook at sunset.

"You just couldn't get enough of the Canyon in there today, could you?" I ask him.

Smiling, Yatika replies, "This is a place you desire to take back with you, my friend."

Looking back to his canvas he continues to paint, and shares, "There's a lot that happens in there for each person. Regardless of the race presenting a physical demand, or not. Some of those people weren't even challenged out there and others could barely manage. But, the course always dictates the experience, you know, and it's a spiritual course. For everyone."

"So, the take-home of the Canyon then?" I ask further.

"The take-home is right here." Yatika puts his hand to his heart. "It doesn't matter what brought these people here, whether or not they wanted to learn about indigenous peoples or if they just wanted to run somewhere for bragging rights. What they get is in here, and the Canyon plants that seed and it makes everyone a better person. You've now got 150 more people spreading-out, back into their day-to-day lives, and they are taking something back which will shine to others."

Back at basecamp, nearly all have left the lot as we begin the breakdown of the tents and equipment. Shaun looks exhausted, finally. He's probably run on less than ten hours of sleep all week. I have no idea how he and the family manage to do it, and probably nobody else does either.

Allen begins the ceremonious closure of the fire, daylight simmers to dark, and the stars make first spark in the coming night sky.

"So, my friend," I share with Shaun, while we load a generator into the back of his pick-up. "Here it is. The end."

He laughs with relief as we drop the generator in and walk back to grab some tarps.

"You, this place, Chinle, the Canyon, you've shown me a lot, man, a ton. Stuff that's going to take a long time to soak in." We pause for a moment, after loading the tarps, and I continue.

"In everything we shared over the last few days, there was one thing I didn't get around to; but I'll ask you now. The First World was dark, the Second World was full of water and was blue, the Third World ended in the great flood, and all these worlds were out of balance for one reason or the other when they ended. Then we got here, to this world. It is said that in this world, the Dine found the Beauty Way and the Earth was at last, in balance. It's also called the White world, or the Glittering World. I've heard some people say it's called that because of all the tinsel and fake shine on shit in the modern age, which I can understand. But for me, it's deeper than that. I've got my own reasons why it shines. But what about you. Why do you think it's called the Glittering World?"

Shaun puts down the plastic table we're carrying and pauses. He looks at the horizon—to the four cardinal directions—with the scope of all his cones and rods, with the whole of his human senses and perception. He closes his eyes and looks deeper still, at the planes of all beings; the human and non-human, holy and sacred alike. I see him look at the world—as the web weaver. He sees a geometric narrative in a pattern of his own weaving. The thousands of students' lives he's touched as an educator; the hordes of souls who've taken something home from their participation in the Canyon De Chelly run; the points on the web which connect everyone not only to each other but to all points in time. All people—the blue people, the sunrise people, the soil people, the bush-people, the wind people, the Cottonwood people, the winged people, the insect people, the earth people. All people. Yourself, included. And, all points in time. All connected. His father running over vast lands for a sense of freedom as a child; the kids in the Hogans with drunk parents and no way to school; the bursting hope in his son and daughter's eyes when they look up to him; that moment you paused and took note of your own breath at the inception of this. The moment before you now. All of it. Sacred.

"Why, is it called the glittering world?" he repeats, slowly.

Shaun takes a deep breath. In his inspiration, he gathers the sum of all he can see and sense. And, on the exhale, he smiles softly with the whites of his eyes completely aglow.

"Just look at it, man. You'll see."

He's completely sure of it.

Allen's fire, which burned not only for the runner's revelations, at last finds its finish.

Indeed, it is, a glittering world.

女人類

WOMAN: KIND.

Perhaps it's best to begin with an admission. I've always wanted to climb like a woman. In many ways, it didn't even begin with climbing. When the realization occurred, I couldn't say. But ever since I could remember; the female form, the feminine energy, the Beauty Way itself, seemed as honorable a path to emulate as the cycles of nature. What I saw in waves breaking across a shore was feminine. What I saw in motion, in the natural order—in seasons changing, in clouds over cliff bands, in subtleties and colors of twilight—all of it, was of the She.

Without fail, there has always been as much if not more, of the yin than the yang. Revelation, for me, has always been a nudge toward that energy. Whether it's an approach I'm taking toward a challenge, or in the ineffable, mysterious part of something beautiful—the revelation, the revolution, has always been feminine. I've always known, far within, that the beauty of life is not only the fact that it is filled with great forces, but that there is a balance which holds those forces together. I suspect in every man's heart there is a pinch of the same awareness. In the ocean, every surfer knows that while men may dig a deeper rail, few of us actually carve, find harmony, and engage with a wave better than a woman. On a wall, there will always be a place for the savage, ballistic roar of will and power; but the most beautiful dance I've seen on stone is and always will be the image of grace under pressure. An image I'd seen more than once from my old friend, and underground inspirational figure, Shanjean Lee.

As many know, climbing well at your limit is determined just as much by what you do in your time off the wall as it is by what you do with your time on it. A 5.14 climber like Shanjean does not spontaneously manifest any more than a garden or a harvest simply appears. Success in one's craft is always the product of much deeper, longer, and interconnected processes. And, at the highest levels of vertical pursuit, any amount of work done on the wall can just as quickly be undone off of it; by any ill manner of living, by mental framework, or by untended landscapes of the inner self. I would submit that the most astounding expression of the female form—and one which I've seen often in Shanjean—is characterized by an abundant and untamable, creative flow. A constant, balletic display of harmony with the forces of life which is only possible through a great and quiet awareness—something of a subterranean, mycelial connection to the higher order..

But Shanjean was not always so alight, like the rest of us she had to struggle to evolve. And just as most of us, she came of age not on the high plains, but precisely in the low points of life, which came without bias, both on and off the wall. One, of many, occurred in 2015.

Neck-deep in her second year—by all measures the hardest year—of surgical residency, Shanjean sat high above the Yosemite Valley floor on To-tok-ah-noo-lah (El Capitan), via the Golden Gate route, dangling off a 9-millimeter rope like a pair of old sneakers swaying from an electric wire. Busted up, head to toe, and frayed by the aggregates of workload and capacity, after two days of shutdown and battle on the wall, she ran hard against her limits. The climbing up there, something she'd dreamt about for years, proved firmly unmoved by the years of sacrifice and time she had dedicated as a surgeon and healer. There was no karmic grace afforded her efforts on and off the wall, only pain. Lord knows it takes a certain composition to square off with the Captain in a free climbing effort; the list of those who do is distinguished.

As far as I know, however, none of the athletes who have given it a wrestle have also had to keep a 90-hour workweek, in a male-dominated, high-consequence field, while navigating a career path as a minority woman. That role was hers alone, as was the setback she faced from it. It was an emotional defeat, Shanjean affirmed. But it was also a moment of truth. In the face of complete failure, on a wall whose gravitational pull is big enough to yank comets out of the sky, she picked up the pieces and went back to work, and training. In so doing she became what I would define as a heroine, someone whose character, and process, are to be modeled for precisely the beauty and feminine nuance they offer.

///

At 5:00 a.m. in Reno, Nevada, and on five hours sleep from the trans-Californian drive the night before, I turned toward my alarm and squashed the snooze function in the soft glow of dawn. Twenty minutes later, while I was prepping the coffee before the morning run, Shanjean texted ahead of schedule. "Can't make it today. Three new cases came in overnight. But have a beautiful morning, and run well!" Today's Tahoe Valley sunrise, it seemed, would be mine alone.

Nine years since our last reunion, in our old Costa Mesa haunts where we began our friendship and often climbed together, we planned to kickstart a week of reconnection in the best way we knew how: putting feet to earth in the morning light with a trail run. But, since three new cases at the Veterans hospital—at least one of which would require almost immediate surgery—rolled in overnight, we put a rain check on our rendezvous. Still, even at that early hour, I could feel the optimism over the phone. Shanjean, one hundred percent, exudes something decidedly calm and yet sincerely excited at almost all times. Sure, everybody eats crow now and again, but there's a preternatural warmth about her, especially considering her life in medicine. This contagious positivity, this assuredness in the face of the difficult and the unplanned, is precisely what I came up to explore.

Right now, Shanjean is not world-renowned, and she'd probably prefer it that way. But to those who do know her, her character is bookended by her trade as an orthopedic surgeon, and as a standout climber. When Gaston Rebuffat once said, "We should refuse none of the thousand and one joys that the mountains offer us. We should brush nothing aside, set no restrictions. We should experience hunger and thirst, be able to go fast, but also know how to go slowly and to contemplate," he may not have had Shanjean or any woman in mind. Take a cursory look at her climbing accomplishments, however, from sport to bouldering, from traditional to big wall and even extending into mountaineering, across continents and some of the highest difficulties, and it's clear: she is incredibly well-rounded in her expertise.

Just the same, when old man Hippocrates declared the tenets of a physician as having wit, order, clarity, and connection to the patient process as much as the disease process, he surely didn't have a woman in mind. But Shanjean's medical practice, coupled with her lightness of being, serve the old man's archetype precisely. Throughout both medical school and her ensuring residencies, her talents and work ethic frequently set her apart from and above her many peers. These hard facts alone aren't what impress the most, however. It's not just that she's supremely good, borderline great at what she does. It's that she remains, by choice, humble and quiet about most of it. But how? As far as I could recall, her childhood was anything but stable.

Born in Taipei, Taiwan, Shanjean was cared for by her grandmother in the early years, until moving to New Mexico, where her mother was stationed for her own schooling. After New Mexico, the family moved to Michigan, where her father studied, and then for a time to Chicago, where work was found. This lasted until the end of middle school, when they uprooted again, moving to California. As an adult, Shanjean then spent her more formative years in North Carolina for medical school, and Portland, Oregon, for her orthopedic surgery residencies. How, in the whirlwind of so much change, had she fashioned enough character to build a life defined not by whim but by a commitment to the long play? Shanjean admitted, "If there was one advantage, it was the family unit." Cultures of the East draw fewer lines between the nuclear and extended family, which tends to provide support in fuller measure. A fullness deeply needed for anyone, especially a minority woman, to forge a path of their own. Family aside, much of Shanjean's success is related to her deep inner balance. And for that inquiry, I figured it may take more than a trail run to discover. Whether it be before work, after work, or on a rare free weekend, I was determined to mine the field.

///

The following day, Shanjean texted from the clinic. It had been another 14-hour go, mostly non-stop. Still, knowing our windows to connect were short, she insisted we get together. And, in a rare show of a divided mind, exhausted from work, she struggled to weigh the options between forcing a twilight run around the Peavine Trails or an extended happy hour and tacos downtown. Settling on drinks rather than sport, forty-five minutes later we found ourselves seated outside an empty brick patio at a downtown joint. She arrived simple and carefree, dressed in shorts and a tank top, with a thin purple windbreaker and the same gentle smile and straight black hair I'd remembered framing her caring and kind eyes.

"Damn," she said as she savored a mezcal and tequila cocktail, "I think we made a good choice."

Bursting into her trademark nasally giggle, she softened the tension from her shoulders and jumped straight into the conversation.

"What I wanted was this chance to relax and enjoy a drink, to catch up! What I probably needed was a workout. But, literally, I never do this," she said.

"When's the last time you had a 'normal schedule'?" I asked. "Like, 4-6 hours in a day, before or after work to choose your activities, with weekends free and reliable time off to socialize and libate as the normies do?"

"My god," she laughed at a seeming ghost of long ago. "I don't know if I ever had that life. If I did it was probably no longer than weeks at a time, and that must have been a decade ago."

"Well then," I said, "from where you're coming in from, all the high performance in both spheres, I think occasions that make you slowdown may be just as needed as the next run you want to take."

She agreed. Truth is, she doesn't get out much, not in the way the common folk do; that's a function of her life as a surgeon as much as it is her life as a climber. Practicing medicine requires as much sacrifice of time as it requires focus within it. Because of that the simple privileges of life are not normally hers to entertain. While that lifestyle isn't for everybody, Shanjean carries little, if any, conflict about it. Instead, it breeds a certain satisfaction in her, visible with one look just by the way she bounces, joyfully, in every step. Surprisingly, even with all her busyness, she is still very outward facing. Shanjean is as much, if not more interested in your life, when you sit with her, than her own.

"Tell me about the podcasts you've listened to on your way up here the other day" she said, curious.

"Well, do you want the whole list?" I laughed.

She did. But from the flock of podcasts in our queues, we quickly ended up on a reflection of Zen Buddhism, ala Wu De, a simple tea master from Taiwan. Unsurprisingly, with her roots in country and her curious mind, thought patterns of the East have a deep appeal to Shanjean.

With the godforsaken heatwave finally cooling into an evening delight, by merit of the thunderstorm clouds sending thermals across the valley, we hunkered in for a conversation that went well beyond our podcasts. In no time we'd covered big terrain, from stitching together the nine years we'd been apart to the plight of women in climbing, to the crown jewels of most physicians and climbers lives: the search for balance and pure motivation.

"Balance in life is not something I've mastered, at all," she shared. "But I think I've come a long way with it. Those things get refined with time and practice, like anything else."

"I know from talking to a handful of women, and men, in my years climbing, that diet and self-perception can be hard issues to maintain a healthy balance around. How has that experience been for you?" I asked.

"Sure," she acknowledged, "I think for climbers in general, when it comes to performance, diet can be tricky to manage. Same with self-perception, if it's only defined by success on the wall. And for women, it's even harder when you throw in the fluctuations of hormones."

"It seems like you've found healthy parameters for those challenges," I suggested.

"I think so," she began. "Everybody is different. But for me, I feel best when I eat well, healthy, and often. I stick to what works for me, which usually means that I eat when I'm hungry and I try to keep it wholesome. Some people find success by losing a quick few pounds for a project, but that's usually less of a sustainable, long-term way to get better. If anything ,it makes it easier to get injured."

"So you focus more on the total package, complete health, perhaps, as you do on just achieving a specific climb or weight?" I questioned.

"Yeah," Shanjean smiled. "I think whether through climbing or practicing medicine, you learn that the best improvements come with time and there's no shortcut to this stuff. That's where real motivation has to come into the equation. I've got to be driven by improvement more than achievement. When it's achievement alone, I can start making the wrong kind of sacrifices. When it's improvement I can get into a better frequency. My self-esteem becomes less tied-up in what I do and more in how I do it. If that's the case, I'll tend to see myself and my body in a better light."

The depth and clarity with which that opening statement floated right out of her was perhaps more exceptional than the idea itself. Snacking down a tortilla chip under a cool sky, with wisps of wind floating about, she looked as comfortable as a person could be in their own skin. On top of that, her answer came straight out of the autopilot. A perfectly formed response born from years of experience in textbooks and medical practice; perhaps exactly what many men and women in this now Olympic sport need to hear. Today, she'll tell you her motivations in life have been an ongoing process of refinement. But she'll also tell you, from experience, that nit-picking the perfect motivation is less important than the action itself. If you're committed to doing good for planet earth, by any form, the motivations will come into clarity as a function of the work. What is important is that you get after it. If it's excellence you are after, practice, more than motivations, will serve you.

///

On Saturday morning, I woke up an hour before dawn and had the pleasure of driving the 395 South from Tahoe to Tuolumne, where Shanjean had already driven out with her partner, Mikey, the previous night. After a sunrise over the Walker River and the final scuff up the Tioga Pass, we rallied together at the Tioga Lake parking pullout; California sun glistening over the rich alpine blue.

Shanjean and Mikey are undeniably fit, and with all their ability I would not have faulted them for wanting to do something far out of my limits. So, I was both pleased and surprised when they suggested, quite invitingly, a morning bouldering session at what they assured would be at a leisurely pace. While that held true, Shanjean's and Mikey's technique was evident. Leisurely pace or not, they are masters of their realm. They each have their own style, but similarities do abound. Precision, acuity, awareness to detail in the smallest plane of the body, and a baffling core stability are made apparent by clean and exact footwork on the wall. It's one of those forms of art that, in any other branch of society, people would pay honest wages to witness.

Before long though, it got hot, and for that reason we quickly shifted gears, packed the pads, and drove over to Py-we-ack Lake. We made our stead on the west end of the shore, where a shallow pool led out at waist-deep level for a hundred yards with the emerald glow of sun-kissed and clear water. Perfect, body-sized banks of granite slabs lay in a natural recliner position, urging us to lay down in a warm Sierra delight, just like so.

"Well," I began, "In terms of sacrifice, orthopedic residencies can be among the worst. What's it like on the other side? What is the practice of medicine like for you today?"

"Oh, boy," Shanjean said after dipping in the lake, "These days, it's so rewarding. You know, residency is kind of like boot camp, and in a lot of ways you feel like you are always failing, 'cause in a lot of ways, you are. But that's all part of the process. You turn a corner one day and suddenly it's just you and these patients. There's a freedom, a beauty, and something incredibly terrifying in that setting."

"Such as being responsible to perform surgeries you haven't yet done?" I asked. "Like the other day?"

"Exactly, that was a bit scary," she laughed. "I mean, I was familiar with the process and I studied for that case completely. But yeah, I hadn't done a case exactly like that. At the same time, I also knew I had all the training and skills necessary to make it work. A lot of residency is about preparing you to have the confidence in your decision making and your ability, which is huge. But I'm definitely happy to have that part of it over with so I can enjoy stuff like this."

What she was looking at as she finished that sentence and smiled, was a pair of Prussian blue dragonflies, flirting in circles around one another in a familiar alpine-spring courtship, just above the banks of the water's edge. Looking around, with all the splendor of a newcomer—she'd only been to Tuolomne a couple of times—Shanjean magnified her delight. "To be able to have a medical practice, and a life, defined by places like this, it's pretty amazing stuff."

About an hour later, just down the road, Shanjean and I warmed up at the Main Wall of the aptly named Tioga Cliff. Between routes, we jumped back in on the conversation about her trust in her skills, her training, and the necessary amount of self-belief when performing operations. No surprise, a lot of those skills transfer to more than one practice in life.

"You know what's incredible?" she started, "I still get completely nervous, like sick to my stomach before an operation. And, I think you have to, to be honest. It's kind of the necessary check in the process. Sort of like if you are rappelling off a cliff, you know, you never want that to feel so normal that you don't check all your systems. I think the day I lose that heightened state is the day I'm more likely to mess up in the O.R."

"Wow, that's pretty honest," I said. "But odds are that at this point, that fear isn't something paralyzing, but something you can use to sharpen your mind for the job?"

"For sure. With time I've been able to use that fear before an operation to toggle me into focus. At the same time, the counterpoint to fear is something like adrenalin, and I'm also making sure I'm not operating from that position either. It's good to have both, but to make sure you aren't controlled by either. Neither would be good for the patient."

As if to demonstrate further, Shanjean exacted this balance of forces right in front of my eyes. We'd just warmed up on a few climbs in the 5.11 terrain, and now, it was her turn to give one of the King Lines of the cliff a burn, her first burn. The routes at Tioga Cliff are long, often requiring more than a 70-meter rope to lower off safely, and here she was about to set off on one of the lengthiest, a 5.12+, onsight—meaning she'd never been on that specific climb and had no prior information about it.

Tying her laces and double-checking her mis-en-place, she readied for the task. She doesn't carry a hard shell around her. In fact, she's very open in energy and conversation, with no signs of internal fracture. Except for that moment, just before the climb. Right before she put her mitts on the wall you could sense just a touch of apprehension, a bit of uncertainty; but only for a moment. Once on the route, Shanjean glowed, fully in her element and composed she took it right to the chains.

Near the top, at the crux, where the crack seam dead-ends to a blocky transition onto an open face, Shanjean moved with a certain grace, but also a noticeable conviction. Conviction can be lost in translation, so allow me to spell it out. From experience, personally, I can assure you that there is a big difference between moving with fear—the desperation of not wanting to fall—compared to moving with conviction. Conviction knows exactly why it's moving, what it's moving toward, and the resources it has to get there. Desperation, to which I can relate, never really knows anything beyond itself. It is just as afraid to find out what the next moment holds, whether it be a triumph or taking the fall, because to do either there is a threshold you have to cross, and for some of us, that is where we flop the nuts.

But Shanjean has done work, all her life no doubt. She met that moment and did so at full attendance, precisely as she had learned from

WOMAN: KIND.

her surgical practice. This might have been the most beautiful expression of the day, except that when she lowered back to the ground, she produced something even better. There's a transgression of the elite at times, and where excellence is an expectation it's easy to lose touch with simple joy. But here, feet planted back to earth, Shanjean boiled over, gobsmacking in delight she erupted into an outrageous, celebratory dance.

That alone, the ability to fully rejoice in life, is just as much a skill as any in her tool kit. As Wu De would say, if you don't know how to celebrate the life that you have right now, no experience, no thing you acquire, no next step will give it to you. Getting, having, or doing things, are all reasons to celebrate, but they won't teach you how to celebrate life. That is something you have to practice, to the point of redundancy like anything else, climbing or surgery alike. By measure of the pure joy, oozing out of every pore, as Shanjean lost herself to the outburst of an involuntary wiggle, I knew she had put in all the practice she needed.

III

Shanjean ascribes much of her success to family. A success, she affirmed, which is not tied to climbing a certain grade or 'making it' in the medical field. "Success is being in the pocket, frequently, it's being plugged in to people, and my fullest capacities," she said. Having the right people around you to lift you up to that aim is fundamentally important, and something Shanjean is aware of. The network of support she keeps is one of her crown jewels, and it's something she learned to be selective about at an early age, probably from her grandmother all those years ago.

At night, accompanied by gales of wind, we made camp at the Windy Bivy, a tiny pocket at the apex of the Tioga Pass, just below Ellery Lake, where winds lash and explode down the Dana Canyon like a spit-wad out of a plastic straw. Nestled in the van, we broke bread, ala shared plates of Mikey's exceptional curry, and an appetizer I'd whipped together.

Sated and warm, we reveled in a conversation on food, culture, and her relationship to family in the face of her busied life.

"When's the last time you visited home?" I asked.

"To Taiwan?" she replied. "It was earlier this year. My grandma was not doing well."

She continued, "In fact, that trip was wild. My flights got delayed and the itinerary was rerouted multiple times, and I only had four days off to make it there and back. But I'm glad I did. It was super important to see my grandma one more time, even if it seemed silly to travel so far only for a couple of days. In the big picture, showing up for family is important to me, even if I'm not with them as much as I want to be."

Touching back on a conversation we'd explored earlier, I asked, "And how does your family feel about your climbing?"

Puffing her cheeks on the exhale, Shanjean answered, "Oh boy. Well, it's complicated."

For anyone with a family, there's a lifelong struggle with risk. In more traditional cultures, and for women in particular, there's a little more footwork in the dance. Men can take risks and be seen as heroes, while women traditionally, are seen as something other. When you do what we do, or better yet, what Shanjean does, the juggling act of life can feel almost impossible. While Shanjean has always lived up to, exceeded even, every one of her parents' dreams for her, her passion for climbing and the inherent risk involved is not well digested.

"You know, those wide pitches on the Freerider," she said, referring to her current project on To-tok-ah-noo-lah, "those pitches are the worst to manage. That's where I have the hardest time consolidating what I'm doing, it's on the climbing terrain that isn't very protectable," she said.

"You mean the overtly runout, big fall-factor stuff?" I asked.

"Absolutely. That kind of terrain is where I struggle with climbing the most. Not physically struggle, but conceptually. I have a hard time with high consequence climbing, with sections where falling is a no-no.

Often the likelihood of falling in those spots is small, and I work my best to reduce it even further, but the chance is never zero."

"So, how do you try to manage it?" I asked.

"Well, I guess I just practice the shit out of anything I feel is dangerous, until it's completely rote. And I try to get better at the types of climbing that I'm not comfortable with. It's not a glamorous process, but in the long run, it allows me to navigate more terrain more comfortably. Also, there are just some routes that I will probably never do. There's no perfect answer, but as much as I can be, I know I'm a safe climber. I take in as much data as possible with every objective, even though I know I can't eliminate risk completely."

"My parents probably learned to ask about it differently," she added, "For a time, their reactions were so bad I found myself lying about it, and that felt terrible."

Rightly so. She adores them, but like many first-generation kids, has found it a life's work to become fully her own person while still honoring the people and the traditions she's born from. For comic relief, she also contextualized that she'd always had to lie to her parents when it came to anything fun, even as a straight-A, junior-high student having a "nerd gathering" with her girlfriends. Just having a pajama party and making mixed tapes of the Spice Girls and Hanson were decidedly rebellious affairs.

The thing about climbing, as I gathered, is that for Shanjean it is a load-bearing structure, not only a place where she executes a craft but an object, a system, and a community she has to lean on. It holds her up in ways she needs to be held, in order to achieve balance and not burn out under the operating light. As a woman, a daughter, and a surgeon, I believe she makes the best choices she can regarding risk, fully considering others while being true to a life of her inner bearing.

In the morning, we convened for an easy sun soak and coffee hour by the lake. With an afternoon session planned for pulling hard at Tioga Cliff, we kept a relaxed pace. And, it's again worth noting that Shanjean and Mikey really could have their pick of the litter. Any route, anytime, they are that good. The fact that they make it a point, rather than an afterthought, to go around and enjoy the classics up here, is unique. The same way Shanjean looks at summer goals in the alpine, notably the Incredible Hulk and its handful of the premiere hard routes, she's also looking at the classics—the Regular Route on Fairview Dome, West Crack on Daff Dome, Tenaya, Matthes, Cathedral, and today, the Great White Book on the Stately Pleasure Dome.

The other day at happy hour I'd asked Shanjean how much the pursuit of beauty influences her choice of climbs—whether there are moments when she is on the wall just for the sake of the view and the partnerships they afford her, rather than the difficulty. She had to think about it because so much of her recent climbing was primarily goal oriented. But right here, at the base of a meager 5.6, it's as clear as the sky is blue over Tuolumne Meadows, she's game for all the right reasons.

What else bears mention, is that Shanjean and Mikey are both stewards. They plug-in to people, not just climbing. In the past 24 hours we climbed and shared laughs with elite company, including one industry magazine editor, two famed route developers, an old sales rep for a national-level brand, a local climbing legend, his wife, and a handful of local kids. The youngsters of the group even recognized Mikey by virtue of the fact that he had recently replaced nearly 50 old quickdraws at the crag on his own volition, for the sake of public service. At almost every spot we parked the van in the last 24 hours, somehow, there was a familiar face to greet. Now at Py-we-ack Lake, under our first climb of the day, it was the same scenario, as we ran into an old friend and Squaw Valley 'snow leopard', Glen Poulsen.

APERTURE ALIKE

"See that guy?" Mikey asked, as we scrambled up the first 100 feet of the slab, "Legend! His family history is totally intertwined with the Eastern Sierra. Back when I used to ski hard, Glen would take me on these ridiculous tours with his friends and family. That guy could out ski Olympians, dude, no joke! We did a tour up and down Mt. Whitney one year and Glen was light-years out of my league."

Mikey, to his credit, is undoubtedly well-fashioned. For someone like him, who is one of a mere handful of humans to free climb the Southeast Ridge of Cerro Torre in Patagonia, to look over at another guy and declare him the model of peak fitness, is really saying something.

About one hundred feet above the floor, at a ledge, we roped up, Mikey on lead, Shanjean and I tied just a few feet from each other at the end of the same rope. Our goal was something of a continuous simul-climb up the 400-foot formation, mostly by way of shuffling into the body size fissures of its single crack system. The advantage of simul-climbing a route like this, as a party of three, was that it allowed constant movement for all involved. Considering Shanjean and Mikey are both 5.14 climbers, and the fact that Mikey protected every crux section, the tactics seemed fair, safe, and efficient. Neither of us was going for speed, just for flow.

While the terrain was decidedly amateur, I was, by far, the weakest link in the chain, and for that reason I focused as much as possible on making all the right moves. That was, until about halfway up, maybe a couple of hundred feet off the deck. Looking down just ten feet below me, I found that while I was climbing face-in, body-oriented to the wall, Shanjean was playing her cards faced-out. With her back to the wall, Shanjean was looking continuously outward and downward at that turquoise bank on Py-we-ack Lake, where just a day before we had been sunbathing. The presence of mind for her to quietly and fully enjoy that ascent was magic. So were the handfuls of moments when she just couldn't contain herself, where she broke out in goose bumps at the sudden realization that we were a part of something so damn picturesque.

After the crack we had been climbing tapered out onto a blank rockface, which defined the final hundred feet of slab to the top, the Northwest face of Tis-se'-yack (Half Dome) and the Valley came into view. It's an angle you struggle to get anywhere else in Tuolumne. From most of the classics out here, you can find parts of the Valley, but it's usually faint or from behind. The straight-in angle, beelining almost exactly to Camp Four, was gangbusters. Following tradition, Shanjean pulled out her phone, gathered the three of us together, and snapped a summit selfie; a tradition she keeps for her record books, because as most of us well know, even on casual days, summits matter. Summits are mile markers of where we've been and with whom, and they should be remembered because it's another statement of Zen, and the feminine, to gather those rosebuds and practice gratitude. Sharing a climb, albeit quite small, in the illustrious curriculum vitae of both Shanjean and Mikey, was an honor.

///

Many of Shanjean's struggles in medicine, and climbing, came in the process of finding her own voice. Even with all her talent, she has no problem admitting, "I also need support and encouragement from others, completely. We all do." These days, that's another point of awareness she carries, something she puts out there for the betterment of the climbing culture, one small interaction at a time.

Just past noon, as the shade shifted over the east-facing Tioga Cliff, Shanjean and I made our way down the switchbacks while Mikey took the afternoon off to rest. To no surprise, when we arrived at the base of the cliff, another handful of climbers who knew Shanjean stopped to chat. It's not that she or Mikey are famed, as much as they are inviting. They always stop and engage in conversation, to laugh with you, to check in with you, to touch on at least one point that has more to do with how you are doing in life than what you are climbing. And that is not by accident.

"I can tell you firsthand," Shanjean began, "that too often, the small victories are not celebrated as much as they should be. So, I make it a habit to put something positive out there for others, you know?"

"You're sayin' this came as a response to experience?" I asked.

"Yup," she said, "I think validation is important for people to grow. And, even if you aren't sending the hardest route at the crag, if you've pushed yourself past a mental roadblock or finished something personally meaningful to you, it makes a huge difference if that is acknowledged by somebody. Even if we know inside of ourselves that we've made personal progress, we are, for better or worse, often influenced by what we are or are not told by others. And sometimes, it's hard when our feelings aren't externally validated."

"So, what did you do when you encountered that?" I asked.

"Well, you can still flip it into something powerful," she replied, smiling. "When our accomplishments aren't externally acknowledged, we can actually end up doing things more for ourselves, and possibly even more for the right reasons. It does take some work to get there, but if we come to the other side of it, we are in a more sustainable place, which is great."

"But, come on," She added with a wry smile. "Everybody likes to feel appreciated by others, and I think it's important for partners, in climbing or romantic relationships, to really focus on that for one another. I guess, in a small way, when I plug into the community, I'm hoping to give some of that to others, too. I want to encourage everyone just for showing up. And for sure, there have been a lot of parallels in medicine. There were just as many times when I doubted myself and needed affirmation in that arena."

In fact, one of Shanjean's only mistakes, perhaps her only regret in her practice of medicine, came a few years back. A male attending physician suggested something during an operation that didn't align with her analysis, and instead of trusting her voice and standing up, she deferred. When the patient returned a few weeks later, with post-operative complications, she understood both the harm it had caused the patient, but also her practice. It did lend her perspective, though. Failing to develop a voice, she said, was just as much a liability as failing to develop an operating skill. It did a number on her for a time, because while she knew she needed to trust in herself, she didn't fully have it yet, and found it difficult to acquire. It took a lot of work, but with enough time and study under a handful of female mentors, it did develop.

Still, as I look back to our old days in Southern California, I can't help but recall that perpetual optimism of hers. She may not have had the validation she needed, but there were always elements of her character which were so self-assured, so well oriented, they couldn't help but shine. There has always been a light about Shanjean that simply could not be stamped out. Where that came from, I'm still not sure, but when you're around her you realize it's not something that needs to be figured out. For measure of its sheer contagiousness, her light needs not be scrutinized, it needs to be celebrated.

///

In one of our earliest interactions, ages ago, Shanjean and I were climbing in Costa Mesa at the old rock gym. She'd been outside climbing a lot that season, even though she was already in medical school and busied by life's obligations. Googly-eyed with a new love for climbing, and her abilities really just taking off, the world was at her fingertips. It was a special moment in life, characterized by the realization that you could both fashion your own dreams and become your own dreamcatcher. Many of us, in one way or another have been there, too, at the precipice of our own becoming. But few have the audacity and the skill to keep those youthful embers alight. Far too many of us, for an honest lack of belief, just let go.

Changing belays, Shanjean and I spoke on our goals. Even then she dreamt of more than just what she could climb, she dreamt of who she could be. Between talking points, as young folks do, we threw ourselves at the only 5.13 in the gym. It was nothing like the outdoors, nevermind the style you find on granite, but it was the best metric of fitness we had at the time.

"You know, if we get this in the bucket that'll build some confidence to start trying this stuff outside again," I said, having come off my own injuries that year. "I got my ass kicked up there a few years back, but I've always dreamt of free climbing parts of El Cap. What about you?"

Shanjean paused, as if she was entertaining something for the very first time, before she answered back with a smile, "What's the Freerider go at? 5.13?"

"I think it's 12d or 13a," I shared, pointing to our project, "but no way it's anything like this. I bet it'll be way harder."

Well ahead of me, Shanjean focused with her eyes closed. It was as if she entered some entire, future-facing meditation, zooming light-years in spacetime, through all the warps and undulations. Like she was downloading the entire zip file of the process. She returned to the present to just a second later, having played out every permutation on the chessboard, completely confident and aglow.

Dumbfounded, I stared at her as she grinned that gentle, assured smile, and said, "That'll be it then. That's going to be the one. I'm going to have to send the Freerider."

Fast forward nine years, and she's rounding what I would call the home stretch in the process that is a big-wall, free-climbing endeavor. She's been on the Freerider numerous times, diligently worked the moves, and cataloged the key pieces of protection along with all the ancillary data points. Nothing is guaranteed in life, but as much as she can be, she is nearly prepared to start composing the final frames of this act. Soon enough, it'll just come down to achieving peak fitness level. The base, the intel, and the belief are all there. And how? As often happens, the discoveries she needed happened off the wall entirely.

The obstacles Shanjean faced in her climbing were exactly mirrored in her experience of practicing medicine. The crucible of her reaching full expression, as both a climber and an orthopedic surgeon, would be less about the work as it would be about the vision in the first place. Her biggest challenge was that she didn't have any obvious role models. She did not know any female orthopedic surgeons, nor, at the time, any females climbing at some of the highest levels. She certainly didn't know anybody doing both. And while Shanjean also had hopes to become a mother at some point in the process, she lacked for models there also.

At a turning point in her life, she reached out to her program director, who thankfully pointed her to the rolodex. Shanjean will tell you that the network of women she chose to emulate and seek counsel from—those who had pursued a less traditional model of a physician's practice—all made indelible contributions to where she is today. This is how she found her voice. Shanjean kept her dreams alive, not by fighting force with willpower alone, but with the help of other women.

When I asked for names, Shajean was happy to give full credit. "Carla Smith," she started, "is an orthopedic traumatologist who works for an organization that provides services to hospitals that lack them. A set up where she works either one or two weeks on, and then one or two off. From Carla I saw you could have a work and life balance, which is a big departure from the traditional physician's schedule."

"Next," she followed up, "Laura Matsen Ko, an orthopedic joints surgeon who was a sponsored runner and triathlete before residency, who continued to run at a high level throughout residency, and who had two kids while continuing full force in her career. She showed me that you could still improve and make gains, in athletic and personal achievement, even in the highest demands of a medical practice."

Third on Shanjean's list, "Kathryn Schabel, another orthopedic joints surgeon who felt strongly about having children went on to have two of them through her residency. She still graduated in good standing and got into the fellowship and career she wanted. She also taught me very methodically how to do a joint replacement and helped me solidify my decision to not attend fellowship, in contrast to the more than 90% of my colleagues who did. When I had doubts, since I was going apart from the norm, she reassured me that my technical skills were sufficient to start my own practice."

Continuing the series, Shanjean pointed to her fourth finger, "There was also Yee Doung, an orthopedic oncology surgeon whose brand of tough love and insistence on doing things right, forced all of us residents to put in the extra effort, always, for the sake of the best practice and best outcome. Especially when she was around."

"Next," Shanjean wrapped up. "Jackie Brady, an orthopedic sports surgeon who was our assistant program director. Jackie might have had a more traditional path, but her unwavering support and just plain kindness, through the periods when I doubted my abilities the most, really helped me through some of the darkest times."

Lastly, apart from the medical field, Shanjean credited two of her largest beacons of support. Unquestionably beginning with her mentor and dear friend, Bailey Speed. Bailey filled the climbing side of the equation. It was Bailey's encouragement, as a woman who had climbed in ways Shanjean aspired to, that gave her the self-belief. If you think back Shanjean's conviction during her onsight of that 5.12+ at the cliff just a day before—her poise, and her capacity to focus on crossing the threshold rather than run from it— that's Bailey's signature on her. Without Bailey, the companionship, the mentorship, and the affirmation, Shanjean wouldn't have made it to where she is now.

While women empowering other women is at the heart of her progression, she was also quick to point a finger at her partner in crime. Shanjean explained that without the love, support, and care of Mikey, the pieces would fall apart. Mikey, as mentioned, has climbed the world over. He's exceptionally fit, talented, willing to work, and able to grind out long-term projects that would empty the well for most. He's built a pyramid of knowledge, awareness, fitness, and craft over a lifetime of adventure and expeditions. He's established routes, climbed on ice and rockfaces of all dimensions; he's learned from the best, kept up with the best, and has seen some of the most dramatic displays of natural light and natural force. Mikey has seen more beauty—at its most rugged and yet most intimate—than perhaps any of us. But beyond what he's seen and done, beyond all the knowledge, experience, and strength he's shared with Shanjean, it's the simplest gifts of love, patience, and unconditional support that have enabled her the most. More than walls and grand ascents, the task of life is an inside job; real partnership, real love, challenges and activates us in our deepest capacities. Above all, that is where Mikey's credit is due.

///

Back to 2015, then. Hanging off the end of that rope, thousands of feet off the deck and beat to hell on To-tok-ah-noo-lah, it hit her. Right there, in the smashed ego, and equally smashed body, Shanjean found what I prefer to call the Great Concession. Work, without end.

Surely, she'd been training for that realization her entire life. Her tools were already sharpened. She had also just tossed out two years of work in an Ear, Nose & Throat residency to be exactly where she was, back at the bottom of a long pecking order. That's what the newly burgeoning self-belief had granted her: more work. But it also gave her clarity. At the end of the day, the ENT trade wasn't what she wanted, it was something she had settled on. Due to a lack of belief that she would fit in, and execute at the level of the boys in Ortho, she chose ENT. But after two years at it, and after receiving the needed affirmations, Shanjean followed her heart. Even if it meant taking steps in what appeared to be in the opposite direction. After more than 20 years in school, since childhood, who among us would walk back to the nearest fork, and choose the longer and harder path? To do so requires a special conviction, and character. Both of which need to be supported by a network of others, because as Shanjean knows, no journey and no success is taken alone.

Those were the years of true fashioning, but also those of the greatest realization. Shanjean found that in staying true to herself and her dreams, she no longer needed to ask if the goals were even achievable. The goals were just targets; the pursuit of them was the important part. She could concede, on paper, that this tangled expedition into her ultimate capacities may not yield the best climber, or the best surgeon. But what mattered most was not the best, only her best. Her best was orthopedics, her best was making audacious climbing goals; it was, as some say, relentless forward progress. To practice for the sake of. To do, more than to achieve.

"I've always noticed that if I'm in it for the right reasons, my work capacity actually increases with challenges, rather than depletes. You start tapping into these reservoirs. And your actual ability expands, not just your drive, to the exact degree you are committed. It's kind of wild." According to her, this always holds true.

I've seen firsthand what an orthopedic residency can do to a person, so it was even more surprising to hear that for her, there were actual, measurable gains in her climbing during that time. Not just in grade, but also in technical awareness, and mental control. Shanjean pushed past thresholds that many climbers only find when they leave every commitment behind and take to the road. That her progression to 5.14 was exactly the opposite of the norm, is completely refreshing to see.

She embraces, fully, the notion that you must participate in all sides of life, that you do not take the easiest path, but rather your truest. She reminds us that your work is never done, that you never arrive, and that practice, that daily submission to something much bigger, longer, and more powerful than you, is the path. A path she'd again demonstrate as we climbed further into the afternoon.

After warming up, we trekked down the cliff to the premiere sector, where Shanjean attempted a 150-foot, 5.13, regional classic up a striking headwall. Steadied and cool, she tied-in and went vertical, easy-riding up the first half of the pitch at a slow, expansive pace. At the headwall, the crucial 60 feet before the finish, Shanjean clocked in. She approached the crux sequence as one approaches the operating space of a surgical site, clearing a path with direct, efficient strokes. Then, at the business end of the grade, she exacted the sum of her skills, grunting but also gracefully dancing through a dozen or more precise, critical movements, in a gorgeous display.

It was an ascent to be proud of, and, to some degree, she was. But even though this climb was harder than yesterday's, for Shanjean, it was not a time for celebration, it was time for work. She came halfway down the headwall, where it intersects with an even harder route, and asked for some time in practice. Pumped to all hell, most of us would've been more likely to come down to ground for some of that affirmation she had alluded to, but not her. Shanjean stayed up there for another 20 minutes, learning, practicing, executing, and then executing again with different methods. Continuously exploring her best sequence, between what little connecting points nature had provided in the way of features, edges, and spans of usable granite, she spun yarn on that wall from some inner fount, some endless reservoir.

At last, back to earth, she didn't even skip a beat when I asked her what drove her to operate with such abandon. "You know, there's balance in life. There are times to celebrate. But there's also work and it's important to do both. What I've learned is that I don't always need to celebrate the small goals, like this climb right now, not if they are just a part of the bigger goal. Up on El Cap, there won't be any onsighting, not like yesterday. I've been on it a bunch, and it'll come down to how consistently I can execute moves at this grade for consecutive, back to back pitches. It'll be about sustaining this level of climbing and hauling our food and supplies at the same time. So, when I got up to the top just now, and I was good and pumped, that was the perfect time to try something even harder. That's when you need to put in that one more lap."

When you see her say it, with the finger strokes of chalk-dust pattered on her forehead, the wisps of hair freestyling in the wind, the satisfaction, and that eternal, kind smile, you understand what she's working on. She is not obsessed, not manic, not driven by some deep insecurity or need to achieve. She's plugged in, lights on, all systems checked, clocking in for craft, for practice, for that long frequency.

///

Our time was short, after all, and life called her back to the clinic as quickly as it called me back to duties at home. With the afternoon on a closing line, Shanjean looked at me and offered I have a go at a damn hard route of my own. When I agreed and took the lead end of the rope from her, she smiled bigger than I'd seen all day.

"I was hoping you'd get on it," she laughed, "Because it's always inspiring seeing your friends try hard, and because I want to cheer you on."

I got about as close as I could to the finish before a pump longer than a chain of DNA raged in my forearms. But with Shanjean's encouragement from below, and with the lessons she'd provided in the past few days, I found myself staring down that moment of truth, face

Lucas Roman

to face with my threshold, all in. It wasn't a grand triumph. In fact, I whipped a good thirty feet, and pulled Shanjean off the ground by force and along for the ride. But it was as good as a fall can be.

Back at ground level, Shanjean was filled with excitement. "That was awesome!" she said, looking up to the new iron in the fire. "You're going to have to come back up here for another trip, now."

"I can see why you'd say that," I laughed.

Because you could. She wanted me to succeed on that climb, to get back up there to square the account, and climb to my best. But it wasn't just that. She wanted me to come back because just as much as she loves finding her own projects up here, she equally wants the chance to cheer you on. To give you support, to be a part of your success, to be a cog in the chain of your life, and to steer you toward your own work without end, that's what she was looking forward to. Outward-facing, at her best.

Two weeks later, on her first trip out to the Incredible Hulk, the High-Sierra multipitch gem, Shanjean got completely knocked around. Was it the incessant workweek, the fact that it was all onsight, or the katabatic winds and hazardous conditions? It didn't really matter.

"I'll just have to keep coming back," Shanjean shared over the phone. "It's such a beautiful place, anyway."

"Is it any harder, or different, dealing with failures these days?" I asked.

"Failure," she laughed, "that's such a needed part of all of this. Whatever the goal and wherever I may be, personally, I'm striving for gains in life skills up there. It's about improvement, more than achievement, like we talked about. Hopefully in doing so, you minimize the failure. But failure is inevitable, so avoiding it is never the goal. What I've learned is that it's a tool, to learn and grow. It's expected along the path."

Chopping wood, carrying water. Shanjean, at her best, is right in the pocket, that sweet spot of flow-state, intuition, and craft. It's a craft that has required long nights and inconvenient turns, but more than anything, it's a craft that has required the right motivation. Calling her a friend and watching her put all the pieces together in her own creative weave, is a gift.

Whether on the wall or at ground level, perhaps the only thing more striking than her soft, fluid movement, is her simple lightness of being. Her unshakeable joie de vivre. By gender, and spirit, she is a much-needed departure from the character norms that have driven the progression of climbing's past. But make no mistake, even with all the beams of light behind her, as a woman, as a minority, as a surgeon, a climber, and a daughter, Shanjean has walked through her own fires.

What she'd want you to know most about the success equation is that where the deepest faith was required of her, when she had to go into places within herself and do things that nobody else could do for her, she could not have done it alone. Community, is perhaps the greatest element of it all. Purpose is unique to each individual, but for any of us to flourish, we need structures to lean on. It is they, our friends, mentors and loved ones who can both light the path, and see within us what we cannot always see in ourselves.

For Shanjean, it all comes down to that ineffable beauty. That's where she seeks her own revelations. In all her travels, in the unfathomable collection of memories and high contrast slides out in nature, where light and force and human will, bleed into one—surely there the unspeakable resides. It always has. And it's completely available for all who seek. Whether nested in the host of alpine sunrises across the Cascade Ranges, where glacial blues you cannot imagine reflect from the ice stacks of distant peaks; to the hundreds of sunset overtones on west-facing granite formations, it's there. And she knows it.

But it's not just there, the beauty she seeks most in the universe is not just that of color and energy, but also that of alignment, balance, and perfect execution. And what she's found is that in order to learn of any of the higher orders, of the divine, we must seek also a craft.

"Mastery," she began, after I asked her to what degree her pursuits relate her to a higher power. "Mastery in any discipline is a thing of beauty—I think, bordering on spirituality. Listen to Beethoven's Fifth. Watch a surgeon flawlessly repair a hole in a beating heart. Witness a climber dance over holds that you know are barely there. It's magical."

"And, every so often," she continued, "when you execute the perfect climb or the perfect surgery. When all the preparation, the failures, the learning experiences— the sleepless nights, the training, the reading—when all that falls into place. When you know you are doing something as well as it can possibly be done, then yes, it feels like you are a part of something greater than yourself. It is the sum of so many tangible and intangible factors, both in and out of your control, that when it does happen, without a doubt, it feels, and is, magical, spiritual, and so much bigger than you.

"That's what all the work is for," Shanjean concluded, "It is to be one hundred percent ready to have a moment like this when it presents itself."

Shanjean Lee, the orthopedic surgeon, the 5.14 climber, the girl next door, left it just like that. What she teaches me is that we cannot, we must not, go at any of this alone. And, that the spiritual experience is not something we fall into, it is something we fashion. It's true that many of us have come out of darkness by the hand of some mysterious grace. That's how many of us begin the path. But strictly speaking long-term, truth and revelation are far too sacred to be stumbled upon. They must be sought. They require work, and preparedness.

Above all, what she teaches me, is that in a world where we long for greatness, what we need, fundamentally, to get there, is more kindness. The old Zen master D.T. Suzuki once said that the Great Awakening, the Great Awareness, is meaningless unless it is also accompanied by the Great Compassion. A truth that resounds in Shanjean's life. Her way has never been about exerting great force as much as it has been about harmonizing it. Where there is pain, she fosters joy; where there are those in need, she brings affirmation. What she teaches me is that lightness of being, the good stuff, emanates from purpose. That's why she's always got that smile, that rosy, curling smile, the one that rises like a rush of champagne bubbles to the highs of her cheekbones. It's tied to her purpose. And, it's tied to gratitude. The gratitude comes because in her still, quiet awareness—in that subterranean, mycelial connection to the higher order—she knows that not only is this universe one of boundless, constant beauty and expression; but that our fortune, is that we are invited, designed even, to contribute those very elements as best we can, right back into the heart of it.

Onward. Together.

Lucas Roman

Lightning Source UK Ltd.
Milton Keynes UK
UKHW020639021222
413181UK00012B/1916

9 781942 549801